Managing the Post-Industrial City

Managing the Post-Industrial City

Ken Young and Liz Mills

Heinemann Educational Books · London

Heinemann Educational Books Ltd
22 Bedford Square, London WC1B 3HH

LONDON   EDINBURGH   MELBOURNE   AUCKLAND
HONG KONG   SINGAPORE   KUALA LUMPUR   NEW DELHI
IBADAN   NAIROBI   JOHANNESBURG
EXETER (NH)   KINGSTON   PORT OF SPAIN

British Library Cataloguing in Publication Data
Managing the post-industrial city.
  1. Cities and towns—Study and teaching—
Great Britain   2. Environmental education—
Great Britain
I. Young, Ken   II. Mills,Liz
307.7'6'0941   HT169.G7

ISBN 0–435–83956–X

Typeset by Inforum Ltd, Portsmouth
and printed by Biddles Ltd, Guildford, Surrey

Contents

List of Figures

Preface

This book arises from a research project, 'Local Authority Interventions in the Local Economy', funded by the Social Science Research Council under grant HR5153. The project ran from November 1977 to October 1979 and was based at the School for Advanced Urban Studies, Bristol University. Ken Young directed the project, and the research team was completed by Liz Mills and Charlie Mason. On completion of the project the members of the team moved to new appointments elsewhere but close contact was maintained. Some further fieldwork was undertaken while efforts to set the study in its context of urban change and to develop the interpretation of the mass of documentary, interview and observational data continued. This work was carried out by the authors in their new posts at, respectively, the Policy Studies Institute and the Department of Geography at Bristol University. At the time of writing, the authors are engaged, with colleagues at PSI and at the University of Kent, on a further study of 'Structural Adaptation in Two Areas of London' which has been commissioned by the SSRC Executive Panel on the Inner City in Context.

In such a study as this it is all too easy to overlook an intellectual or practical debt. The authors want first to record their appreciation of the contribution made by Charlie Mason, who helped both to gather material on the development of local economic policies and to unravel the course of policy change in the two case-study authorities. The support of other colleagues at the School for Advanced Urban Studies must also be acknowledged, as must the special help willingly given by Alison Sims, the school librarian, and, latterly, Susan Johnson, her opposite number at PSI. The manuscript was typed at PSI by Mari Girling, Stephanie Maggin and Dorothy Bennett.

A considerable debt is also owed by Ken Young to his colleagues on the Inner City Working Party of SSRC and its successor, the Inner City Executive Panel, of which bodies he was a member from 1978 to 1982. Without doubt, the debates which took place there under the chairmanship first of Professor Peter Hall and latterly of Professor Gordon Cameron did much to inform the thinking in this book. So too did the comments made at seminars held at, in particular, Lanchester Polytechnic, Nuffield College, Oxford, the School for Advanced Urban Studies, the Centre for Urban and Regional Studies of Birmingham University, Downing College, Cambridge, the Universities of Kent and Liverpool; at meetings of the urban politics group of the Political Studies Association; and in discussions at Bogazici University, Istanbul. Thanks are also due to Liz Mills' colleagues in the Department of Geography at Bristol University, particularly to Allan Frey, and to Peter Haggett, Michael Morgan, Tony Hoare and Glen Norcliffe. The data presented in Figure 4.1 are made available by Steve Fothergill of the Department of Land Economy, University of Cambridge.

This book centres on the close study of the development of economic policies in two London boroughs, which appear here simply as 'Westborough' and 'Southborough'. For obvious reasons, proper acknowledgement cannot be given to the many patient individuals who co-operated in the research by allowing us to read their files, attend their meetings and question them persistently. To all of them, to the chief executive officers and directors of planning and to the council committees who agreed to this collaboration we offer our most sincere thanks.

Ken Young and Liz Mills,

London and Bristol,

September 1982.

1 Introduction

THE recent emergence of an urban economic crisis in advanced industrial nations has attracted widespread attention from policy-makers, academics and the media. In Britain, the adoption of an inner cities programme by the last Labour government and of a more discriminatory regional framework by its successor suggest that we are edging our way towards a specifically *urban* as distinct from regional policy. In the meantime, far from being sanguine about the ability or the willingness of national governments to stem the flow of wealth creation from the cities, many local authorities have taken their own initiatives to bolster the urban economy through the provision of industrial sites and premises, through financial assistance to firms, or through measures to enhance the employability of the urban population.[1] This book attempts to bridge the gap between the wealth of descriptive material on the extent of urban change on the one hand, and accounts of the programmes introduced by local authorities on the other; it asks *how* de-industrialisation arrived on local policy agendas, and *why* local authorities felt obliged – and able – to respond to it.

Far from being a handbook for urban managers, this is instead an interpretative study of the crucial first stage of the management process: the identification of urban change as a problem for policy. The apparent narrowness of that concern belies its wider significance, for it is only through analysis of the organisational processes of problem identification that we can begin to understand the complex relationship between urban change and public policy. The pursuit of such understanding necessitates a case-study approach, and two key chapters of this book describe how economic change became a policy issue in two London boroughs during the late 1970s. Our approach, and our focus on the relationship between external change and internal politics, has been developed in a series of separate but linked research projects; we feel that it may be applied to many situations in which the aim is to unravel the relationships between environmental change and organisational response.[2]

Our basic argument is set out in Chapter 2, where we claim that there is no determining mechanism by which the stresses of change evoke a policy response, and that the decision processes, policies and programmes of governments cannot be directly explained in terms of external forces. Rather we see adaptation to change as resulting from an internal process of bureaucratic politics, a process which is led by participants who, for varying and essentially private reasons, see

environmental change as their cue for action. Intervening in the decision processes of their organisations the policy entrepreneurs (as we
shall call them) argue a new account of local environmental conditions,
one which (they will seek to persuade) makes better sense of changing
circumstance.[3]

To identify a key role for entrepreneurship is not, however, to
confine our attention to the internal politics of local governments, to see
local economic management as no more than a bright idea, or as
something dreamed up by a planning profession in search of a role.
Instead, the changing environment is mediated by the images, myths,
power relationships and routines that prevail within the organisation,
factors which may make a local authority more or less inclined to
recognise actual shifts in economic circumstance, more or less inclined
to assume the role of manager of change, and more or less able to be
effective in that role.

To understand how changes come to impinge upon the everyday
worlds of policy-makers and junior officers we need first to identify
what is changing. This, too, is something which we could have chosen
to do on a case-study basis, presenting the reader with a detailed
account of street–level changes in the two boroughs whose responses we
consider. However, we are concerned to stress the generality of the
change/response linkages, and to show that urban economic decline is
no localised phenomenon, but part of a massive and continuing shift in
the spatial structure of the economies of industrialised nations. To
place the local changes in two areas of London into a broader international and national context enables us to set aside the question of the
impact of policies and programmes upon the urban economy, for, by
implication, that impact is unlikely to be significant and can hardly be
expected to reverse the tide of urban de-industrialisation.[4] The
phenomenon of urban change at an international level is then the focus
of Chapter 3, where we examine both the evidence for and the analyses
of what is loosely termed *the counter-urbanisation thesis*.

Alleged culprits for the urban crisis abound, and government
policies for urban containment and peripheral growth are foremost
among them. Our own reading of the evidence compels us to turn our
attention elsewhere, to the other factors which bear upon the establishment, expansion, contraction, survival, collapse, relocation or
retention of the urban industrial base. For us, the urban crisis is a
confluence of forces which bear upon the decision processes of firms;
the industrial enterprise in the urban milieu is the proper unit of analysis
and we therefore devote the whole of Chapter 4 to a review of the
evidence on current patterns of change in the manufacturing metropolis.

Images of urban change are shaped both by generalities and by the specific local impacts of decisions taken by individual firms. Typically, planning officers experience local changes through unwelcome pressure on the development control system, but in interpreting these changes they have recourse to their wider appreciation of what is happening to the city, the region, or, in a more sketchy and impressionistic way, the national and international economy. In Chapter 5, therefore, we turn to examine the recent history of Greater London, bearing in mind not only the compact interdependence of metropolitan life in which labour market areas challenge the logic of administrative boundaries, but also the notable mobility of London's planners, whose progression from one authority to another serves to delocalise their images of metropolitan character. Inner and outer London have experienced rather different patterns of change during the last decade and we consider the fortunes of each as a means of setting our two case-study boroughs in their metropolitan context.

The two case-studies occupy the next two chapters and they need little further introduction here. Chapter 6 is an account of the pressures in an outer London industrial suburb which experienced a transformation from a manufacturing to a predominantly service-based employment centre. We focus particularly on the ways in which the stresses of change were felt and interpreted within the council's own organisation, and the factors which led first to the formulation and then to the revision of an industrial strategy for the area. In Chapter 7 we turn our attention to an inner London borough where the mid-1970s contraction in inner London's manufacturing base stimulated a number of officers to challenge the prevailing policies of the council which, until that date, had favoured housing and environmental improvement over the maintenance of the local economic base.

In Chapter 8 we return to our main theme in an attempt to draw together both the experience of and the responses to urban change in the two authorities. Aware of the need to transcend merely idiographic case-studies, we concentrate our attention on the ways in which the case material addresses the general theme of intervention as a response to the stress of change. Confined by our data-base to a speculative account, we argue that intervention is the outcome of, first, a threat to the prevailing and valued image of the locality and second, of the propensity to intervene. This last draws our attention to the differences between the two cases, and in the final section of the book we suggest that the propensity to intervene is just one facet of a powerful set of intersubjective beliefs, values and orientations which characterise an organisation and which may be termed its *culture*.

Finally, some remarks on method.[5] Chapters 6 and 7 are highly condensed abstracts of a mass of research material accumulated in the course of two years' association with the two authorities, during which we traced their economic policies back to their origins in the early 1970s. Owing to the nature of the material and to our privileged access, we have not followed the customary scholarly practice of providing source citations for each quotation, since we do not wish to identify our two authorities. We have trespassed heavily upon the patience and tolerance of a large number of busy people, intruding into their every-day worlds in ways which must have seemed at times perplexing to them. We appreciate the openness of the two authorities and we must in turn respect the confidences of their staff.

The problem of responsibility arises with special force in organisa-tional research, for unobtrusiveness on the part of the transient observer encourages informants to drop their guard.[6] While formal interviews were important to us as a means of clarifying issues, exploring perceptions and pursuing topics in depth, we enjoyed a far larger number of informal encounters, casual chats, unexpected confi-dences and revealing remarks.[7] To a large extent, then, our character-isation of the two authorities is based upon material which could not be presented without an unfair violation of trust.

That constraint lies less heavily upon us in relation to two other main components of our research strategy which, while they depend equally upon the privileged access to sources, do so in a more explicit fashion. These techniques, upon which we place special value, are unrestricted access to documentary sources, and attendance at the periodic officers' meetings at which issues are discussed and programmes formulated. Little need be said here as to the first, save that we profited greatly in both authorities by being able to backtrack through the files and glean thereby a sometimes wider understanding of events than any single participant could give us. If we sometimes allude to an issue rather than document a source, we do so in order to leave the social peace of the organisation intact by not revealing all of what was recorded to those who would not normally have access to their colleagues' files.

We also placed considerable emphasis on transient observation, a technique of regular informal visiting that escapes some of the more telling criticisms of the deeper involvements of participant observation. The (formally) non-interactive technique of sitting in on group discus-sions is one which the first author has developed further since the study reported here, but we learned a great deal from these first explorations in the role of group observer. Once simple group techniques – and the art of very rapid writing – have been mastered it is possible to obtain a verbatim account of at least the key junctures of a meeting, along with notations of nuance and expression. As a technique, sitting in is both highly productive and (we believe) low on bias.[8]

Bias is of course the heart of the methodological issue. It is the essence of organisational research practice to employ, in a complementary fashion, a range of techniques that might otherwise be seen as alternatives. Each has its own strengths and weaknesses, and the pressing reason for employing a mix of methods to approach a single focal issue is that each one 'is potentially biased and has specific to it potential validity threats.'[9] The account which we have constructed is then to be seen as the final result of a series of data overlays, the stronger lines of which have been built up from an assessment of evidence from different and (so far as possible) independent sources. At the end of the day, the researcher builds a picture from this accumulation of material, seeking a confluence of evidence and – inescapably – weighing it and exercising judgement. With the judgement comes an element of subjectivity, which is not entirely compensated for by constant critical discussion within the research team.

This is, then, an interpretative study at two levels. First, the case material represents our own interpretation of events, interactions, motives and interests as displayed in organisational politics. Second, our concern was with the interpretations which the participants *themselves* made of their own experience of urban change. This is not the place for a debate on validity in the social sciences. Suffice to say that the accounts which we have constructed are grounded to some extent in the life-worlds of the organisational members themselves, as we were continually seeking to test our own interpretations with them, to check our own constructions of events and, ultimately, to hold a mirror to their experience.[10] In so doing, we tacitly acknowledge their status as choice-making agents, concerned, as we all are, to make sense of circumstances, to cope with change, and to impose a cognitive order on life in the post-industrial city.

2 Understanding Policy Change

POLICY-MAKING, we are often told, is a problem-solving activity. Policies and problems are inextricably linked in ordinary usage by an implied stimulus – response relationship; problems are the stimuli to which policies are responses. Naturally, neither commonsense notions nor the more formal cybernetic theories of public action suppose a perfect or instantaneous match between manifest problems and remedial policies,[1] and even the vaguest conceptions of policy-making acknowledge that a critical threshold must be crossed in order for a situation to be accorded the status of a problem and thus recognised as a legitimate claim to public attention. These lags and thresholds qualify, but do not detract from, the basic conception of government as an exercise in equilibrium.[2]

We might call this loose association of assumptions *the evocative theory of policy-making*. Its mechanistic views have proved popular in comparative and quantitative studies of input/output relationships, in which the allocative decisions of governments are related to the material circumstances of their immediate environment.[3] In such studies, human agency – in the form of a disposition to choose – is but a literally intervening variable, a source of friction or distortion in a system which is otherwise driven by force of circumstance.

Against the mechanistic assumptions of evocative theory may be set a range of dissenting views, each of which accords a more central place to human agency. Koestler, for example, responded passionately to what he saw as a behaviourist elimination of human values in social explanation, and insisted on the reinstatement of the free agent as the intermediary between pressing circumstances and a chosen response.[4] A similarly critical view of the elimination of politics by organisation is presented by Sheldon Wolin.[5] Both writers accord a central place to thought in the explanation of human action; thought moreover which is itself independent of circumstance.

Within the narrow field of public administration resistance to mechanistic theories flourishes. The biographical tradition in the study of public policy helps sustain this resistance by personalising policy; sceptical of schematics, it instead elevates the particularism of 'insider accounts'.[6] So too do the new administrative historians who portray government officials as engaged in a competitive struggle for position, identifying new 'problems' to sustain their dwindling roles or to gain tactical advantage.[7] These diverse (and otherwise divergent) views share no more than a common conception of policy-makers as the architects of the very problems they seek to solve.

According to whichever view we adopt, we may see men and their governments as either borne along on the stream of material events, responding as promptly or prudently as they are able to the exigencies of an ever-changing situation, or as shapers of events, demonstrators of the power and autonomy of human agency. Each view has theoretical underpinnings in the philosophy of history, in historical sociology, and in the theory of organisations. Ultimately, each may claim still deeper roots in, respectively, the materialist and idealist views of human action.

It is to these deeper foundations that we turn in this chapter in order to appraise their respective strengths and shortcomings. We consider first the materialist view of public action as conditioned by force of circumstance, before going on to review the idealist objections to such a denial of human agency. Neither view will be found to provide an ultimately satisfying account of how men intervene in a changing world. We therefore consider the ways in which the agent, as a social being, makes sense of his circumstances in order to act upon them. Finally, we turn our attention to the politics of urban policy and consider the processes by which credence is gained for public problems.

The force of circumstance

The two basic positions which we wish to contrast here are those which portray policies as, respectively, dictated by force of circumstance or, alternatively, as freely chosen by independent agents. The long-standing controversies as to the nature of historical explanation exemplify this contrast and conflicting theories of historical interpretation have become an important source of historical disagreement.[8] The naturalist or 'materialist' interpretation (as we shall term it here) is characteristic of the attempt to formulate a scientific history in which the explanation of events is grounded in material forces, often, though not exclusively, of an economic nature, whose inexorable logic and pressures 'dictate' the responses of government.

The premises of materialism emerge most explicitly in the critiques offered by its opponents. Hannah Arendt argues that the materialist view sees historical forces as natural forces and historical laws as examples of (rather than analogous to) the laws of nature.[9] For Pieter Geyl, materialists see the historical process as 'a concatenation of events, one following upon the other inevitably, caused as they are by a superhuman force or by impersonal forces working in society independently from the wishes or efforts of individuals'.[10] Thus it implies 'the impotence of deliberate human action, whether individual or concerted, to alter the course of human history, since historical changes are allegedly the products of deeper-lying forces which conform to fixed, although not always known, patterns of development'.[11]

According to such a prospect, the beliefs, images or intentions of policy-makers are, in Gardiner's apt term, mere 'vapour' arising from material foundations.[12] As Marx himself put it:

The phantoms of the human brain . . . are necessary sublimates of men's material life processes which can be empirically established and which is bound to material conditions. Morality, religion, metaphysics, and other ideologies, and their corresponding forms of consciousness, no longer retain therefore their appearance of autonomous existence. They have no history, no development; it is men, who in developing their material production and their material intercourse, change, along with this their real existence, their thinking, and the products of their thinking. Life is not determined by consciousness, but consciousness by life.[13]

The intentions of statesmen, social reformers, or citizens are thus no more than pretensions; their impact on events is illusory. According to Sir Isaiah Berlin's glittering caricature, they live in oblivion upon the precarious slopes of the volcano of history.[14]

If uncompromising materialism invites the response of the caricaturist, it may be argued in defence that Marx sought to reconcile materialism and idealism for 'while materialism makes consciousness a reflection of external reality, idealism makes reality a product of consciousness. Materialism splits up into two separate worlds what Marx thinks to be a unity whereas idealism dissolves one world into the other'.[15] The determinism of brute materialism is none the less readily apparent in recent writings on social policy. Contemporary Marxist commentators portray the development of the welfare state not as the gradual ascendancy of a caring philosophy, but as 'a lubrication of the social mechanism',[16] as 'functional to capital accumulation',[17] as arising from the tension between capitalist state structure and working-class struggle,[18] or as expressing a concern with the legitimation of class dominance in the face of revolutionary threats.[19] The actions of local governments are similarly interpreted, for all governmental institutions are seen as possessing a 'functional unity' in 'the overall determination of their policies'.[20] It is for this reason that 'the local state' has been accepted into the currency of concepts.[21]

Materialism has also been influential among non-Marxists, as reflected in those functionalist theories that elevate the 'integrative needs' of societies above the independent power of values and concepts of social justice.[22] Such a crude non-Marxist materialism has proved especially popular in explaining the origins of social policy in nineteenth-century England. This important 'Tory interpretation of history' exemplifies some of the problems of the materialist account of policy development.[23]

The rapid rise of urban-industrial society was followed by the growth of state and municipal intervention to regulate and ameliorate the urban condition. This intervention has been variously interpreted. The publication in 1958 of MacDonagh's 'reappraisal' of 'the nineteenth-century revolution in government' promoted an intense debate on the relative influence of changing circumstances and changing thought in bringing about these developments.[24] MacDonagh's iconoclasm is a classic statement of the 'evocative' theory of policy; 'pressures working within society' and the 'exogenous' exposure of social evils 'set an irresistible engine of change in motion'.[25] Its workings were eagerly charted by others. Writing of central-local relations in the period between 1858 and 1871, Lambert concluded that ideas of centralism or 'a priori notions' mattered little in comparison with the 'more impersonal forces which operated widely in the growth of Victorian government'.[26] Roberts' study of the Victorian origins of the welfare state stressed the necessity of social reform and the 'unconscious' creation of new interventionist agencies *'in almost absence of mind'*.[27] Kitson Clark portrayed urban-industrial development and the felt need for social reform as arising from 'impersonal historical forces which possibly no man can control'.[28]

City authorities played a major role in attempting to manage the growth or assuage the evils of Victorian urbanisation, promoting private legislation to increase their own powers and adopting local improvements under a fluctuating central tutelage.[29] Fraser, in his general survey of Victorian urban politics, concludes that these developments

> simply evolved out of the purely pragmatic response of the Victorian state to urban social problems. And so it was with municipal welfare . . . it was on the practical plane rather than the theoretical that municipal reform was measured . . . the pragmatic rather than the ideological continued to spur municipal endeavour.[30]

Fraser goes beyond this judgement to a more general espousal of the 'evocative' theory: because the ancient corporations had been created 'to meet problems different from those facing an emerging urban industrial society', so 'reform of urban local government became a pressing necessity'; in particular 'the growing problem of law and order . . . was to be a compelling force for local government reform'.[31]

Pressing needs and compelling forces are the familiar apparatus of the materialist account. Yet it seems that they need not be confined to the external environment of cities, people and their problems. They may equally be internal to government; among the more potent of

MacDonagh's 'blind impersonal forces' are to be found the dynamics of bureaucracy itself. The growth of intervention and of the whole fabric of social policy on this view followed from the unintended growth of agencies: 'administration may be, so to speak, creative and self-generating . . . it may gather its own momentum . . . it may reach beyond the control or comprehension of anyone in particular'.[32] Lambert concurs: his study of one important agency found it to be 'a prime instance of that force which occasioned so much state expansion – the self-sustaining and self-generating impulse of administration itself'.[33]

The idea that the dynamic forces of history inhere within agencies and that agencies – as organisations – are driven by a functional dynamic that transcends particular human purposes is a familiar precept of organisation theory. The more general propositions of Mac-Donagh and his followers would seem unexceptionable to the readers of the *Administrative Science Quarterly*, whose contributors have for some years discounted the notion that organisations (or their leaders) possess independent goals, purposes or principles.

The sociologists' concept of 'organisational goals' often attributed simplistic purposes to undifferentiated organisations;[34] Yuchtman and Seashore had little difficulty in demolishing 'the goal perspective',[35] while later studies are held to demonstrate 'the fruitlessness of understanding organisations as goal-attaining devices'.[36] Since Silverman's influential *Theory of Organisatons* was published in 1970, references to goals have been viewed as something of an intellectual *faux pas*; goal theorists committed the cardinal error of 'reification' – 'the attribution of concrete reality, particularly the power of thought and action, to social constructs'.[37] Latterly, a fastidious concern to avoid reification has deterred some writers from any consideration of human agency in organisations, at least until Mohr contrived to resuscitate goals and avoid reification by the simple expedient of referring to the 'dominant coalition' within an organisation.[38]

While interest in bureaucratic purposes had been sustained by a tendency to consider organisations in abstraction from their operational mileux, its eclipse has been hastened by a shift of attention in favour of organisational *environments*. This more recent perspective further 'depersonalises' institutions, and introduces a new variant of determinism by substituting organisational function for human purpose. In this way the materialist assumptions of 'the Tory interpretation' of nineteenth-century policy development are given a sociological imprimatur by organisation theory. The scope and content of policy are now seen as constrained by what one modern writer terms 'the major environmental factors that shape the behaviour of the organisation', factors of which organisational decision-makers may be unconscious.[39]

According to this very important strand in organisation theory, the actions of policy-makers in public agencies are characterised by their dependence on *other* agencies, in particular for their necessary statutory, financial or political resources. The outcomes of the policy process are on this view shaped not by manifest problems in what might be termed the 'operational environment' of the agency, but by the functioning of an inter-agency network.[40]

Such a network of agencies represents a web of constraint, and little emphasis is placed upon such loopholes as may exist for the pursuit of particular purposes. Instead, 'while there is a strain towards organisations maximising their autonomy', they are none the less 'pushed into . . . interdependence because of their need for resources'.[41] In subsequent versions of this account a general drive to resource maximisation and the management of dependence take the place of discrete goals or purposes.[42] In a competitive world of governmental agencies resources are portrayed as a prerequisite for survival.[43] Moreover, organisations compete not just for resources but also for territory or clientele; they seek to extend their 'policy space' to achieve hegemony within their 'domain'.[44] Purpose is reduced to function by the competitive 'interdependence of complex organisations';[45] policy-makers are borne along by the logic of events in a material world of other agencies. Interorganisational life is portrayed as vaguely nasty, occasionally brutish, yet (except in the case of individual leaders) apparently interminable.

There is then a striking if unremarked convergence between those historians and sociologists who regard the argument from 'force of circumstance' as a powerful explanatory tool. Necessity, pressing needs and compelling forces, rather than human purposes or intentions, drive the engine of policy change. While Marxist and non-Marxist materialists proceed from different premises and adopt contrasting lines of explanation they share the view that human agency – beliefs, intentions, principles – are secondary to and derived from the underlying realities of political life. As Quentin Skinner has pointed out, Namierite, Marxist and behavioural analyses – 'the most powerful currents in modern social theory' – share the common presumption of human agency as a residual category and human purposes as illusory.[46] Such analyses, if applied to the question of governmental responses to urban change, would respectively account for policy in such terms as 'underlying forces', 'accumulation needs', or 'resource dependency'. In some cases their style of inference and their handling of evidence may strike one as cavalier. But even the best of such accounts would fail to persuade those who see the circumstantial constraints of the material world as existing largely in the minds of the policy-makers themselves; for the idealist historians and sociologists 'reality' is itself a product of consciousness, and the reforming politician or administrator is an independent agent.

The independent agent

Amongst both historians and sociologists, materialism gives causal precedence to the force of circumstance in the explanation of action. Given the impotence of human purposes, developments in policy are driven either by the pressure of external events which 'come of themselves', or by the internal functional dynamics of agencies *qua* organisations. There are, however, dissenting voices within both disciplines, expressed with varying degrees of force and clarity.

The idealist historians – Dilthey, Croce and Collingwood – take the precisely contrary view of human agency; for them history is 'the life of mind itself'.[47] They prefer to portray the human mind 'in predominantly active terms: they treated it, in other words, as creative and self-determining, playing a constructive role in life rather than passively responding in a mechanical fashion, to the promptings of external or internal stimuli'.[48] Of these, Collingwood has been the most directly influential: in his famous attack on 'naturalism' he wrote that

the processes of nature can therefore be described as a sequence of mere events, but those of history cannot. They are not processes of mere events but processes of action, which have an inner side, consisting of processes of thought; and what the historian is looking for is these processes of thought. All history is the history of thought.[49]

Because thought is autonomous, 'the activity by which man builds his own constantly changing world is a free activity. There are no forces other than this activity which control it or modify or compel it to behave in this way or that, to build one kind of world rather than another'.[50] Man acts in situations which are not of his own choosing, yet ultimately 'the hard facts of the situation, which it is so important for him to face, are the hard facts of the way he conceives the situation'.[51]

The idealist view and the idealist rebuttal of materialism are also conveniently illustrated by the debate over state intervention in the urban-industrial society of Victorian England. According to the idealist interpretation, the growth of state intervention reflected the mounting ascendancy of progressive ideas. In the classic treatment, Dicey's *Law and Public Opinion*, these ideas, in particular the rise of a collectivist ethos, were disembodied currents of thought which somehow transformed the nature of state action.[52] In later versions, influence was attributed more specifically to particular thinkers, most notably Bentham; or, in closely-focused studies of actual policy development, to such men of action (in particular Chadwick) who were committed to translating Benthamite theory into administrative practice.[53] The biographical method which figures prominently in political and administrative history tends to stress the importance of ideas when they are embodied in the great innovators in social policy.

Yet the link between ideas and action need be neither direct nor recognised; as Hart argues of nineteenth-century reform:

most social evils are not removed without fierce battles against absurd arguments, vested interests, obscurantism and timidity, and . . . their removal required considerable effort and determination on the part of the men (even if only obscure men) who realised that it was worth while making a conscious effort to control events. And in this enterprise many of them were assisted, whether they know it or not, by Benthamism in spite of all its shortcomings . . .[54]

Moreover, 'while many officials who were responsible for administrative and other changes had probably never heard of Bentham, much less read his works', nevertheless 'ideas can influence people who are unconscious of their origin'.[55] Even the materialists were obliged to concede this point, and introduced a degree of human agency in order to explain how the urban and industrial conditions of Victorian England evoked a governmental response. They pointed to the shifting definition of what constitutes 'intolerable' social conditions, reducing the point at issue to the relative influence of specific ideas on the one hand, and 'humanitarian sentiments' on the other.[56]

We need not pursue this issue further here, but merely note that the idealist historians were unimpressed by the vague diffusionism of the 'intolerability' thesis.[57] Its weakness lies in its account of the mechanism by which social conditions are translated into 'problems', and hence into issues for decision. Materialists anticipate that tensions in society at large will eventually permeate the policy agenda of the governing institutions; government is seen as inherently responsive to changing conditions or shifts in the climate of opinion. Impedance is to be expected, but is only temporary; 'because of the inertia present in any system, the institutional agenda will always lag to some extent behind the more general systemic agenda'.[58]

The idealist response is to deny that these linkages are necessary to public action. Idealists draw attention away from material conditions and popular feeling and point up instead the propensity of governments – at all levels – to determine their own agenda. Policy-makers define their own issues: 'social problems were what [such] people think they are',[59] and 'if men believe situations to be real they are real in their consequences'.[60]

In taking this position, the idealists deny the significance of any distinction between the actions of statesmen and the general category of social acts. Collingwood in particular ranges far beyond 'high politics' to elaborate the conditions of all meaningful social action. In his version, the actions of agents may be seen as flowing from the ways in which they define their everyday situations. If the perspective has a remarkably familiar ring to the contemporary sociologist it should not be surprising; Collingwood extended and elaborated the insights of

Wilhelm Dilthey whose work has also had a powerful and independent influence on 'interpretative' sociology and is particularly marked in the 'idealist' stream of organisation theory.[61] What the historians and the sociologists share here is an indifference to such abstractions as 'the state' or 'the organisation', and a close concern with the human agents who act in their name.

The dispute between materialists and idealists in the field of organisation theory centres upon a single issue: the specification of the 'significant environment' of the organisation. The significant environment comprises those aspects of the external situation which are relevant to decision-making.[62] While materialist writers emphasise the imperatives of dependency, idealists portray decision-makers as engaged in a process of *strategic choice* in which the most pressing needs may be recognised or ignored at will.[63] That policy-makers define their own realities has been a recurrent theme among this second group of organisational theorists, from Dill's emphasis on the *perceived* environment, to Duncan's conception of the organisational environment as 'the totality of physical and social factors that are *taken into account* in the decision-making behaviour of individuals in the organisation'.[64]

The phenomenon of selection from external realities has been particularly stressed by those writers who have portrayed circumstances as complex and unpredictable.[65] While the drive to reduce uncertainty is tempered by the varying ability of individuals to tolerate it, any decision-maker is inclined to simplify his situation by selective perception.[66] The greater the uncertainty in the external world, the greater the decision-makers' need to engage in 'strategic choice' in reacting to it.[67] In particular, given the complexity and unpredictability of the external world, decision-makers exercising strategic choice express their own priorities, purposes and definitions of the situation. This 'selective attendance' to environmental problems is held to explain why 'organisational decision-makers may not react to observable environmental changes'.[68]

In achieving this 'shift of focus from the characteristics of the objective environment to the characteristics of the decision process',[69] the idealist theorists frequently drift into solipsism. Weick, for example, in an influential and widely quoted passage, asserts that organisations 'enact' their environments;[70] their leaders 'create and constitute the environments to which they react; the environment is put there by the actor within the organisation and by no-one else . . . environment is a phenomenon tied to the process of attention and . . . unless something is attended to it doesn't exist'.[71]

Even Weick has difficulty in maintaining this position which is based on an unconsidered reading of W.I. Thomas's famous dictum that 'if men believe situations to be real, they are real in their consequences'.

Robert Merton had little difficulty in refuting Thomas by the simple expedient of inverting the statement: if men believe a situation to be unreal, do they thereby ward off its consequences?[72] In the event, even the most extreme idealists qualify their position. Weick himself concedes lamely that 'while it is true that enactment refers to the constituting of an environment by actors, it remains true that actors live in situations'.[73] Pfeffer and Salancik, who start from the same questionable premises, also ultimately concede that organisations 'depend' on their environments.[74]

A similar shrinking from the implications of unqualified idealism is to be found among the historians. Even such a master-work as Collingwood's *Idea of History* is riddled with ambiguity: on the one hand, a situation 'is always a thought-situation' in which 'hard facts' are facts of the mind; on the other hand, man is not free 'to do what he chooses' for the situation 'is what it is, and neither he nor anyone else can ever change it'; that while he may neglect it, 'the situation will not neglect him'.[75]

The entirely independent agent is then inconceivable. Governments may be free to 'create and constitute' an objectively non-existent 'problem' of witchcraft or subversion, but the existence of a real and objectionable condition cannot be defined away. 'Selective attendance' to environmental forces carries its own risks, for no policy-maker is invulnerable to turbulence or the relentless contraction of domain – be it political support, clientele, market share or empire. Men are constrained both by circumstance and by their own appreciations; they 'make their own history, but not under circumstances chosen by themselves'.[76]

Making sense of circumstance

If the solipsism of the extreme idealists is not credible, the weaknesses of the materialists are more subtle. Their inherently mechanistic assumptions and their implicit presumption of an equilibrating tendency reduce purpose to function and so reduce human agency to an aspect of the system.[77] More generally, materialists mistake the meaningful actions of individuals for externally accountable behaviour.[78] In so doing they confuse causal forces with the reasons for actions.[79] Acts are not performed 'in absence of mind'; agents cannot avoid defining their situations, and the barest pragmatism is itself a way of accounting for the immediate situation. Policy-makers – like all social beings – commonly see themselves as doing *something*, sometimes (if rarely) as pitting great ideas against an intractable reality.

Were we to encounter the 'unconscious' agent promoting policy change 'in almost absence of mind' as a response to external pressures, his activities would still accord with Collingwood's notion of action as expressive of thought, as having 'an inner side' of thought. Unable to account for his action in terms of some 'design', he may still be recognisably pursuing a purpose, one perhaps that has yet to crystalise in his consciousness, as in the case of Eugene Wrayburn's growing involvement with Lizzie Hexam in *Our Mutual Friend*:

'Eugene, do you design to capture and desert this girl?' 'My dear fellow, no.' 'Do you design to marry her?' 'My dear fellow, no.' 'Do you design to pursue her?' 'My dear fellow, I don't design anything. I have no design whatever. I am incapable of designs. If I conceived a design, I should speedily abandon it, exhausted by the operation'.[80]

The 'unaccountable' action may still be intentional and expressive. In order to produce acceptable accounts of how public policy is created in its organisational context, both materialism and idealism are forced to make concessions to 'thought' and 'circumstance' respectively. Neither concession however takes us very far. Materialists have yet to show *how* circumstances shape, impinge upon or constrain consciousness.[81] On the other hand, the dictum that action is expressive of thought provides a weak defence on the independent agent, for beyond the truism that action is intentional it remains unclear *whose* thought is expressed in the taken-for-granted actions of the agent.

   Culture, ideology, 'the spirit of the age', and similar constructs all refer to shared values and meanings.[82] Personality or character on the other hand have a more particular referent, while 'organisational climate' occupies an intermediate position.[83] At which of these levels of aggregation is thought supposed to possess an explanatory power? Of *whose* thought, we might ask, is history made? The answers are not obvious. It would, for example, be a gross mistake to infer the values and intentions of an actor from his intellectual environment, as in the case of 'the influence of Bentham'. Still less, as Brian Barry has shown, can they be inferred from his actions without risk of tautology,[84] although (where there is sufficient evidence) it may be permissible to speak of an actor's 'dispositions' to act in a 'characteristic' way.[85] This is no small matter. A great deal of historical dispute is grounded in disagreements as to how far particular actions – policies, legislative initiatives, executive acts – may be explained by vague if recognisable 'societal' or 'élite' or 'class' values rather than by the often unascertainable values of the individuals concerned.

   Neither orthodox materialism nor orthodox idealism can assist us beyond this point, for the attribution of meaning to circumstances is both a social *and* an individual process. First, the world is socially constituted: the purposive agent encounters it as having all the solidity and intractability of the materialist's world of 'irresistible forces', despite its being composed of the actions and meanings (that is of the *thought*) of others both past and present.[86] This is the basic paradox, or, as Berger and Luckmann prefer, the 'dialectic' of a socially-constructed reality: 'man is capable of producing a world which he then experiences as something other than a human product'.[87] To say that the individual experiences the social world as 'constituted' is not however to attribute its constitution to the operations of the collective will or reason of his fellows; it is rather an *historical* accretion of individual acts. As Oakeshott portrays the constituted world: 'this so-called "social inheritance" is an accumulation of human understandings and is compiled of the moral and prudential achievements of numberless individuals expressed in terms of the rules and conditions which specify a multiplicity of practices. *It is a collected, not a "collective" achievement.*'[88]

Second, the social world is 'expressive' as well as 'impressive'.[89] The agent responds to the world of his subjective understanding as if it originated in his own experiences; it is his own *assumptive world*.[90] As such, it incorporates and internalises the direct experience of the individual in his transactions with the world, transactions which are bounded by the limits of experience, by what Lewin called 'the life-space'.[91] Thus 'every individual lives in his subjective understanding and looks out at the world from it and through it'.[92]

While the world of immediate experience is chaotic, randomised, in flux and ultimately incomprehensible, the assumptive world – the product of a mediating consciousness – imposes order by simplification, selection and generalisation.[93] It condenses raw experience into meaning.[94] It provides 'a map of problematic social reality' which codifies and transmits workable interpretations,[95] and meets the existential need 'to assess one's place in the world . . . to place oneself in the social universe of reference'.[96]

The symbolic representations of the assumptive world enable the actor to model the relations between things. He is able to 'make sense of circumstance' by stabilising, ordering and ultimately making manageable such relations. Such simplifications enable the actor to cope with uncertainties by providing acceptable accounts which he brings to situations 'to give them order and hope'.[97] In providing predictions about the relations between things the assumptive world thereby provides 'guides and bases for future actions';[98] the past is condensed and projected so as to order the future and thus provide an expectable environment.[99] As Vickers comments:

whatever else we learn, we surely learn what to expect. Creatures much simpler than man detect regularities in their milieu and act on the assumption that these will recur . . . From such simple beginnings to the predictions which made moon landings possible, men have progressed by building ever more complex and reliable models of their environment, projecting them into the future and acting on the faith of them.[100]

This last is particularly important. Our mental models encapsulate past experience and anticipation; moreover, given the uncertainties of circumstance, there will be alternative expectations: 'the assumptive world not only contains a model of the world as it is . . . it also contains a model of the world as it might be (these models represent probable situations, ideal situations or dreaded situations)'.[101] Action arises from the mismatch of these models with one another and with felt experience. Individuals act upon their situation according to their *diagnosis* of its potential for change from a state of lesser to a state of greater acceptability, or to avert a further deterioration; in Oakeshott's rather cumbersome prose 'what predicates action is an agent's understanding of his own situation as, in some respect, unacceptable to himself . . . that is, the spring of conduct is a situation in respect of its being recognised to contain a specific unacceptability'.[102] The implication is a profound one: social action, in the sense of interventions in the world of experience, is an inherently conservative response.[103]

The assumptive worlds of individuals vary in their depiction of common circumstances, for experience may be differently construed by uniquely different personalities giving rise to 'multiple realities'.[104] Accepted accounts confer common meanings and stability but may prove fragile when rapid social change (as in the transition to and beyond industrial society) undermines traditional accounts of social reality or when a clash of cultures corrodes the stabilising myths. Then 'the individual is aware of many different contradictory and unrelated . . . schemes. Thus he has come to confront life and experiencing directly'.[105] Yet individuals may vary not only in their images of the situation, but also in their discernment of 'problems' within it, in their sensitivity to change and in their beliefs as to their power to manage it.

We now have the outlines of a relationship between the material world and imagination, between experience and image; one, moreover, that establishes the conditions of action. Yet, as it stands, it is unable to predict the ways in which individuals in either their private or their public roles cope with the experience of change. The assumptive world not only represents circumstances in symbols, it provides a cushion between changing circumstance and felt experience. Changing situations need not evoke intervention nor need stable situations preclude it. Consciousness mediates between experience and action and includes the perceptions not only of change itself, but also of the threat of change and of the feasibility of intervention to forestall it.

The indeterminacy of the relationship between circumstance and imagination (as we construe it here) generally leaves human action as an open question. Our specific interest, however, concerns the agent as a policy-maker, operating within an organisational context which is strongly oriented to the condition of the external world. There is in this case both a presumption to act and an institutional setting in which the uncertainties of the social experience have to be resolved into collective accounts. The starting-point of any inquiry into policy change must then be the process by which such accounts are framed: the organisational processes of problem definition.

The politics of urban problems

Men make sense of their circumstances. The everyday world is an expectable world, one which generally confirms the predictions and supports the hypotheses which 'inquiring man' erects the better to manage his transactions with it.[106] Social stability is a condition in which expectations are broadly fulfilled, in which circumstances conform to familiar and acceptable patterns.[107]

Change is a dislocation of the pattern, a denial of expectation. Some changes are, however, assimilable to experience and there are well-known processes of bolstering and denial that enable us to resist discontinuity and maintain our cognitive balance.[108] Equally, the ways in which we appreciate our circumstances may be sufficiently fluid and flexible to accommodate change without psychological costs.[109] Beyond a certain threshold, however, change creates an unacceptable condition; the mismatch between image and experience generates increasing stress as denial continues.[110] Either we progressively lose touch with the world of our experience, or we manage to achieve a fundamental cognitive realignment.[111] The possibility remains that in certain circumstances stress provides the springs of action; we intervene in our changing world in the hope of restoring a balance between image and experience by attempting to manage the experience itself.[112] Such a theory of intervention, based as it is upon the potency of loss, is of course inherently conservative.[113]

While the managers of organisations do not experience change in their operating environment in an immediate sense, they nevertheless have a sharper need than most to account for their circumstances and to make defensive adaptations. In the special case of public policy-makers, there is also a sense of obligation (admittedly, rather a variable one) actively to intervene in the interests of welfare, howsoever defined. Changing circumstances are not in themselves a signal to intervene, however. Social and economic conditions only become *problems* – and thus calls to action – when they are so construed by policy-makers.

It follows from our earlier argument that problems do not 'arise full-blown, commanding community attention and evoking adequate policies'.[114] For a condition to achieve the status of a problem or issue, it has to undergo a social process in which it is transformed from a condition of unconcern to one of established and continuing presence on the policy agenda of government. It has to achieve recognition and the status of an issue. It is not difficult to recognise this transformation when it occurs, for the very language in which the condition is described undergoes a change. As Solesbury points out, 'water quality describes a situation but water pollution describes an issue, traffic density a situation, traffic congestion an issue. The language of . . . issues revolves around a number of key words like congestion, despoliation, ugliness, decay, pollution, overcrowding'.[115]

This linguistic transformation also marks a distinction between the material condition itself and the way in which it is appreciated by policy-makers: 'every social problem . . . consists of an objective condition and a subjective definition. The objective condition is a verifiable situation which can be checked as to its magnitude . . . by impartial and trained observers . . . The subjective definition is the awareness of certain individuals that the condition is a threat to certain cherished values'.[116]

This analysis draws our attention away from the observable conditions or objective situations to inquire into the processes by which situations come to achieve the status of problems.[117] In particular, the assumptions of those who are in a position to secure recognition for 'their' issues on the policy agenda, the claims which they make and the techniques which they can use for enforcing claims are crucial to the career of a social problem. As Blumer notes, 'many budding social problems are choked off, others are avoided, others have to fight their way to respectable status, and others are rushed along to legitimacy by a strong and influential backing'.[118] Some issues occupy a privileged place on the policy agenda without regard to current circumstances. Other conditions may encounter such obstacles as to be systematically excluded from status as issues claiming 'the right to responsive action'.[119]

The two key variables in determining the fate of the would-be issues are what we have elsewhere termed *the appreciative and organisational contexts of policy*.[120] Let us look first at the appreciative context, the variable set of assumptions within which any one organisation's policies are framed. Any particular condition is capable of an infinitude of possible appreciations and interpretations, for one man's social problem may be the next man's satisfactory situation.[121] Our own portrayal of the ways in which actors make sense of their circumstances recognises this propensity to 'multiple realities'.[122]

On the other hand, within a given organisational setting, there are likely to be only a limited number of plausible accounts competing for legitimacy, as well as a strong drive toward finding a single accepted account. The resolution of this competition 'results from an interaction and conflict between the perceptions and interests of the groups involved'.[123] However, it is often weighted in favour of a stable set of prevailing definitions or (as we have elsewhere termed them) dispositions. The disposition to regard as satisfactory a situation which other participants see as a problem and to resist the shift toward describing it in the language of issues is the most potent obstacle to those seeking to change the agenda of policy. Dispositions

may be best understood as very general and taken-for-granted assumptions about both the facts of a situation and its evaluation. Within a broad corpus of more or less consistent assumptions certain phenomena, relationships, qualities and values are held to be self-evident. Certain other issues, if they present themselves, are held to be undiscussable.[124]

Dispositions, then, establish 'the parameters of credibility'.[125]

Prevailing dispositions may prove more robust than any particular account of a problem, and may continue to shape the pattern of routine decision-making despite the apparent victory of some new issue as embodied in a formal policy statement.[126] The resilience of existing dispositions possibly owes much to the well-documented phenomenon of 'post-decision dissonance'. The need to reduce the psychological costs of decisions (in this case the outcomes forgone by a particular choice) leads decision-makers to seek out consonant or supportive information and avoid or (if it is presented) discount information that does not seem to square with that formal choice.[127] This phenomenon of 'consonance' or 'balance-seeking' provides stability in policy, maintains the appreciative context, and serves to damp down the fluctuations that are engendered by the activities of those participants who seek to change the accepted accounts of the situation in order to redirect policy and action. There is then an inbuilt resistance to change in the appreciative context; authoritative decision-makers tend not to change their minds.

The organisational context also works to favour stability and the maintenance of existing problems which are readily institutionalised within bureaucracies. Beyond a certain threshold, officials have a powerful professional or managerial interest in seeing their favoured issues kept securely on the policy agenda. While in the longer term new issues generate new policies and can lead to the emergence of new professions, stable issues secure prestige and resources for those who are identified with them. In either case, those professionals who can successfully articulate a claim – literally, a *profession* – to the better understanding of an issue[128] come in a real sense to 'own' it, to 'build their lives and careers around it, even to become attached to "their" problem and view anything that threatens to make it disappear or diminish its importance as a threat'.[129]

Against such claims and interests *'policy entrepreneurs'* – the proponents of new problems – struggle.[130] Their marginality to the mainstream of policy demands of them an unusual degree of skill in 'gatecrashing' the policy agenda. Participation in the process of problem definition is limited to those who are in a position to articulate claims and counterclaims as to the key issues facing a community. However, in English urban government the organisational context retains a degree of openness which may account in part for its more developmental style in comparison with Whitehall. The complexity of organisational and inter-organisational networks and the dual channels of political and administrative authority provide the would-be entrepreneurs with multiple routes to the policy agenda. Successful policy entrepreneurs are skilful and strategically-located officers or (perhaps less often) elected councillors who can use the organisational resources at their disposal to secure a place for new issues on the policy agenda. Their accomplishment is to *transform a situation* hitherto regarded with neutrality into an *issue* and a *commitment* to action. However this is not to say that success in this enterprise necessarily implies influence in shaping subsequent particular decision outcomes. That, paradoxically, requires a different, and more formalised, variety of organisational power. Yet policy entrepreneurs, if sufficiently motivated and resourceful, can shift the frame of reference within which specific decisions are taken.[131]

We argued in the preceding section of this chapter that change in the external circumstances of actors tends to be discounted until a critical threshold is reached beyond which cognitive adjustment or active intervention may occur. This marked discontinuity or 'step function' in human appreciation is reflected in the organisational politics of problem redefinition. A hitherto accepted account of a problem is succeeded by another as a group of policy entrepreneurs bring off a successful *coup*.

Such events are, however, only the turning points in policy development which is not only episodic but also continuous. Having achieved recognition, a new issue continues its career in a sequence of further elaborations. We can hardly improve on the sketch of this process offered by Bossard in some remarks published in 1941. Bossard argued that following the initial recognition of a situation as problematic, initial interventions are usually 'intuitively arrived at, often ill-advised, prompted by the "well, let's do something folks" '. This stage is followed by a successful demand for more careful – and possibly survey-based – appraisal. A change in participants occurs at this point, and policy then proceeds on the basis of some new account of the basic problem factors. Further refinements of programmes and concepts are brought about and similarly bring about further changes in personnel. From this iterative process follow further adaptations and refinements of the basic issues which action is intended to address.[132] Bossard's portrayal of the progressive redefinition of problems through action, monitoring and intelligence, drawing in successive cohorts of new participants, broadly corresponds with the observable realities of organisational life. Policies and problems are stable but not static and are subject to successive elaborations.

How, finally, do changing circumstances set off this complex process of organisational adjustment? As we have depicted the process, the redefinition of issues is unlikely to begin at the top of the hierarchy, where prevailing dispositions make for issue stability. Such dispositions are not of course immune to exogenous change, the most common form of which is the displacement of one group of leaders by another as a result of the electoral process. A particular regime – in the sense of a set of institutionalised dispositions – may none the less survive a succession of parties and the stability of the top officials tends towards such continuity.[133] Accordingly, the more common threat to established policy is that posed by the web of entrepreneurs in the middle ranks of the organisation, where creative energy has yet to be tempered by the rewards of routinised power. But while issues may be promoted as claims to action at this level they have often originated at the field or operational level itself.

The changing realities of urban dynamics are sensed first by planning, education, housing, highways or valuation officials through their involvement in day-to-day operations. They are in an unrivalled position to monitor the disjunctures between existing policy commitments and real world change, and are the first to feel the discomfort of maintaining stable images in changing circumstances. Moreover, early adaptations to policy in the wake of the recognition of a new issue are first monitored by those who operate the policy. Unintended consequences and areas of oversight come initially into their view. Operational officials are the first onto the learning curve and their access to new experience enables them to control and shape the learning of their superiors.[134]

While it may seem counterintuitive to suggest that this might be the case, it is no more than a departure from hierarchical habits of thought engendered by classical theories of organisation, habits that support an often unquestioned notion of a downward flow from 'policy' to 'implementation'.[135] In the relatively fluid and multiplex forms of urban government in England, the pressure for policy adaptation in the face of changing external circumstances may come as often from the periphery as from the centre of the organisation.

Implications
The relationship between the world of material circumstance and the 'assumptive world' of interpreted experience is an indeterminate one.

Experiencing and the creation of meaning are private processes, publicly conducted. It is no easy matter to enter the assumptive worlds of others. While individuals' material conditions are accessible, the significance attributed to them remains elusive to interviews, observation, simulation or even the most sophisticated techniques for the 'measurement of meaning'.[136]

If meaning is elusive, so too is the propensity to act for, as we have argued, action is but the expression of intention and purpose. It can be understood but not explained; it can be reconstructed but not predicted.[137] It can be interpreted, but the action we interpret itself derives from the actor's own interpretations of his own circumstances. Imaginative identification with policy-makers – what Money-Kyrle termed the anthropomorphic approach of empathising with the actor's experience – is required.[138]

The major pitfall of interpretive policy analysis, as of all interpretive social science, is to concentrate upon 'the actor's point of view' to the exclusion of the real world in which he is located and by which he is constrained. Any account of how policy-makers 'make sense of circumstances' must also establish what those circumstances are. Our foremost concern in this study is with the *process* by which change in material circumstances – in particular the far-reaching de-industrialisation of cities – is taken account of in the formal policies of city governments. We begin, then, with those circumstances, looking first at the patterns or urban change in the advanced industrial countries of the West before turning to examine the forces making for decline of the manufacturing cities of England, and of London in particular.

3 The Urban Exodus

IN this chapter we provide a broad-brush description of recent urban economic change. We consider some of the more salient aspects of change in the structure of the 'space economy', that is, change in the organisation of economic activity upon a spatial surface.[1] The structure of the space economy at any one point in time refers to a territorial division of labour and capital. We know that at an *international* level the world's economic system is undergoing rapid changes, and is restructuring to the potential disadvantage of the older industrial nations, and of Britain in particular. The vehicle, shipping and electrical consumer goods industries offer just three examples of change at this level. Restructuring also operates at an *inter-regional* level, manifested in the US in the shift 'from Snow Belt to Sun Belt' and in the UK, for example, in the perhaps analogous shifts to the high amenity regions of the south-west and East Anglia. The space economy is also changing at the *urban* level, with suburban and fringe growth and the desolation of what we loosely term 'the inner city'.

Here we attempt to summarise some of these structural changes, in particular reviewing the evidence for the proposition that the decline of the older industrial cities is part of an international trend towards population decentralisation and towards non-metropolitan growth, a trend that has been rather dramatically dubbed 'counter-urbanisation', and which amounts to a reversal of long-held expectations of the urban future.[2] The assumption that urban change follows a unilinear path towards greater concentration arose in past years of rapid growth. 'Urban problems' were viewed as the (temporary) costs of agglomeration itself. As early as 1901 it was feared that London would stretch from the Solent to the Wash, a fear that underlay the planning debates of the middle decades of this century.[3] Urbanisation in the north-east US lagged behind the British experience, but soon caught and surpassed it, and the assumption was the same: progression towards Megalopolis, impeded only by the relative costs of location and the politics of containment.[4]

In the US, analysis of the 1970 Census and later Current Population Reports of the US Bureau of the Census shattered that assumption. Something had happened during the 1960s and early 1970s that was to transform urban expectations and, to a lesser degree, urban politics. It was a turning-point. As Berry put it:

To those who wrote about nineteenth- and early twentieth-century industrial urbanisation, the essence was size, density and heterogeneity in an atmosphere of continuing growth. 'Urbanisation is a process of population concentration' wrote Hope Tisdale in 1942. 'It implies a movement from a state of less concentration to a state of more concentration.' But since 1970 American Metropolitan regions have grown less rapidly than the nation and have actually lost population to non-metropolitan territory. A new low-slung, far-flung pattern is emerging as we move from a state of more concentration to a state of less concentration, i.e. as a process of *counter-urbanisation* runs its course.[5]

While the source of this, as of so many images of the future, is rooted in North American experience, there is evidence that the process is a more general one. These indications have prompted the hypothesis (which we consider further below) that some of the more advanced industrial nations are experiencing a new stage in what might be termed the 'life cycle of the manufacturing metropolis'. If this is indeed the case, then the experience of urban change in the US may contain significant pointers for the future of cities in other parts of the world. In the following section we look at aspects of change in the US space economy, first reviewing the shifts away from the metropolitan regions of the north-east and north-central states, and the recent phenomenon of peripheral growth, then going on to examine changes in metropolitan structure. We consider the implications for the central cities of this movement towards decentralisation. We review the general evidence for the proposition that non-metropolitan growth is an international trend and consider some of the implications of this for Britain, going on briefly to discuss some of the developments in the search for a satisfactory explanation of these trends.

Changes in US metropolitan structure

From Snow Belt to Sun Belt
There is no doubt that the US has recently experienced inter-regional shifts of both population and economic activity away from the north-east and north-central states to those of the south and west.[6] In an era of steadily decreasing population growth, with declining birth-rates throughout the US, inter-regional migration has become the most important factor in population redistribution. Since 1955, net migration has accounted for an increasing share of the population gain in the growing regions of the south and west. As Weinstein and Firestine point out,

the migration gains in the South are largely the result of net outmigration from the North East and North Central regions. Between 1970 and 1975, nearly a million more persons left the North East for the South than moved [in] the opposite direction.[7]

Population change, though significant in its patterns, is the least dramatic of the indicators. The disparities are highlighted by employment change between 1960 and 1975 when there was relatively low growth (21.7 per cent) in the north-east states and buoyant growth (around 70 per cent) in the south and west.[8]

The wider recognition of the magnitude and pace of the inter-regional shifts in American demography and in economic life owes much to Sternlieb and Hughes who, in characteristically racy manner, outlined the 'monumental' changes in the US space economy. 'A very powerful momentum has built up over the past fifteen years, sweeping employment and population growth away from the older metropolitan centres of the North East and North Central states to the newer growth poles of the South and West.'[9] Basing their observations on Census Bureau and Department of Labor statistics, they chart the hitherto 'unnoticed . . . long term downward slide' of 'the industrial belt from Boston to St. Louis' and the rise of centres in the so-called Sun Belt states.

Figure 3.1   *Percentage change in manufacturing employment, real personal income and retail sales, United States, 1960–1975*

Region	Change manufacturing employment	Change real personal income	Change retail sales
	per cent	*per cent*	*per cent*
New England	−9.0	65.5	162
Mid-East	−13.7	57.8	132
Great Lakes	3.2	65.1	154
Plains	24.0	70.5	144
Rocky Mountains	45.6	93.2	130
Far West	19.8	89.7	193
South-West	67.3	105.8	246
South-East	43.3	114.3	254
US average	9.2	77.5	n/a

Source: Compiled from various tables in *Business Week*, 17 May 1976, pp. 93, 104.

Changes in the location of manufacturing industry and, more recently, in services, have been particularly striking, and Norton and Rees summarise them as follows. The northern industrial region, or 'core' area,

entered a period of relative industrial decline after World War II, a decline which became absolute in character after 1969. Between 1966 and 1977, virtually every state in the core lost manufacturing employment. In the aggregate, the core region lost 1.7 million industrial jobs, against 700,000 gained in the periphery – including not only the Sun Belt, but also the Mountains, Plains and Far West. Moreover, contrasts in state growth have been amplified by corresponding changes in tertiary employment.[10]

Figure 3.1, showing a breakdown by area for manufacturing employment, for real personal incomes and for retail sales, illuminates the situation. Other indicators, among them unionisation rates, tax indices and living costs, support this general picture of regional differentials. The effects of the regional changes seem to be cumulative. A *Business Week* special report summarised the processes underlying this new 'War between the States':

Once under way, the process of migration gathers momentum that becomes self-sustaining. The migration itself shifts incomes, spelling accelerated market growth in the favoured region. As new markets spring up, the region begins to attract a broad array of industries – from manufacturing to all its financial, advertising, wholesale, printing and other support services. The rapid growth of taxable economic activity ensures adequate resources for maintaining or even increasing public services without increases in the tax rates. As people and companies realise this, the lure of the fast growing regions intensifies.[11]

The notion of the Sun Belt as a distinct regional entity extending across the entire southern half of the US and containing the areas of fastest growth has been called into question:

The Sun Belt is now a part of the American vocabulary. The term has been eagerly embraced by the media, it appears in corporate reports which tout the advantage of doing business in the Sun Belt, it has increasingly been accepted by the academic community, and it has become a symbol of regional favoritism to some Northerners. All of this has occurred quite recently and without any serious discussion of the adequacy of the Sun Belt as a valid or useful regional entity.[12]

A careful review of the evidence suggests that the Sun Belt does not emerge as a distinct geographical region, and that the greatest differences are not between north and south as the second 'War between the States' would suggest, but between east and west. Yet the critics conclude, somewhat ruefully, that 'we may quarrel with the delimitation of the Sun Belt, question its homogeneity, and caution against the often misleading impression the term conveys, but no matter. It is a notion whose time has come. The Sun Belt has become fixed in the minds of many Americans; the image is the reality'.[13]

The urbanising suburbs

The inter-regional shifts obscure what is happening *within* metropolitan areas, for here the central cities have been experiencing a steady loss of population relative to the suburbs for some time. Throughout the 1960s the suburbs grew in enumerated population terms at more than five times the rate of the central cities,[14] while the basis of enumeration probably understated the even greater real disparities.[15] By 1970 more than half of America's population lived outside the central cities and close to three-quarters of the nation's population growth was generated there. Moreover, by the mid-1970s many central cities were seen to be experiencing *absolute* population decline for the first time, those of the 20 largest metropolitan areas losing an estimated 1.2 million people between 1970 and 1974.[16]

Not only has population decentralised, so too has economic activity. In general, the absolute decline in employment opportunities in the central cities is observed to occur later than a similar decline in population, and writers have tended to see this phase in the evolution of metropolitan spatial structure in two distinct parts. Yet there is little doubt that the two processes are closely connected and become mutually reinforcing.[17] For example, evidence that the redistribution of employment opportunities leads to further population shifts has been provided by a number of writers. Hecht examined the changing residential location of employees as a result of the movement of industrial firms from the central area to the urban periphery of Worcester, Massachusetts and found that the movement of firms tended to encourage employees to find homes nearer to the new work locations, even though the firms' moves were frequently of only a few miles.[18] Muller's work reinforces these findings. 'Much . . . intra-metropolitan population dispersal can . . . be attributed to the suburbanisation of economic activity, especially employment opportunities. The deconcentration of these activities appears to be one of the strongest forces in sustaining the current urbanisation of the suburbs.'[19]

The exodus of manufacturing has attracted particular attention. High land values and tax rates, transportation difficulties, shortages of skilled labour and problems of obsolete premises are among those factors which have tended to push manufacturing out of the city, while inter-firm linkages have tended to maintain a centripetal pull. It is none the less apparent that many industries have become less dependent on traditional location factors, and that technological changes, particularly those affecting transport, have led to an 'evaporation' of the advantages of central locations and a more rapid decentralisation to suburban sites.[20] Moreover, it has been argued that the rise of the industrial suburbs is due in part to self-generated growth, the significance of migration having been overestimated because of the tendency of high growth firms to concentrate their subsequent investment there.[21]

Nor is this process confined to the movement of manufacturing, for the advantages of suburban locations become cumulative also for offices and for retailing. The original prestige and linkage attractions of the CBD, previously of overriding importance in determining the location of offices, become less crucial, at least for the more routine functions, than such factors as the improved quality of life that the suburbs have to offer to young executive staff. In retailing, there has been a period of rapid 'take-off' during the 1960s in the previously gradual process of suburbanisation 'with the recognition of the full economic potential of the suburban market place, increasingly settled by the more affluent segment of the metropolitan population'.[22]

While explanations of the industrialisation and commercialisation of the suburbs tend to be couched largely in economic terms, suburban governments are also playing a part in the process. Traditionally, residential suburbs have restricted the growth of economic activities, but Logan, in a rare but welcome discussion of the social organisation of growth, pointed to the profitability of industrialisation for real estate developers, local businesses and residents and found that there are actually remarkably few instances of continuing suburban resistance because this is something that only the most affluent areas can afford.[23]

The urbanisation of the suburbs represents a new economic independence which undercuts the classic model of the monocentric city. So widespread has been the process in metropolitan areas of the US that old stereotypes – the dormitory suburbs, the CBD – are no longer appropriate. As economic activities gravitate towards each other in the new suburban location, new nodes of activity or 'mini-cities' are emerging to confer a greater degree of spatial order on the distribution of production in the suburbs. There has been 'a shift from the tightly-focused single-core urban region of the past to the widely-dispersed multi-nodal metropolis of today'.[24] In the US, the trend towards the suburbanisation of industry, offices and retailing, towards suburban population and employment growth – in sum toward a more dynamic suburban economy – are mutually sustaining and may be expected to continue.

Decentralisation and urban decline
Closely linked to these trends towards decentralisation are the problems of the central cities, where 'rising costs and static incomes',[25] and a basic 'lack of economic value'[26] describe the predicament of both the cities and the citizens. The social and economic effects of the outward movement have been considerable, not least because of the selective nature of outmigration from central cities. The younger, more able and more affluent have tended to move out, while a poorer, less skilled and increasingly dependent population has remained. One of the effects of selective migration has been to lower *per capita* incomes, reducing the purchasing power of central city residents by almost 30 billion dollars in the brief period between 1970 and 1974.[27] It is not surprising that in a study of unemployment, dependency, education, income, housing and

poverty in 55 of the United States' largest cities, Nathan and Dommel found a very close relationship between population decline and an income-related measure of hardship.[28]

Further, a great deal of attention has been focused on changes in the racial mix of US cities and suburbs. As Cameron has commented, for example, 'Discrimination in the private owner-occupied sector and a poorly-developed public housing sector meant that very few . . . blacks were able to find a house in suburban areas. In contrast, the wealthier whites flowed out of the central city'.[29] Changes in purchasing power are closely associated with this selective population movement for in central cities white populations have declined faster than black, and black incomes are roughly 60 per cent of white.[30]

The selective outmigration of population from the central cities achieves further significance when set against changes in economic activity and employment. In certain metropolitan areas the number of jobs lost to the central city during the 1960s exceeded those lost over the previous six decades. Levels of unemployment now tend to be much higher in central cities than in metropolitan areas generally. Unemployment also has a racial dimension, with higher rates amongst non-white groups, although these racial differences have recently been obscured by the national economic recession and by the accelerating loss of employment opportunities as firms have migrated or closed.

Of particular consequence for urban governments has been the decline in the tax base resulting from the outward movement of population and economic activity at a time when central city populations are becoming increasingly dependent on government aid, and a large literature now exists on this topic alone.[31] As more residents and businesses move to the suburbs, the city's tax base is driven down and, as US urban governments are heavily dependent on local funds, property or other taxes must be increased to compensate, thus (it is argued) causing more people and firms to leave.

The most rapid rates of urban decline, and the severest social and fiscal problems, are displayed by the older north-eastern cities. A specific example from New York illustrates the wider problems:

The surface cause of the financial problems of New York is the 542,000 jobs lost in the central city between 1969 and 1976, a rate of job loss that was twice that of the preceding seven year period. For each job lost, the city loses between $651 and $1035 in tax revenues, and if the jobs that disappeared during the 1970s were providing tax income for the city there would be no financial crisis. The real, or sub-surface, causes of the crisis are the forces that give rise to the migration of people and jobs from the central cities to the suburbs, non-metropolitan parts of the urban regions, and to other parts of the nation.[32]

To summarise, the US has experienced major changes in long-established patterns of movement: the net movement from the north and central states to the Sun Belt and, at the urban level, from central cities to suburbs. With these changes has come an increasing catalogue of problems for the central cities. These may be seen as but a few aspects of a more general process of metropolitan to non-metropolitan movement. In Hall and Hay's terms, urban growth is passing not only from older, industrialised and urbanised regions dominated by manufacturing to newly industrialising and urbanising regions dominated by service industry and outwards within metropolitan areas from cores to rings, but also 'downwards through the urban hierarchy from larger to smaller urban systems' and 'outwards . . . from urban to rural areas'.[33] In particular, much of the new growth is occurring in small places, with lower population densities and high amenity value.

In the following section we go on to examine evidence from a number of countries that the linked processes of metropolitan decline and non-metropolitan growth are not unique to the US, but are occurring elsewhere, and that they may be part of an international trend towards 'counter-urbanisation'.

International trends
As Hall and Hay note, no other country has produced systematic analysis of change in the urban system on quite the American scale.[34] However, a number of writers, particularly those associated with the International Institute for Applied Systems Analysis (IIASA) at Laxenburg, Austria, have in recent years produced a great volume of comparative information.

Canadian experience provides an interesting comparison with that of the US, for although Canada logically forms an extension of the US urban system (and indeed Yeates has chosen to link the two and to examine urban development in North America as a whole),[35] there are a number of differences in the observed patterns. Internal migration in Canada has 'shifted away from the . . . major metropolitan areas . . . toward medium-sized cities and to smaller centres just outside the metropolitan region',[36] and later analysis of the 1976 Census shows more dramatic changes in population dispersal as the rural areas, which formerly experienced net outmigration, gained population for the first time.[37] There was substantial growth in Canada's small towns and villages during this period, attributable to both the suburbanising effect of metropolitan development and the movement of population to towns and villages well beyond the metropolitan orbit.[38]

Yet there is no consensus that Canada is experiencing 'counter-urbanisation' on the US pattern. Rather, Bourne and Logan stress that trends in Canada have been remarkably similar to those in Australia, with considerable movement of population from major urban centres, but continued metropolitan growth resulting from the high rates of foreign immigration.[39] This, together with the pursuit of more inter-ventionist urban policies, has meant that the problems of central cities tend to be those of congestion rather than stagnation or decay. Also, the racial dimension, so striking in US cities, is much less marked in those of Canada and Australia.

Despite the differences, Hall and Hay are of the opinion that the Canadian and Australian trends broadly reflect those operating in the US. Such differences as are apparent, and notably the continued via-bility of the inner city, are attributed to 'the relatively late development of the space economy of the two countries, and its still less mature evolution'.[40] This view also finds support in Little and Carter's study of Melbourne. They conclude that 'the processes which have been described as impacting upon US cities are likely to be experienced here. The only reason they have not been felt more markedly to date is the lag in the development process between Australia and the United States'.[41]

Similar assumptions are used to explain the somewhat different trends observed in Japan.[42] Here, high concentration of population and economic activity is still evident, although since 1970 there have been signs of decentralisation within the largest metropolitan zones as sub-urban growth has begun to exceed that in central city areas. Vining and Kontuly refer to 'a sudden and precipitous drop in net migration into Japan's three major metropolitan regions', and a corresponding rise in net migration into peripheral regions, including the islands, during the mid-1970s.[43] Reviewing some of the work on Japan, Hall and Hay note 'the slowing down of the rate of increase in the largest cities, the growth of medium-sized cities near to major centres and even of medium-sized cities in more rural areas', and draw the inference that 'all these trends suggest that increasingly Japan will come to resemble North America . . . Japan's urban evolution has simply been later'.[44]

There is a growing body of research evidence on population and employment trends in other parts of the world. Vining and Kontuly, in their comparative study of population trends in 18 countries, conclude that in several European nations (Hungary, Finland, Spain and Poland) the major metropolitan regions are still gaining in population, while in Third World countries generally the concentration of population con-tinues apace.[45] Despite the data difficulties which seem bound to occur in such an exercise,[46] and despite Vining and Kontuly's reluctance to attempt any causal explanation for their findings ('we prefer to let the facts stand by themselves, unadorned by theoretical discussion'),[47] their study succeeds in pointing to certain regularities in the process of population movement away from the major core regions in the other countries studied, and in western Europe in particular.

Change in Europe has, on the whole, been less well and less evenly documented than that in North America, particularly because 'the statistical base for this analysis is nationally fragmented, with very different geographical data collection units, with data that vary in amount and range and quality, and even with different Census dates'.[48] Following Vining and Kontuly's efforts, more detailed research material has recently been amassed by members of the European Urban Systems Study Team (based jointly at the University of Reading and at IIASA), in addressing themselves specifically to the question of how far European trends follow the North American pattern.[49]

Until 1970, Europe presented a most varied picture, failing to demonstrate a general tendency towards decentralisation on the American model, yet experiencing a movement of population from cores to rings in some metropolitan areas. There was a change in the early 1970s when the process of decentralisation within metropolitan areas accelerated, but there remain important differences between one part of Europe and another.

The decentralisation of population is most marked in the larger urban areas of the British Isles, West Germany, Switzerland, Austria and the Low Countries. In the Netherlands, for example, the three largest cities – Amsterdam, Rotterdam and The Hague – together lost about 110,000 people to suburban locations between 1971 and 1974. In Scandinavia these trends have been rather less apparent. In Sweden and France, as in Canada and Australia, foreign immigration into the major metropolitan areas remains strong, bolstering the position of these largest cities, but in France there has also been a marked growth in non-metropolitan areas. Southern European experience appears at first completely to contradict that of the US, with continued centralisation, at least until the late 1960s. Again, however, the 1970s brought something of a change, and while the metropolitan cores continued to grow, the 'rate of core growth dramatically slowed, and the rings by this time were growing twice as fast'.[50] There was then little evidence of a transfer of people back to the remoter rural areas.

European employment trends are more difficult to ascertain, but the available evidence for the early 1970s suggested that employment decentralisation was not especially marked, at least in mainland Europe, and an important feature was the continued strength of Europe's industrial heartland, in contrast to that of the United States. 'It appears that only in Britain – and to a limited degree in the Franco-German coalfield and the Ruhrgebiet – is there more serious evidence of the decline of the older industrial-urban regions.'[51]

These conclusions should now be re-examined in the light of fresh evidence. In Italy, for example, there are tentative indications of a reversal in rural-urban migration as the southern immigrants of the 1960s return home from the stagnating 'industrial triangle' of the north between Genoa, Turin and Milan.[52] Recent evidence on migration trends in western Europe has been carefully reviewed by Fielding. He concludes that neither western Europe as a whole, nor any country in western Europe, has made the simple straightforward change from a situation in which net migration is positively correlated with settlement size (in other words, in which a process of spatial agglomeration is in operation) to the reverse, in which net migration and settlement size are inversely correlated. Nevertheless, he concludes that 'there is enough evidence of change in the patterns of migration to assert that urbanisation has ceased in most of Western Europe and that counter-urbanisation is in the process of emerging as the dominant force'.[53] It is in Britain that the most recent evidence suggests the new attraction of the countryside and the freestanding towns beyond the metropolitan rings. It seems that here, at least, non-metropolitan growth on the American pattern may become a significant feature of the space economy during the 1980s.

The British experience

At an urban level, the British evidence largely arises from work carried out by Hall and his colleagues,[54] and extended by Drewett, Goddard, Spence and their research team in their investigation of urban change in Britain.[55]

A central task in these studies has been the derivation of a satisfactory functional definition of urban areas, one that allows both the description of major trends and a comparison with US studies, and in this they have made use of the concept of the urban field or daily urban system. Their analysis is based upon labour areas of two sizes, first, on a number of Standard Metropolitan Labour Areas, each a core plus metropolitan ring, intended to reflect the spatial extent of a local labour market, and secondly on Metropolitan Economic Labour Areas, in each the total urban system centring on a particular area and consisting of SMLA plus outer metropolitan ring.

The dominant trend which their work reveals has been one of accelerating population decentralisation, initially (in the 1950s) from urban cores to suburban locations within commuting hinterlands, then, in the 1960s, to outer metropolitan rings with relatively weak links with urban cores. Thus, through a period of two decades, 'the frontier of most active population change has moved progressively from the urban cores'.[56] While the cores grew slowly during the 1950s, in the 1960s their relative decline was transformed into an absolute decline.

In the case of employment, we find that the pattern is repeated after a time lag, so that during the 1960s employment too reversed its relative movement and began to decentralise outward – thus following the population trend.[57] The 1960s presented a great contrast to the previous decade and while core areas as a whole lost almost ½ million jobs, metropolitan rings greatly increased their share of employment, while the outer rings showed modest gains which reversed the previous pattern of employment concentration; 'overall a process of metropolitan decentralisation of jobs in the late 1960s can be clearly detected'.[58]

As in the American case, the fortunes of individual cities and indeed whole regions have varied widely. Generally, the largest metropolitan areas have experienced the largest declines of both population and employment, and the strength of this negative relationship has increased over time, thrown into sharp relief by the continuing fall in the birth-rate. Greater London lost 472,000 people, over 6 per cent of its population, during the six years 1971-77 alone. Merseyside lost 92,000, or 5.6 per cent. Greater Manchester and the West Midlands each lost around 60,000, or just over 2 per cent.[59]

Preliminary results of the 1981 Census of Population suggest that every large city has suffered further substantial population losses; in fact, 'the bigger the city the bigger the loss'.[60] In England the largest percentage decrease was for inner London, about 18 per cent. Manchester, Liverpool and Birmingham each lost between 90,000 and 100,000 people, declines of 17, 16 and 18 per cent respectively. Scottish cities suffered similar dramatic changes, and in Glasgow the population dropped by 22 per cent between 1971 and 1981, from 982, 317 to 763, 162.

Figure 3.2   *Percentage population and employment change by urban zone, Great Britain, 1951–1961 and 1961–1971*

	Population change		Employment change	
	1951–61	1961–71	1951–61	1961–71
Urban cores	+1.88	−2.77	+6.72	−3.06
Metropolitan rings	+13.33	+17.17	+6.33	+15.04
Outer rings	+3.13	+9.76	−0.43	+3.91
GB total	+4.97	+4.95	+5.06	+1.69

Source: Compiled from Drewett, Goddard and Spence, *Urban Change in Britain*, p. 52.

These trends are not limited to the conurbations. In the non-metropolitan districts, all but one of those containing large cities showed a decrease, the largest being about 10 per cent for, respectively, Bristol, Nottingham and Portsmouth. Smaller cities were less susceptible to the decline, some of them, including, for example, Durham, Gloucester and Norwich, showing small increases rather than decreases and, as was to be expected, the New Towns continued to grow, in fact experiencing the largest population gains of all. Milton Keynes, for example, showed an increase of 85 per cent. The case of the urban centres of the south-east region is particularly illuminating. While the commercial centres around London (like Reading, Crawley and South-end) have continued to grow, this growth has not been big enough to compensate for the capital's total loss of 756,000 people, and the south-east has therefore suffered a net decline in population of about 1.2 per cent. In general, however, the percentage gains in population were not in cities at all, but in the non-metropolitan areas, and it is readily apparent that the pattern of decline and growth is heavily dependent on the location of the largest urban concentrations.

At a regional level, until the early 1970s the established population trends in Britain were relative losses from the northern regions, Scotland, Wales and Northern Ireland, and relative gains in the Midlands and southern regions. Since then there has been a shift in the pattern of migration away from the 'drift to the south-east' in favour of a new pattern of losses from the core and gains in the marginal regions.[61] The 1981 Census has revealed that the most rapidly growing regions between 1971 and 1981 were Wales, with a net gain of 2.2 per cent, the south-west, which has grown by 6 per cent, and East Anglia with an increase of as much as 11.7 per cent. It is striking that these are the three regions which do not contain metropolitan counties. In fact it is the more remote and largely rural districts – a sort of British Sun Belt – that have experienced the largest net immigrations.

OPCS confirm that the remoter rural districts experienced faster growth in the period 1971-1981 than they did during the previous decade; in other words, there was an 'upward shift' in the pattern of population change in those areas:

In some cases, upward shifts may be a further expression of looser urban structures identified during the two decades before 1971: smaller centres on the fringes of metropolitan areas gained jobs and population in the 1960s while the metropolitan cores declined. During the 1970s places more distant from the cores enjoyed the growth – a characteristic now labelled 'counter-urbanisation'.[62]

OPCS are careful to caution those commentators who might interpret these findings as evidence of 'a rush to the country'. They point out that, in terms of *absolute* numbers, the gains in the remote rural areas are modest compared with those in the areas of planned growth such as the New Towns, and on the outer margins of the main urban centres. They doubt whether a growth rate of about 10 per cent over ten years can be truly described as a 'rush', and remind us that growth may be due just as much to a reduced outward flow of migrants as to a greater inward flow. Significantly, however, they go on to conclude that 'there are indications that, when the more local and detailed results of the census are analysed, population growth in the main will be strongly associated with the smaller towns and accessible settlements in the countryside – the areas most suited to economic growth in recent years'.[63]

In several respects the British urban system differs markedly from that of the US,[64] yet the similarities in their recent experience are becoming more and more striking. In Britain, as in the US, the forces for decentralisation so apparent during the 1970s have been linked with accelerated decline of the central areas of the largest cities. Migration has been highly selective, and the central city areas have come to be populated increasingly by those who do not have the option to leave.[65] As we go on to discuss in later chapters, there has been a massive loss in employment, particularly in manufacturing. Overall, the seven British conurbations lost about 700,000 jobs between 1961 and 1971, and over 80 per cent of this loss was caused by a fall in manufacturing employment.[66]

Central city problems are not reduced as a result of population and employment decline. The associated fall in the tax base has been accompanied by the need to maintain the social and physical infrastructure of the central areas.[67] Public services cannot necessarily be scaled down to match a declining population since many services are provided in indivisible units.[68] There are indeed strong indications that 'the era of the central city dominating its hinterland is undoubtedly over; the cities of the Victorians, like their seaside piers, are lingering artefacts, and the pains of change remain'.[69]

Metropolitan to non-metropolitan growth: the search for explanation

Today's urban policy problems are now recognised as originating in the enormous structural changes in the British space economy.[70] To demonstrate the processes of suburban and peripheral growth in the space economy and the associated problems experienced by the central cities, and to highlight the parallels on an international plane, is no difficult task given the wealth of data presented by a number of commentators. To explain them is a very different matter. The processes have clearly been in operation for some time, but their recognition has been recent and there is considerable debate as to how they are to be interpreted. Some writers see the difficulties of explanation largely in terms of data shortages; others consider that the answers to the questions raised by non-metropolitan growth will require more than statistics and are more concerned with problems of theory-building.[71]

Initial efforts at explanation have concentrated on population change, and two main schools of thought, largely arising from work carried out in the US, are evident. The first interprets these recent developments simply as a continuation of past trends, 'a continued wave of urban decentralisation'[72] from inner cities to suburbs and from suburbs to adjacent non-metropolitan areas, powered by the forces of urban growth. Renewed rural growth is noted, but not held to be overly important. The other school places much greater emphasis on 'rural revival', and holds that the changes amount to a reversal of past trends – 'a "clean break" in the traditional pattern of rural-to-urban migration dominant since the Industrial Revolution', now reversed 'as Americans move in increasing numbers from the metropolitan areas to quite remote, sparsely populated rural areas'.[73] While it is tempting to argue that the so-called 'clean break debate' represents a digression from more important issues,[74] it has served to emphasise the search for explanation of the observed patterns, a search which has assumed further importance since it has become apparent that the changes taking place in the US are not specific to that nation, but have parallels elsewhere in the world, particularly in Europe.[75]

There are currently several competing explanations of these changes.[76] For example, there is the simple view that the observed changes may be no more than the artefacts of inappropriate boundary locations, as metropolitan fields have spread beyond their censal limits. Equally simply, non-metropolitan growth has been held to be at least partly due to an upsurge of interest in outdoor recreation. More significantly, there is a growing tendency for the increasing numbers of elderly people in the population, some returning to their places of origin, to seek pleasant, low-cost environments in which to live, especially as sources of retirement income are no longer tied to specific locations. On the other hand, increased investment in environmental conservation, and also in resource exploitation, in the more sparsely populated areas may be a major contributory factor. Government departments, military installations and universities have continued to provide a basis for growth in service employment in some of the more remote places.

One further factor seems to be cited with increasing frequency. 'To a degree we do not know, hard economic times in the 1970s have encouraged people to return to more rural environments to weather personal economic difficulties.'[77] Current trends have been likened to those of the 1930s when many areas of the US which had previously lost population showed a period of growth, 'a measure of the greater unemployment and depression in the city than in the home county'.[78] Hall and Hay also consider this worthy of discussion, and they note that the return migration to Italy's Mezzogiorno, brought to light in their analysis of changes between 1970 and 1975, 'offers a foretaste of what could happen if a prolonged recession were to limit job opportunities in the larger industrial cities of Europe'.[79] Common to many lines of explanation such as these is a concern with the images and preferences of migrants, both demographic and economic. Thus some writers claim to have identified a rural renaissance, 'a movement in search of amenity and easy living, even at the expense of an obvious economic base and a good money income; truly a post-industrial phenomenon'.[80] With some caricature, others ask 'Is the city now vanquished, its vanity crushed in the dust, while the homely and steady virtues of the country begin to reap their just rewards?'[81]

The less speculative, if unromantic, explanations are couched largely in economic terms, and link population movements very closely with changes in industry and employment, pointing up such contemporary developments as the emergence of nationally integrated societies, in which movement is relatively easy; the increasing role of communications rather than transport in locational choice and the emergence of a post-industrial economy.[82] These are clearly unilinear developments, and Hall and Hay accordingly suggest that 'all industrial nations fit somewhere on to a path of urban evolution, but at very different points along it'.[83] They envisage four stages in the development of the urban system in any industrial nation. Population first concentrates into metropolitan areas and centralises within them. Secondly, concentration continues but decentralisation of people begins in the larger metropolitan areas. Thirdly, 'the outward movement of people begins to wash outside metropolitan area boundaries while jobs too begin to move out with a time-lag effect. Finally, metropolitan areas (particularly the larger and older ones) tend as a whole to stagnate and decay, as people and jobs move out to the inter-metropolitan peripheries'.[84]

The main differences between countries in terms of urbanisation patterns are held to be related to the stage of industrial and urban evolution reached by those countries. According to this model, the US is the first nation to reach 'stage four', and it has been suggested that the British space economy is also rapidly entering the final stage as the postulated time-lag between US and British urban phenomena becomes shorter. We suggest that the primary value of this essentially descriptive (and arguably tautological) model lies in drawing attention to the fundamental shifts which are occurring in the pattern of economic activity, and, in particular, changes in manufacturing activity, for the model is essentially one of *the life-cycle of the manufacturing metropolis*.

The life-cycle thesis does not, however, identify the nature of the dynamic forces which produce the evident pattern. Fielding's analysis, firmly rooted in a discussion of economic and industrial changes, goes a stage further, and comes to the specific conclusion that counter-urbanisation in western European countries (and indeed in the other countries of the world in which this phenomenon is occurring – the US and Canada in particular) is to be seen as a stage in the development of the mature capitalist society:

> From this perspective, counter-urbanisation is seen as a product of the rapid deindustrialisation of the largest cities and old industrial regions . . . of Western Europe, accompanied by a stabilisation of rural population levels following the long process of 'restructuring' in agriculture, and by a growth of manufacturing in small and medium-sized towns in rural and peripheral regions.[85]

In particular, 'firms have acted as the major agents of change in the distribution of population' and are 'the principal generators of counter-urbanisation'.[86] It is then to a more detailed consideration of recent changes in manufacturing firms in metropolitan locations that we now turn.

4 Change and the Manufacturing Metropolis

OF the several aspects of metropolitan decline in Britain, none has been so striking, nor has attracted so much attention, as the decline of manufacturing industry. Manufacturing decline, seen as part of a complex process of 'de-industrialisation', has a prominent place in official diagnoses of British economic problems.[1] At the urban level, falling employment in manufacturing industry is seen as one of the major causes of the 'inner city crisis',[2] while according to Keeble, the significance of manufacturing industry for regional policy 'can scarcely be overestimated'; from the 1920s to the present time, 'politicians and regional planners have viewed the location of manufacturing activity as the most important single variable controlling the country's economic and population goegraphy'.[3]

The general accounts of change in the space economy on which we have drawn in Chapter 3 clearly indicate that the larger and older cities have experienced, in addition to population loss, the largest and most rapid manufacturing decline. If local economic policies are aimed at stemming or reversing that decline their chances of success must be slender. Indeed, they are confounded by the long-standing recognition of a trend towards industrial dispersal in Britain at all geographic scales – national, regional and local – and there is mounting evidence to show that the fastest growing regions, in manufacturing employment terms as well as in population terms, are the small towns and rural areas of Britain.[4] We accept Fothergill and Gudgin's argument that the location of employment change in the manufacturing sector is now the dominant influence on the pattern of urban and regional growth in Britain,[5] yet the links between manufacturing change and, for example, population decentralisation and inner city unemployment, are not simple ones and the mechanisms for change remain poorly understood.[6]

A number of explanations have been advanced for the decline of manufacturing in cities, all of them plausible and yet none of them entirely satisfactory. There seems to be general agreement that there are several causes, and indeed as to which causes these are. It has nevertheless proved difficult to find a common framework within which these various factors may be linked and examined beyond an acknowledgement that many industries have in the past found it favourable to locate in metropolitan areas, that certain types of activity rather than others have tended to be located there, and that these associations are markedly weaker today.

We have chosen to concentrate on three major aspects of change in the British space economy which bear upon the issue of the 'de-industrialisation' of cities: relative rates of new plant formation and of firm closure, changes in the concentration of industrial ownership and control and thirdly, and more generally, locational trends in manufacturing industry. This is not to deny the particular significance of other factors such as improvements in transport technology or the role of regional and planning policies for the changing pattern of industrial growth and decline. But we hold the view that in seeking to interpret changes in the space economy as a whole, an examination of these three factors and of the links between them will be fruitful. Moreover, these three prove to be of particular significance for the account of change in London presented in the following chapters.

Births and deaths in the manufacturing sector

The process of employment change has usually been examined in terms of its components: the new jobs provided by plant openings and expansions set against jobs lost through plant closure or relocation or through *in situ* contractions of the labour force. We begin with births, and review the claim that cities are 'natural' locations for new enterprise before considering, more briefly, the impact of the pattern of plant closures.

Metropolitan areas have traditionally played a seedbed role in industrial growth. Their inner areas, in particular, have had a taken-for-granted part in the birth of new enterprises. The inner city is seen as an attractive location for external economy industries – those which seek especially to minimise the costs of access to suppliers and to customers through the use of a close network of linkages – and for other small new firms seeking urbanisation economies including, for example, the availability of premises, skilled labour and good transport links in an environment in which a free of exchange of information can take place.[7] The availability of premises has been seen as a particularly important factor. Land costs in inner city locations tend to be high, but property costs may still be kept low due to the poor condition or layout of small, old and often multi-storey buildings.[8]

These observations underpin the hypotheses, generally ascribed to Hoover and Vernon, that the inner areas may be expected to have an industrial birth-rate above the average for the metropolitan areas as a whole, and that as new plants grow they will tend to shift outwards from the inner areas as they require more production space and seek internal economies of scale rather than external or urbanisation economies.[9] Thus the inner city has been seen as the incubator of new firms which, once 'hatched', would move outwards to suburban or outer urban locations. Furthermore, there is a second strand to this argument, for according to the traditional view, the firms themselves have been regarded as seedbeds of entrepreneurship from which larger enterprises have developed. Thus by extension the small firm sector has come to be seen as vital to national economic growth, despite academic scepticism about the relationship between scale, newness and innovativeness, and recent evidence that new firms in conurbations tend neither to be located in the fastest growing sectors of the economy, nor to be a major source of technological innovation.[10]

The inner city incubator hypothesis has been described as 'one of the major integrative hypotheses of urban economics'.[11] In particular, when linked to the concept of a product cycle it plays a central part in the filter-down theory of industrial location.[12] However, work in the US and in Britain has cast doubts on its validity. The authors of a study of four Standard Metropolitan Labor Areas in the US (Boston, Cleveland, Minneapolis-St Paul and Phoenix) conclude that the evidence 'provides little support for the simple incubator concept of urban growth', and that 'there is very little support for the view that new plants which incubate in the CBD, after a brief period of incubation, relocate in less dense areas outside the central city.[13] In his study of births, deaths, movements and *in situ* change in manufacturing industry in central Clydeside from 1958 to 1968, Cameron found that although a large number of new establishments located within the area defined as the inner ring, the *birth-rate* of plants there was low in comparison with the average for the conurbation as a whole, and most of these establishments were very small.[14] Also, these new firms did not bring much in the way of new industry to the inner city since most of them tended to be of the same type as those already there. Altogether, the inner area attracted relatively few jobs. Cameron also concluded that the 'inner area is neither an incubator zone in the sense that it has an above average birth-rate nor [is it] an area of major growth of new location employment',[15] finding as he did little evidence that growing firms seek to move outwards to suburban and outer locations from the supposed nursery of the inner city. Most moves originating within the inner areas also ended there.

More recently, Nicholson and his colleagues carried out two studies of new firm formation in London designed to test the incubator hypothesis. In the first they examined data on Establishments New to Manufacturing set up in Inner London between 1966 and 1978. There was no evidence to suggest that new firms other than those in what they term 'inner city industries' like printing and clothing found the inner city a favourable location.[16] In a second study they interviewed the founders of independent new firms in non-inner city industries locating in inner south-west London, and found no evidence that they had located there so as to take advantage of the 'external economies' of the inner city, although they *had* all located in old industrial premises available there. However, 'urbanisation' economies seem to have some relevance, since the most important factor affecting the location decisions of this second set of firms appeared to be the close proximity to local markets for their products.[17]

The one positive piece of evidence in favour of the incubator hypothesis is provided by Fagg's study of new firm formation in Greater Leicester for the period 1957 to 1970.[18] Fagg points out that many 'incubator' studies do not distinguish adequately between the creation of new firms and the opening of new branch plants. His own approach is to compare the locations selected by new firms with those chosen as destinations of single-plant company transfers during the same time period, arguing that 'both groups of establishments will be competing for vacant sites or factories in the same market, so that any significant difference in the pattern of choices should reflect the attractive qualities of one zone for one type of decision-maker'.[19] Significant differences were indeed found:

> The method of comparing the distributions of new firm origins and transferred company destinations has proved strong support for both the simple and complex incubator hypotheses when applied to Greater Leicester. New firms show a greater affinity for the inner area of the city than for the outer suburbs, although smaller zones of older buildings near to the periphery also perform a 'seedbed' function. The incubator hypothesis appears to be applicable to most industrial groups.[20]

The Leicester evidence introduces a new dimension, raising the possibility that urban incubator effects, formerly thought to be industry-specific, may be place-specific. Attention is therefore shifting away from the somewhat threadbare issue of whether cities have ever served as industrial seedbeds to the separate questions of *which* cities (if any) continue to do so, and the distinct factors which support that role. There is some evidence, for example, of the loss of a seedbed function in the West Midlands over a period of several decades. Beesley, in a pioneering study, examined the formation of new firms in the West Midlands for the period 1923 to 1938 and concluded that the inner city represented a favourable environment for new establishments.[21] In sharp contrast are the more recent findings of Firn and Swales from their comparison of new firm formation in Clydeside and the West Midlands between 1963 and 1972. They concluded that by 1972 the West Midlands conurbation as a whole was performing particularly badly in this respect, with 'the local industrial base . . . becoming even more dependent upon the firms already in existence in the region'.[22]

In a recent study of the contrasting rates of new firm formation in different areas of Britain Mason points out that most research on this topic tends to focus on very recently established firms, whereas significant regional contrasts in new firm populations only emerge some years after firms have been in business, since firms are better able to adapt and diversify as a response to changes in the local economic environment in some areas than they are in others.[23] There is then a major deficiency in work of this type: existing studies reveal little about what happens as small firms mature into larger ones, and we remain largely ignorant of the processes of growth and movement which relate to changes in individual firms over time. It may then be argued that spatial variations in the birth-rates of firms are less significant than the operating environments in which those firms flourish, stagnate or die.

Despite the advantages of inner city locations, there has always been a high 'infant mortality rate', partly, perhaps, because 'the establishment of a concern and entrance of an individual into business are usually accompanied by the naive optimism of inexperience'.[24] Certainly, the evidence suggests that 'establishments are most vulnerable in their first five years of operation when their susceptibility to closure is significantly higher than at any other time',[25] and also that the smaller the firm the more liable it is to closure. Such 'deaths' were not formerly seen as a cause for alarm; initial failures are thought to 'play a useful role in both releasing resources for other uses and providing signals to others that certain markets and/or products are not viable'.[26]

Inner city deaths also signal the declining appeal of such locations, for with the exodus of population and firms the market and linkage advantages of centrality have diminished. While the industrial birth-rate has been falling nationally for some time, small urban manufacturing firms have experienced a much higher rate of failure, reflecting in part the negative multiplier effects of the outward movement of (generally larger) mobile firms. Moreover, when small manufacturers have themselves attempted to emulate the larger by relocation, or have been required to do so by local authority or private redevelopment, they have often failed to survive the experience.

Overall, the enormous loss of manufacturing employment from metropolitan areas is attributed to plant closures rather than to a fall in the rate of new firm formation. For example, in Greater London net losses of employment (openings less total closures) amounted to 170,000 jobs between 1968 and 1974, when 69 per cent of the total manufacturing employment loss was attributed to the excess of closures over openings,[27] and in inner Manchester plant closures led to a loss of more than 35,000 jobs between 1966 and 1972, while openings provided only 11,000.[28] A study of manufacturing employment change in the Central Clydeside conurbation between 1958 and 1968 found that 'in the case of Glasgow, ninety per cent of the total net employment decline can be attributed to the closure of manufacturing plants within the city, whilst relatively few jobs were lost through plants moving out to the periphery'.[29] Finally, a wide-ranging review of recent studies providing evidence of the scale of employment losses concluded that 'in every case it is the influence of plant closure that dominates job losses in the urban areas'.[30]

A central question in the examination of plant closures is the relative significance of firms which have ceased trading against those which have moved to new locations. Lloyd and Mason attribute manufacturing decline in Greater Manchester largely to closure, concluding that 'only 3000 jobs were . . . actually lost to the inner city through plant migrations'.[31] A similar pattern was observed by Gripaios in his very detailed studies of south-east London.[32] Further work has been carried out by the Department of Industry in London; the results are dramatic, although measurement difficulties suggest that some caution should be exercised in interpreting them. About two-thirds of the job losses resulting from plant closure were due to complete closure rather than to moves. The most significant figure, however, is that which indicates the relatively high proportion of employment lost through closure once the number of jobs created by new firm formation have been taken into account – some 44 per cent of London's net employment loss between 1966 and 1974.[33]

From the foregoing discussion of new firm formation and of closure and decline three main conclusions emerge. First, it is clear that while some cities may have lost, by whatever process, a seedbed role which they previously enjoyed, some retain such a function. Secondly, high rates of firm closure and of *in situ* shrinkage of manufacturing employment appear to be of overwhelming importance in accounting for the observed decline of manufacturing employment in the largest British conurbations. Thirdly, while all of the largest cities are undergoing employment decentralisation, the same *processes* are not necessarily at work in each.[34] While some are experiencing decentralisation through closure and *in situ* shrinkage in the inner areas, in others it is a decline in the rate of plant openings in the central areas and the growth of suburban manufacturing employment (a topic to which we return in the closing section of this chapter) which largely account for the observed decentralisation of manufacturing employment.

We may conclude that cities, and indeed different areas of particular cities, vary in their industrial fertility, and that each may be viewed as a milieu favourable or unfavourable to firm formation and growth, indeed to firm survival. The concept of industrial milieu is not a new one. For example, in 1968 Steed suggested that milieu or 'geographical setting' of an individual firm is composed of two closely-linked features – 'those factors external to the firm which actually affect it in one way or another' and, often quite different, 'those factors which the firm itself thinks to be important'.[35] As Steed pointed out:

Whether the firm's external milieu is facilitating or restraining is a function not only of the nature of the objective environment but also of the way that milieu is perceived by those responsible for making decisions within the firm. And the way the decision-makers see the external opportunities or constrictions before them undoubtedly, in turn, depends on what they view to be their own internal resources.[36]

Steed envisaged a continually changing relationship and concluded that 'to grasp at the . . . milieu of an industrial firm . . . is to seek a continuously moving object'.[37] In a time of rapid and traumatic change for manufacturing industry the identification of a favourable or unfavourable industrial milieu is particularly difficult.

It must be admitted that of the external factors forming part of the industrial milieu those that are unfavourable to firm growth spring most readily to mind. They include, for example, the decline of local markets and the atrophy of linkages, problems of capital supply, skill shortages and unsuitable premises and the effects of regional policies. Unsympathetic local planning policies also contribute to an unfavourable milieu, not just directly in the sense of policies towards non-conforming industry and the handling of industrial planning applications, but also indirectly through the priority given to, for example, housing and amenity uses.[38] In addition, in recent years rising local rates have attracted more criticism from industrialists and have been explicitly cited by them as determining factors in closure decisions; here, particularly, it is the perceived and not the 'objective' milieu that must be considered. Overall, it would seem that unfavourable factors are currently at a maximum in the inner city areas, while in suburban or non-urban locations external factors are much more favourable to industry and are *believed* to be so.

The attractiveness of the milieu argument has increased with the failure of more traditional explanations to account for the observed patterns of industrial change. In particular, while the possession of an adverse industrial mix was hitherto thought to underlie the poor performance of the inner areas of conurbations a number of studies using shift share analysis have suggested that industrial structure does relatively little to explain the decline of employment in manufacturing in the areas studied.[39] Indeed, recent work reveals a continuing *favourable* industrial structure in many inner city areas and a large negative differential effect, suggesting that other 'local' factors are bearing upon the performance of city economies.[40]

The concept of the milieu is a useful means of bringing into focus the spatial patterning of the many factors, internal and environmental, 'objective' and perceptual, economic and psycho-social, which bear upon the fortunes of the enterprise. For example, the attributes of new firm founders are of some importance, and there appear to be slight regional differences in their characteristics. Mason's evidence suggests that new firm founders in south Hampshire used more start-up capital and had greater business experience than those in Manchester and Merseyside examined by Lloyd.[41] The motives of founders in setting up in business may also show some regional variation. The decision-making structure of the firm and the availability of capital would seem to be of particular importance and, in the small firm sector at least, decisions to invest or disinvest are crucially affected by entrepreneurs' beliefs as to the appropriateness of the city as a location; beliefs which result from the experience of the changing environment and from the subjective interpretation of that experience.[42]

The elusive quality *entrepreneurship* is perhaps the most discussed of the features of the industrial milieu. The CBI has maintained that recent population shifts have drained the inner cities of 'natural leaders and entrepreneurs'[43] so that the firms remaining suffer from a dearth of entrepreneurial capacity. In any particular area there may be links between entrepreneurship and 'external' features such as housing tenure or the informal sector. In particular, entrepreneurial capacity has been tentatively linked to the corporate structure of urban firms: cities whose economies are dominated by large multi-plant corporations are seen as unfavourable to entrepreneurship.

Leicester, for example, with only 38 per cent of its manufacturing jobs in plants employing 500 or more, does appear to act as a new firm incubator, for the city and its environs have a rate of new firm formation 'considerably greater than the estimated national rate'[44] and four times higher than in Derby, for example, where the proportion in large plants is 68 per cent.[45] Low rates are found in the Teesside, Tyneside, Merseyside and Clydeside conurbations and several studies have sought to associate the very marked inter-urban and inter-regional differences with the preponderance of large plants, arguing that large plant milieux 'are an inadequate training ground for entrepreneurs and in the long run this undermines their capacity for adaptation and growth'.[46] This variant of the milieu argument seems to have considerable explanatory power when combined with a separate set of arguments which link the de-industrialisation of cities to the rise of the large multi-plant firm and the increasing concentration of industrial ownership, arguments which we shall consider in the following section.

What implications do these various factors have for local policy-makers who seek to improve the operating environment of local firms and, in particular, to stem employment losses? First, since the significance of particular factors varies from place to place, an understanding of the configuration of local economic forces is a prerequisite of effective action. Second, local planning policies may themselves contribute in unintended ways to fostering or undermining a favourable industrial milieu. Thirdly, however, while positive policies to support small firm creation or bolster failing firms are feasible in the sense of lying within the action space of local government, their effectiveness in overall employment terms is likely to be slight. Ultimately, the scope for effective local action is constrained by two of the most powerful forces operating upon the fortunes of cities: the pronounced shift toward a greater concentration of industrial ownership, with its consequent 'delocalisation' of investment decisions, and the tendency for much industrial investment to favour suburban or non-urban locations.

The impact of concentration

The second strand of argument as to the significance of large firms for the urban economy encompasses the processes of industrial concentration and rationalisation and the increasing tendency for inner city plants to be controlled from outside the area in which they are located. It is argued that ties to inner city sites have been weakened by the tendency of large firms to internalise economies and linkages,[47] and further that firm closure and employment shrinkage have resulted from the processes of merger and acquisition through which concentration occurs. Such arguments have their basis in the concentration of ownership in manufacturing which occurred during the 1960s and which is still in progress. The 1960s saw 'a great acceleration in take-over and merger activity', especially during the second half of the decade.[48] The result was a marked increase in industrial concentration, particularly noticeable in the metals, electrical engineering, vehicles, textiles, leather, clothing and footwear and brick-making industries. Although the nationalisation of the steel industry in 1967 was undoubtedly the major factor explaining the big increase in concentration in the metals industry, in the other sectors 'mergers almost certainly played the dominant role' in bringing about increases in concentration.[49] The spatial significance of these developments is of particular interest, and three features of the concentration process stand out: the effects of merger and acquisition on subsequent employment change, the 'delocalisation' of control, and the spatial separation of function so apparent in the multi-plant firm.

There have been several studies of the effects of external take-overs on manufacturing employment change. One examination of 120 externally acquired manufacturing concerns in the northern region of Britain between 1963 and 1973[50] concluded that most of the acquired firms exhibited faster than average employment growth before take-over and, following take-over, a decline in growth performance, although it was also the case that establishments surviving merger or acquisition had relatively higher rates of growth than non-acquired firms. More recently, Healey's study of the closures made by 64 multi-plant enterprises in the textile and clothing industries between 1967 and 1972, found a high rate of post-acquisition plant closures, mainly because managers sought to achieve economies by concentrating production in fewer plants. Also, plants which were acquired in horizontal mergers (that is, the acquired firms were classified under the same Minimum List Heading as those acquiring them) were more liable to close than plants acquired in mergers of other types. The size of plant was also a major factor influencing plant closures, since there was a propensity for larger plants to close, but the nature of the enterprises, including their organisational structure and the extent of diversification, was 'a relatively unimportant factor in differentiating between the closure behaviour of the companies examined'.[51] As Healey points out, while the majority of employees affected by plant closures work for multi-plant organisations 'this is not surprising given the estimate that in 1972 approximately three-quarters of employees in the private sector of manufacturing industry in the UK worked for multi-plant enterprises'.[52]

Further evidence on the effects of merger and acquisition on plant closure and employment loss has been provided by Leigh and North in their work on regional aspects of acquisition.[53] Using Department of Industry data, they examined acquisitions by firms in the food, chemical, clothing and textile sectors between 1973 and 1974. 'Somewhat contrary to initial expectations, it appears that expansion of output was a more common consequence of acquisition than was plant closure', although 'employment increases were not very commonly associated with output expansion'.[54] Like Healey, they found that the plant closures that did occur tended to be associated with the rationalisation of the production process rather than with such activities as asset-stripping, or with unintended closure. Unemployment through redundancy averaged 95 jobs for every acquisition involving closure, and 'the typical situation was where a medium or large public company acquired a multiplant firm with the intention of rationalising and consolidating production at the "best sites" in order to achieve scale economies'.[55]

More positive evidence is provided by Dicken and Lloyd who studied the industrial milieu (or 'enterprise characteristics', to use their term) of inner Manchester and inner Merseyside for the period 1966 to 1975. They identified a large increase through mergers and acquisition in the share of inner Merseyside's workers employed in multi-plant firms and also an increase in the proportion of the total workforce employed in plants controlled from outside the Merseyside region. They found that if closures and *in situ* changes in employment were taken together, just over 30 per cent of all job losses from inner Merseyside between 1966 and 1975 were in some way associated with these ownership changes.[56] Inner Manchester, too, experienced some very large acquisitions and mergers:

the most widely publicised were, of course, those resulting from the government-encouraged merger between GEC, AEI and English Electric in 1967. Almost 1000 jobs in inner Manchester were lost in the aftermath of this major corporate upheaval in plant closures alone, quite apart from employment reduction in acquired plants which survived. Large job losses were also associated with the Johnson and Firth Brown merger, with the takeover of English Steel by the British Steel Corporation, and Allied Polymer's acqusition of Greengate and Irwell and by other major ownership changes.[57]

Nevertheless, inner Manchester is judged to be 'much closer in almost every respect to the archetypal inner city area with its particular industry mix' and emphasis on smaller, locally headquartered plants, although here too there was clearly some move towards increased external control. On the whole, the most important contribution to job loss in Manchester was 'the closure and outmigration of manufacturing plants'.[58]

Thus the research evidence on the effects of merger and acquisition on plant closure and employment loss in particular cities is somewhat variable in its conclusions.[59] Less equivocal conclusions are reached by taking a sectoral rather than a local view of the impact of concentration. For example, Massey and Meegan examined the impact of the intervention of the Industrial Reorganisation Corporation into the electrical, electronics and aerospace equipment sectors.[60] The intervention took the form of the encouragement of mergers and reorganisation. Their results are striking:

The restructuring processes which were analysed resulted in an overall net employment loss, in the survey firms, of 36,016 jobs: a decline of 16 per cent. In terms of its geographical distribution, this overall change was dominated by three regions (the South East, the North West and the West Midlands) which experienced major declines in employment in absolute and percentage terms. Together they accounted for 94 per cent of the net overall loss . . . Further disaggregation of the data, however, showed that 89 per cent of the losses suffered by these regions could be explained by the significant declines which occurred in the four major cities located within them, namely Greater London, Liverpool, Manchester and Birmingham. These four cities together lost 30,315 jobs in the sector, or 84 per cent of the overall net decline in the survey firms' employment.[61]

One of the more striking features of this study of sectoral restructuring is that it exemplifies the very processes of modernisation which successive governments have sought to promote throughout the manufacturing sector. In the light of present-day scepticism as to the effectiveness of regional policy, it might be thought that sectoral policies have had more profound (if unintended) spatial consequences than spatial policies themselves. Publicly-sponsored change apart, the corporate strategies pursued by the large multi-plant firm may have unwelcome effects on the metropolis in terms of the loss of manufacturing employment.

The delocalisation of control is also seen as increasing the vulnerability of areas (especially inner cities) whose indigenous firms have fallen under the control of distant, and hence inaccessible, decision-makers. The evidence from inner Merseyside, for example, would certainly suggest that this is the case, although most of the concern with delocalisation centres on the (postulated) loss of local influence over investment decisions rather than on closures and employment loss *per se*. In this version, the spatial concentration of control involves a corresponding loss of community control over local industry and an increase in 'the social distance between top executives on the one hand, and workers and the community on the other'.[62] Conflicts between the two groups become more pronounced because they 'lack the bond of mutuality' which is presumed to exist in the case of local ownership.[63] Problems of industrial relations are, of course, frequently cited as factors making for an unfavourable milieu and encouraging firms to move elsewhere.

The phenomenon of delocalised control has been most marked in Scotland and the North of England:

in the Northern Region the number of independent companies headquartered in the region has declined significantly over time, while branch plants and extra-regionally controlled subsidiary companies have increased, the former due to in-movement of mobile industry and the latter due to merger and take-over activity. Thus in 1973, 48.1 per cent of all employment in manufacturing industry in the region was controlled from the South-East and 21.2 per cent from elsewhere in the UK . . . In the UK as a whole, in 1977 nearly 83 per cent of turnover from the top 1000 companies was controlled from the South-East.[64]

Other studies have adduced further, if 'fragmentary', evidence to reinforce this picture:

A very considerable proportion of manufacturing activity in [Scotland, Northern and north-east England] is controlled from outside. In the case of Scotland, for example, 58.8 per cent of the total employment in manufacturing in 1973 was controlled externally, of which English based companies (39.8 per cent) and North American based companies (14.9 per cent) were most important . . . plants controlled by non-Scottish based companies were, in general, very much larger than indigenous plants.[65]

While evidence as to the operations of UK domestic multi-plant firms continues to accumulate, multi-*national* corporations have attracted fewer precise analyses. This is at first sight surprising, given the dominance of multi-national firms in aggregate employment terms. There is a sizeable body of work on the trend towards the urban 'branch plant economy' and it has been asserted that the 'problem of external control can be exacerbated when the controlling corporation is [a foreign] multi-national, since then its headquarters may not even be in the UK'.[66] However, as far as foreign-owned multi-national enterprise is concerned, the spatial pattern of costs and benefits of their operations is unclear. There is evidence as to the beneficial spin-offs from the presence of US-owned corporations in diffusing innovation and raising efficiency,[67] and it has been argued that similar assumptions as to corporate behaviour *may* not hold for both multi-national and national multi-plant firms particularly as regards their locational choices. Many of the larger British manufacturing companies are themselves multi-national producers, and a recent survey of company reports depicts falling employment in the UK while overseas employment increased.[68] This suggests a deterioration of the fortunes of British metropolitan areas in favour of low-cost operations overseas.

While not all writers are of the opinion that the economic effects of the concentration of industry and the growth of multi-plant organisations are necessarily adverse[69] there is a greater measure of agreement about the spatial consequences of organisational change in manufacturing industry, especially since the weight of evidence suggests that the consequences of restructuring may be particularly bad for the inner urban areas, while favouring suburban or outer urban locations. There is an increasing awareness of the growing spatial separation of function within multi-plant firms, accentuated by merger and acquisition activity. In Britain, 'many multilocational firms appear to rationalise their activities in such a way that there is a concentration of head offices, marketing and research in the South East, with production facilities designated to peripheral areas'.[70] The spatial centralisation of control resulting from acquisitions has not brought about a corresponding centralisation of production. 'If anything, the net effect is probably the reverse; a relative decentralisation of productive capacity to certain provincial/peripheral regions'.[71] These developments have suggested to some writers a distinction between 'central' and 'peripheral' functions in the space economy, the relationships of dominance and dependence within firms and within industries being expressed in spatial patterns. Not surprisingly, the metaphor of 'internal colonialism' comes readily to hand.[72]

Keeble has summed up the importance of the argument concerning multi-plant firms and their contribution to the decline of the metropolitan economy. If correct, it could imply that the forces responsible for manufacturing decline in inner city areas are chiefly of a locational rather than a historical nature. Put another way, industrial emigration to areas perceived as possessing a better environment for growth and profitable operation, *plus* closures as part of conscious multiplant locational evaluation, may be more important factors in most conurbations than deaths reflecting simply a historic concentration of now derelict, aging firms characterised by outmoded organisational and technological methods or inadequate entrepreneurship.[73]

If, then, decline is a response to rational locational evaluation, we must pause to ask which aspects of the inner city environment are seen as disadvantageous and, conversely, what are the factors leading to an increasingly observed phenomenon, the location of new, fast-growing industrial activity on the periphery of urban areas, or even in non-urban locations?

Locational trends in manufacturing

Trends in manufacturing location during the 1950s and 1960s corresponded closely to the shifts in population and employment in those decades. Indeed, the early 1960s are 'likely to become recognised as a watershed in the country's industrial location history'.[74] Whereas the 1950s witnessed 'massive absolute and relative manufacturing growth in and around the central industrial conurbations of London and Birmingham', the 1960s saw the reversal of this trend. In the later years of that decade in particular 'the spatial pattern of manufacturing employment change in the UK . . . was dominated by the dramatic decline of the country's five greatest industrial conurbations',[75] and more recent studies have pointed to the associated growth of manufacturing employment in suburban or non-urban locations.

At the national level, Fothergill and Gudgin's examination of UK manufacturing employment trends identifies a strong urban-rural contrast in growth, with the highest growth rates being recorded in those areas such as East Anglia and the south-west of England which do not contain a conurbation.[76] Manufacturing employment growth has been especially marked in the country towns and rural areas. As figure 4.1 shows, the figures for growth and decline in manufacturing floorspace show a similar clear inverse relationship between size of place and growth. To provide a regional example of the shift in locational preferences, Mason's evidence suggests that 'the distribution of new manufacturing firms within south Hampshire has clearly favoured locations outside the two city areas' while 'the contribution made by new firms to total manufacturing employment has similarly been most significant in suburban and rural local authority areas'.[77]

Although, as we have seen, the closure and contraction of manufacturing firms have played an important role in the decline of inner city employment, more recent analyses focus rather on the location of

Figure 4.1   Changes in industrial floorspace in England, 1974–1980

'000 square metres

	Stock 1974	Demo- lition	Other loss	Exten- sions	New units	Change of use	Stock 1980	Change
London	24,261	−1051	−3443	+1051	+836	+642	22,296	−1965
Other conurbations	64,129	−2052	−7106	+3626	+3242	+1588	63,427	−702
Freestanding cities	38,796	−1026	−3538	+2650	+1386	+1201	39,469	+673
Large towns	25,172	−711	−3128	+2152	+1736	+622	25,843	+671
Small towns	47,226	−873	−4428	+4248	+4244	+1671	52,088	+4862
Rural areas	25,443	−489	−3294	+3543	+2364	+1106	28,673	+3230
England	225,027	−6202	−24,937	+17,270	+13,808	+6830	+231,796	+6769
% change 1974–1980		−2.76	−11.08	+7.67	+6.14	+3.04		+3.01

Source: Unpublished figures kindly made available by S. Fothergill and colleagues of the University of Cambridge Industrial Location Research Project. In this table, freestanding cities are those with in excess of 250,000 population, large towns are in the range 100–250,000, small towns 35–100,000, and rural areas are areas with less than 35,000 population in any one settlement.

employment growth.[78] It has been argued that in shaping the overall pattern of change in manufacturing employment 'the location of new factories and the expansion of existing ones are probably more important than the location of contractions and closures'.[79] The cumulative weight of the push-and-pull factors which produce these shifts 'are by now so powerful that it is no longer necessary to ask industrialists, as surveys once did, why they choose to leave the city for the smaller towns, but rather to inquire what it is that keeps them in their present locations'.[80]

Many factors have combined to overcome the inertia of industrialists and to loosen the ties of manufacturing industry to the conurbations, and their cumulative effect on patterns of locational advantage has been to change radically the relative costs of metropolitan and non-metropolitan operations. Here we explore three which are frequently cited by industrialists themselves: the incentives provided by government policy for the regions and for New Town development, problems of labour recruitment, and the physical drawbacks of location in traditional urban industrial areas.

Regional policy, along with the dispersal of industry to the New Towns, has frequently been cited as a source of metropolitan manufacturing decline. For example, in a paper written in 1976 Keeble agreed that 'the dominant reason for the recent shift in the balance of manufacturing locational advantage in favour of the [geographic] periphery was government industrial location policy'.[81] Local industrial development officers in metropolitan areas seem to attribute much of the blame for inner city problems to these policies,[82] and this view may be supported by the evidence that regional policy has done something to equalise regional imbalances.[83]

However, in the light of more recent evidence, policy is no longer held to be an important factor. In a regression analysis of county variations in the change of manufacturing employment in the UK between 1971 and 1976, Keeble found that the government policy variables were not statistically related to rates of differential manufacturing employment shift.[84] After a detailed discussion, he concludes that 'by 1976, regional policy had ceased to exert a measurable impact on the spatial pattern of manufacturing employment change in Britain'.[85]

A similar scepticism exists in relation to the effectiveness of New Towns policy. In a recent paper, Fothergill and Gudgin conclude that policies for the New and Expanded Towns 'have made little difference to the scale and direction of the urban-rural shift'. Though these towns managed to increase their manufacturing employment while employment in this sector fell in the country as a whole, since 1967 their growth has not been a great deal better than that of other small towns which have not had special status. 'The number of jobs which can therefore be attributed to the New and Expanded Towns Programme itself is modest, particularly in the case of New Towns.'[86]

In the specific case of London, the decentralisation of manufacturing industry to the ring of New Towns is now seen as 'spurious' evidence of the achievement of planning goals. As Keeble puts it: 'New Town manufacturing growth, the decline of industry in London, and substantial within-region dispersal of firms owes less to direct location or regional planning action than to natural forces, coupled with central government pressures and controls.' He concludes that 'labour availability, not planning, if of crucial importance in explaining the recent dispersal of manufacturing'.[87]

The arguments surrounding labour availability are, however, equally contentious. In an important paper, Massey has invoked structural developments within the capitalist mode of production to account for such regional changes as may be discerned.[88] According to the 'restructuring hypothesis', a new spatial division of labour is occurring as multi-plant companies, especially, seek 'to rationalise their production systems in an effort to maintain profits by taking greater advantage of peripheral region, low-wage, less unionised and above all female labour'.[89] Massey and Meegan argue vigorously that the decentralisation of production represents a pursuit of the less-skilled labour required by modern production techniques. In the electrical, electronics and aerospace equipment industries at least, 'It may be that the balance of location factors is changing to release such industries from their previous requirement for highly skilled labour. This, in turn, may loosen their existing spatial ties to the major, established industrial cities.'[90]

The picture presented in much of Britain's 'urban systems' work examined in the previous chapter has a rather different emphasis, and suggests that population decentralisation has prompted employment change. Jones and Warnes, for example, explicitly portray a suburbanisation of skilled workers seeking improved residential amenities, followed by an outward shift of manufacturing industry.[91] There is some evidence for this view. Massey and Meegan's analysis may overstate the deskilling effects of changing production technology, for some types of manufacturing industry evidently require a high level of skill among their workforce and are particularly vulnerable to the tendency for highly paid workers to implement their own anti-urban preferences. Significantly, in a series of GLC surveys of manufacturing, food and distribution firms, 'only in manufacturing groups were the problems [of skill shortage] considered sufficiently important to constitute a relocation factor'.[92] It is possible that these two opposed views of the relationships between changes in manufacturing employment and labour availability may each be valid for different firms and products.[93]

However, in so far as the outmigration of skilled workers may be a factor in industrial relocation in the London region, it may be encouraged by the high cost of housing and by the limited supply of housing for owner-occupation in the inner areas. There is evidence to indicate that non-commuting population flows have increased since the mid-1960s with net decentralising effects and 'a tendency to move upmarket in housing'.[94] The continuing shift towards owner-occupation is likely to increase this mobility and the structure of the urban system may be transformed by an increasingly 'footloose' population.[95]

The final set of factors we consider encompasses the drawbacks of location in traditional urban industrial areas. The period since the mid-1960s has seen the evaporation of locational advantages formerly associated with metropolitan areas. Changing transport technologies and costs have produced 'substantial scope for decentralisation . . . among firms with sizeable markets outside London and with supply linkages that can operate efficiently over long distances'.[96]

Population movement and falling freight costs must each serve to increase this effect,[97] which may be reinforced by inter-firm linkages, for in so far as there are any discernible external economies accruing to separate firms in proximate locations they are increasingly unlikely to be found in the declining metropolitan areas, but are apparently achievable in the new, more dispersed pattern of location.

In this respect the London evidence of linkage change is illuminating. Keeble's study of manufacturing firms in north-west London[98] revealed surprisingly low levels of linkage, except among engineering firms, where inter-firm linkages none the less failed to act as a barrier to migration. While larger engineering firms have played a very important role in migration from London,[99] their relocation has followed a distinctly radial pattern along the major lines of communication, thus widening yet maintaining the network of linkages. Improvements in transport, particularly in the major radial roads of north and west London, allow linkages to be maintained over greater distances than had previously been possible, enabling manufacturing firms to improve their site and labour positions without weakening their associations with suppliers and contractors.

Further factors encouraging the outward movement of manufacturing growth are the congestion of sites and the obsolescence of premises in inner areas. In the suburban or non-urban areas, in contrast, there are greater opportunities for location in more spacious single-storey modern factories, and extensive one-storey factories in suburban locations enjoy significant cost advantages per unit floor area in comparison with multi-storey factory buildings in sites towards the city centre.[100] In particular, many manufacturing firms demand single-storey premises in order to incorporate modern production technologies, and these needs rule out even the factory buildings of the inter-war suburbs. Moreover, while smaller companies might settle for older premises there remains a severe shortage of suitable sites and premises for the larger firms.[101]

The arguments about the spatial restructuring of capital and the drawbacks of location at inner city sites have been drawn together by Fothergill, Kitson and Monk. They suggest that the explanation for the observed shift in the location of manufacturing employment from cities towards small towns and rural areas during the late 1970s lies in the combined effects of two factors: the falling number of workers per unit area of factory floorspace as industry becomes more capital intensive, and the lack of space for expansion in the cities.[102] Some structuralist writers – for example Scott, in an exemplary review essay – take the analysis a stage further and argue that the factors making for decentralisation (unfavourable aspects of inner city sites and the attractions of peripheral locations) and changes which appear to arise from incubation, product cycle and hierarchical filtering processes are essentially secondary to the historical process of the substitution of capital for labour.[103] Such analyses, with their emphasis on the dynamics of development, pose real dilemmas for those urban policy-makers who seek to retain employment in the cities.

We have attempted to present a synoptic view of those counter-urbanising forces which bear upon the manufacturing sector. Space precludes our citing more than illustrative examples of the extensive literature which appears to us to support this broad thematic review, and our selectiveness in this chapter is in part a deliberate device for achieving, in the following chapter, a closer focus on Metropolitan London. We turn at this point to see just how these various trends in openings, closures, moves, contractions and births and the factors which underlie them – rationalisation, the spatial separation of corporate functions, problems of labour, sites, access and premises – come together to create, for outer and inner London, a massive manufacturing job loss and a major challenge to the adaptive capability of the capital city.

5 London: Towards a Post-Industrial City

In Chapters 3 and 4 we examined some of the powerful forces for change in the urban space economy, forces that have already had a profound impact upon the form and function of the older industrial city. While these changes are common to the more mature industrial economies, their impact upon particular cities varies. The processes of deconcentration and peripheral growth have been more marked in their impact in Greater London than they have been in other metropolitan areas of the UK. At the same time, London enjoys a special prominence within certain service industries, being a major focus of both public administration and professional services, as well as serving as a location for the headquarters operations of many large multi-plant firms. We would argue, then, that the recent experience of London is a reflection of the powerful trend towards de-industrialisation of the largest metropolitan area in Britain, accounted for in large part by the closure and contraction of plants, and in part by the movement of firms to more favourable locations. In this chapter we consider the impact of this trend upon outer London, the location of one of our two case-studies, and upon inner London, the location of the other. But first, a brief review of change in Greater London as a whole is called for.

The changing function of Metropolitan London in the UK space economy is highlighted by the steady decline of its manufacturing role. The rate of decline of manufacturing employment has been higher in London than elsewhere, and although it has coincided with a rise in service employment, particularly in the 'growth' sectors of banking, insurance and professional services, this rise has been at a slower rate than in other conurbations.[1]

The rapid growth of office employment in Greater London has been striking, and cannot be attributed solely to the growth of the service sector. In Great Britain in 1971, nearly 3 million people were employed in office and other non-production occupations within the manufacturing sector.[2] Neglect of this feature, associated in the case of London with the increasing spatial separation of corporate functions, has obscured the magnitude of the shift from blue-collar to white-collar work. While manufacturing employment has declined rapidly, this has been most marked for the blue-collar workers. (Figure 5.2.)

The extent to which white-collar jobs are substitute openings for a

Figure 5.1   Changes in manufacturing and total employment, 1961–1978

	1961	1966	1971	1974	1978	% change 1961–1978
Manufacturing employment			*thousands*			
Greater London	1429	1309	1093	940	769	−47
Rest of SE Region	990	1142	1200	1194	1092	+10
England and Wales	7626	7848	7442	7248	6513	−15
Total employment						
Greater London	4386	4430	4084	3990	3679	−17
Rest of SE Region	3240	3775	3900	4149	3612	+12
England and Wales	20,913	22,325	21,562	22,186	20,186	−4

Sources: For 1961–1974, L. Weatheritt and A.F. Lovett, *Manufacturing Industry in Greater London*, GLC Research Memorandum RM498 (1975); for 1978, '1978 Census of Employment: Further Results,' *Employment Gazette*, (March 1981).

Figure 5.2   Greater London Occupation Groups, 1961–1981

	1961		1971		1981 (est.)	
	No. (000s)	% of total employment	No. (000s)	% of total employment	No. (000s)	% of total employment
Manufacturing						
Operatives	877	20.0	623	15.3	367	9.9
Office workers	383	8.8	354	8.7	318	8.6
Others	167	3.8	116	2.8	59	1.6
Total	1427	32.6	1093	26.8	744	20.1
All industries and services						
Operatives	1507	34.3	1164	28.4	844	22.8
Office workers	1404	31.9	1527	37.4	1606	43.4
Others	1475	33.8	1393	34.2	1251	33.8
Total	4386	100	4084	100	3701	100

Source: London Council of Social Service, *Employment and Industry in Greater London: A Background Document* (1977), p. 27.

local population previously employed in blue-collar activities is a question of some importance. During the 1970s many commentators expected the vitality of the metropolis to continue into the post-industrial era, service employment being substituted for manufacturing as the centralisation of service and control functions continued. Gottman, for example, argued that 'a few central cities particularly dependent on their industrial function have been declining, but the majority of old centres continue to thrive and . . . new centripetal forces . . . propel urban concentration in this modern post-industrial age'.[3]

Others were less sanguine, pointing out in particular that the inter-sectoral shifts in the economy involve massive costs in terms of unemployment for existing metropolitan residents.[4] Until recently, London's office growth was seen by many local policy-makers as the answer to the decline of manufacturing employment. Others have been more anxious about the 'mismatch' of skills and opportunities which might result from such replacement activities.[5] While the process of adaptation is far more complex than simple 'mismatch' models would suggest, assumptions of this kind underlie the evident resistance to office development in some of the older industrial boroughs.[6]

Above all, the broad patterns of sectoral change and of change in occupational categories obscure the unevenness of their impact. In some areas of London the decline of manufacturing has been associated with high and persistent levels of unemployment, while in others the growth of service jobs has provided new opportunities. Generally adaptation, in the sense of structural shift without high unemployment, has been more characteristic of west London than of east. West London, with its high level of demand for office workers and buoyant land market in the commercial and warehousing sectors, contrasts sharply with east London, where the derelict docklands are just the most visible and symbolically potent aspect of the loss of economic function. The marked skew in the spatial pattern of unemployment is readily apparent in Figure 5.3. We now consider the impact of these changes, first, in suburban areas of west London, and secondly, in less favoured inner city boroughs, as a preliminary to examining the responses made by policy-makers in those areas.

The transformation of the suburbs
The experience of west Middlesex, one of the most studied areas of outer London, provides a clear illustration of recent suburban change. With its pattern of 'ribbon' industrial development along the major arterial and radial roads – Western Avenue, the Great West Road, Edgware Road and the North Circular – west Middlesex is the quintessence of inter-war London. Reviewing London's rapid industrial

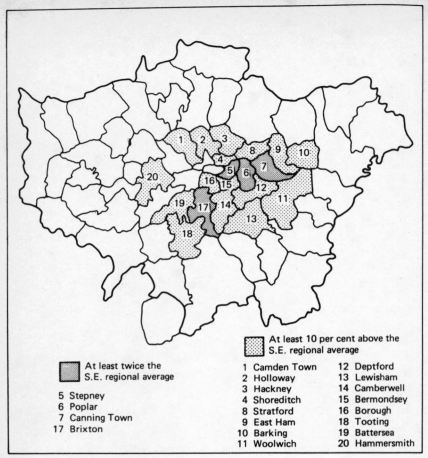

Source: GLC Planning Committee Report, 26 February 1976

Figure 5.3   Unemployment in London by Employment Office Area, 1976

development in 1933, *The Economist* commented that:

The development of the new factories has followed a clearly marked radial plan
along the main arteries of transport. It is transport which has made West
Middlesex the favoured area for industrial development . . . The Lea Valley
was the earliest industrial area of Greater London. It has obvious advantages in
that it provides room for expansion while retaining contact with the labour
supply of East London. Some of the heavier industries are settling on the
Medway, and small miscellaneous industries in southern London between
Wimbledon and Croydon. But the largest developments have been in the
triangle enclosed between lines drawn from London to Watford on the north-
west and Slough on the west. The advantages of this area can be seen at its new
industrial centre, Park Royal . . . which . . . also has the Grand Union canal,

two 'tube' railways to bring its labour and a brand new arterial road. The arterial road is perhaps the greatest attraction, to judge by the factories that line the Great West Road, the Edgware Road, and the North Circular Road.[7]

In the speed, magnitude and novelty of its transition, the industrial growth of Middlesex was unparalleled.[8] Describing the factory growth in the outer London region between 1933 and 1936, Richardson and Aldcroft note that 'the most outstanding example of extensive industrial development was the Great West Road. Within a two-mile stretch more than fifty factories were established employing 11,000 people, and the road became one of the principal industrial centres of the outer London region'.[9] Here the frenetic pace of development was aided by the introduction of new building techniques; the astonishing Art Deco Firestone building on the Great West Road was producing motor tyres within eighteen weeks of the contractors going on site to begin construction.[10] Factory developments like these were particularly characteristic of Middlesex, a consequence both of London's relative prosperity, especially in light industry, during the inter-war years, and of industry's need to escape its own congestion costs.[11]

While the growth of the west London suburbs during the 1920s and 1930s was rapid, their decline, equally rapid and dramatic, if barely noticed by commentators, underlies the transformation with which we are concerned. By 1973, the press were observing that

during the last decade, the aptly christened 'Golden Mile' of industry along the Great West Road . . . has been showing signs of tarnish. Industrial premises which had housed internationally famous manufacturing industries have been standing derelict – the former occupants have taken advantage of government grants aimed at encouraging companies to move out of London, and for some other sound economic reason (like the difficulties of recruiting labour) sought pastures greener.[12]

The great factory buildings for the most part still stand (although the Firestone building was recently demolished by the Trafalgar House group), yet many of them stand empty, while others have been converted to warehouses, cash-and-carry retail centres or to office uses.[13] The predominant characteristic of Middlesex's workforce as producers of tangible goods – consumer durables, mechanical, electrical or motor engineering products – has similarly faded. The persistence of factory frontages notwithstanding, this is post-industrial London; the airline terminal buildings of Heathrow are better symbols of Middlesex's contemporary character.

Three aspects of change deserve special attention: the pattern of employment, the closures and moves of firms, and the changing economic function of this part of west London.

The pattern of employment

The unemployment rate is the indicator of economic well-being most readily available to local policy-makers, and in this respect west London has fared relatively well until quite recently. Figure 5.3 showed that the areas of high unemployment tend, for the most part, to be concentrated to the east of the City of London. A breakdown of the figures for the several sectors of metropolitan London illustrates more clearly both the spatial skew and the recent sharp deterioration overall (Figure 5.4).

Many areas of outer west London have had consistently low unemployment rates and sudden increases due to the closure of large employers have tended to be fairly swiftly absorbed by redeployment.

Behind the favourable employment conditions lie marked changes in the structure of employment, in terms of both industrial sectors and occupational categories. In Hounslow, for example, the proportion of men employed in manufacturing fell from 62 per cent in 1961 to 45 per cent in 1971, of women from 51 to 34 per cent, and of both to 23 per cent by 1976. The total number employed in manufacturing fell from 61,292 in 1961 to 38,484 in 1975. At the same time, the number employed in the service sector more than doubled to reach a total (excluding air

Figure 5.4   Greater London: sectoral unemployment rates, 1972–1982

Sectors of London	Male resident unemployment rate (per cent)				
	April 1972	October 1973	April 1975	January 1978	January 1982
Greater London	3.2	1.8	3.3	5.8	11.6
Inner London (excluding central area)	4.3	2.4	4.4	7.8	15.7
inner north-east	4.7	2.6	4.6	8.1	17.2
inner south	4.2	2.4	4.4	7.3	14.7
inner north-west	3.7	2.2	4.1	8.4	15.1
Outer London	2.4	1.3	2.4	4.1	8.6
outer north-east	2.8	1.8	2.8	4.3	8.8
outer south-east	2.6	1.6	2.5	4.5	8.7
outer south-west	2.1	1.2	2.3	3.8	7.4
outer west	2.3	1.1	2.0	3.8	8.7
outer north-west	2.3	1.1	2.4	4.2	9.6
Great Britain	4.7	2.7	4.5	6.5	12.6

Source: GLC, Industry and Employment Committee Reports IE112 (Ferbruary 1979), and IE193 (February 1982). See IE112 for a discussion of the bases of the figures.

transport) of 69,241. The relative significance of the two broad sectors was therefore inverted in a period of less than 15 years, and the projections to 1981 indicated a continuation of these trends.

In Middlesex, as in Greater London as a whole, the occupational structure shows a trend from blue-collar to white-collar work. Offices decentralising from central London have shown very strong tendencies to concentrate in certain outer suburbs. Croydon alone took 30 per cent of relocated office jobs between 1963 and 1973 and west London has taken a further 28 per cent of these. The attractive pull of west London, with the simultaneous advantages of proximity to the central area and to Heathrow, has been reinforced by the existing distribution of office workers' houses.[14] The relative proportions of operatives and office workers once again show this broad trend in outer west London (Figure 5.5).

Figure 5.5   Employment in occupational categories in Outer West London, 1961–1981

	1961	1966	1971	1981 (est.)
Operatives	170	167	146	109
Office workers	98	122	131	161
Others	114	121	128	129
Total	382	410	405	399

Source: P.M.H. Kendall, D. Williamson and W. Alexander, *Employment, Housing and Local Economic Consequences of the Proposed Fourth Terminal at Heathrow* (London, Metra Consulting Group Ltd, 1978).

Positive planning policies underlay the earlier phases of this shift in outer London. The original County of London Plan provided for a substantial decentralisation of office employment, and Middlesex County Council responded by designating areas of office growth. However, by the early 1960s the initial receptivity to offices had already begun to wane as new firms were attracted into suburban areas and new office developments generated volumes of local traffic in excess of the roads' capacity. By 1962 the several suburban country councils had reversed their policies, and only Croydon continued to attract decentralising offices.[15]

Closures and moves of firms
The shift in the employment structure of west Middlesex reflects the reversal of the inter-war patterns of rapid industrialisation. As Keeble remarks:

as early as 1937 discerning observers of industrial 'boom' areas such as North-West London were beginning to detect the development of certain hindrances to continuing industrial growth. By and large, these hindrances were the natural result of unrestricted and massive industrialisation within a relatively small area. Since 1945, with continual industrial development and pronounced change in national economic conditions, they have intensified to a marked degree.[16]

Keeble introduced the notion of a 'ceiling to growth', a phenomenon which encourages expanding firms to migrate, and his evidence shows a strong correspondence between industrial migration and the subsequent growth of migrant firms in their receiving areas. Thus, north-west London has become, in recent years, a victim of its own earlier success. Between 1940 and 1964 no less than 266 factories were established by north-west London firms at distances of ten miles or more from their main factories. Of these, 148 represented complete closure of operations in north-west London 'transferring production lock, stock and barrel to another area'.[17] In all, 71,000 jobs were created in the reception areas as a result of this movement, amounting to a loss of 30 per cent of north-west London's industrial employment. The continued contraction of industrial activity after the early 1960s has then to be seen against this background of migration in which the inter-war period represented just one stage in the progressive relocation of successfully growing firms.

Most of the available figures relating to firms deal with the larger enterprises, and there is no direct evidence of the fate of the very large number of smaller firms which not only comprise the majority of local enterprises but which are also less likely to favour relocation or indeed to survive a move. In the case of the larger firms, the pattern of movement exemplifies our initial argument as to the significance of concentration of ownership, subsequent rationalisation, and the separation of metropolitan corporate headquarters from peripheral production. Much of the industrial exodus from west Middlesex has been due to the processes of corporate rationalisation and expansion by large firms seeking low-cost production conditions and a number of specific examples serve to illustrate this process.

In several cases the parent companies of firms leaving the area have been multi-nationals. This was the case at Sperry Ltd, producers of business machines and a subsidiary of Sperry Corporation of America, and also at Siemens Ltd, a subsidiary of Siemens AG, which moved to Sunbury. Reckitt and Colman, one of the larger British-owned multi-nationals, retained a headquarters office in the area and moved production to the modern factory which they had developed at Hull for that purpose. In some cases, relocation followed rapidly upon acquisition of the firm by a multi-plant enterprise. Fluidrive, an engineering firm specialising in automatic transmissions, was acquired in 1978 by the automotive plants conglomerate, Amalgamated Engineering. During 1979 the operations of the firm were consolidated in modern premises at Bracknell New Town, and the entire production process transferred there. During 1978 Unilever decided to rationalise the laboratory operations of their research division and moved more than 300 staff from their London site to their laboratories in Bedfordshire and the Wirral.[18]

Just as the rise of the Great West Road was the most tangible expression of outer London's development in the inter-war years, so too does its decline exemplify the changes which have taken place since the 1960s. Typical of the changes was the case of Pyrene Chemical Services, a specialist in paint pre-treatments located in one of the factories on the Great West Road. In 1973 Pyrene was bought by a locally-based multi-plant firm, Brent Chemicals International Ltd, which had, in addition to several local enterprises, more modern sites in the outer parts of the south-east region, at Iver (Buckinghamshire) and Dunstable (Bedfordshire). Within twelve months, the parent company found it possible to 'concentrate the group's main offices and laboratories at Iver . . . the Brentford site has been . . . freed by transferring production to other facilities'.[19]

A second example is that of Brentford Nylons, a locally-based and rapidly growing textile firm specialising in artificial fibres, which in 1965 moved into large factory premises on the Great West Road.[20] Throughout the next decade Brentford Nylons continued to expand, building new factories in the development areas – two in County Durham with a total of more than ¼ million square feet, more modern establishments in Scotland and Northern Ireland, and, finally, a massive single-storey factory at Cramlington, Northumberland. The Cramlington mill employed more than 2000 people in the largest vertically integrated textile plant in Europe. Associated with this growth was a 1974 turnover of £50 million, and a network of 46 retail outlets. Brentford Nylons were hoping to double their number of retail outlets and were planning a major export drive from their new mill, both operations being controlled from the corporate headquarters in the Great West Road. However, these developments did not materialise, and the likely next stage, that of closing production in London, was arrived at sooner than expected when the firm, plagued by production difficulties at Cramlington, went into receivership in 1977. The Cramlington mill was bought by the multi-national corporation Lonrho and the Great West Road premises were sold to an adjoining manufacturing firm mainly for conversion to offices.

The third and best-known example concerns the US-owned Firestone Motor Tyre Company. Firestone was of particular importance within west London, being one of the longest established and indeed the largest of the private sector employers in the area.[21] The symbolic significance of the famous Wallis Gilbert Firestone building on the Great West Road was evident in the central position which it occupied in the cover photograph of the local council's *Guide to Industry and Commerce*. The Great West Road site accommodated manufacturing and storage facilities as well as the UK headquarters of Firestone, a multi-national operation controlled from Akron, Ohio. Firestone's recent history exemplified the process of 'unequal growth', for while the London site had been expanded in the years immediately preceding and following the war, subsequent expansion took place in newer premises in North Wales. While the North Wales factory concentrated upon the production of radial-ply tyres the London premises were still specialising in cross-ply production for which the market was rapidly shrinking.

The obsolescence of their product, the intensity of domestic and foreign competition, and local labour shortages had long plagued Firestone's Great West Road operation. In November 1979 a new company president was installed in Akron, and a £32 million retrenchment programme announced for the European companies.[22] The London plant was rumoured to have lost £6 million in the previous year, and there were few surprises when Akron announced the closure of the plant. Nor were there many hopes of a resumption of manufacturing activity on the site; one local union official, surveying this latest of the changes in west London, commented that 'Britain has become one giant warehouse'.[23]

A *change of function*

The closure and movement of many large manufacturing establishments has left many other industrial cities in a derelict state and with high unemployment. That the local economic conditions in outer west London remained favourable was due to the marked shortages of skilled labour and to the employment-generating substitution of office functions for production. Indeed, the very desire of multi-plant corporations to maintain headquarters operations in west London was often displayed in pressure from them for a change of use to increase their office content and reduce production floorspace and workforces on their existing sites. For example, during the early 1970s Gillette established a right to increase their office space by 100,000 square feet. This concession led rapidly to similar pressures from Pyrene, Beechams, Rambler Motors and Agfa Gaevert.

Of the several examples of an *in situ* change of function, that of Brentford Nylons is particularly revealing. In March 1974 the firm applied for planning permission to convert 92,000 square feet of their factory to office use to supplement the existing 19,000 square feet; the plan was to centralise the administration of their London factories, and to turn the vacated buildings into warehouses, accompanying these changes with the recruitment of an extra 385 office staff. Such changes often drew implicit support from the local press, who attacked the local council's practice of resisting changes of use as 'short-sighted and disastrous' – a 'mad hatter situation':

Concerned about the effect of vanishing factories on employment in the area, Hounslow Council sternly refused applications by newcomers who were prepared to take over the buildings for office, warehousing and transport depots and insisted on their being re-occupied by similar manufacturing industries . . . Far from protecting the jobs of workers it has led to the owners of site after site on the Great West Road nailing up 'To Let' notices.[24]

After an initially unfavourable reaction the application was approved.

The changing pattern of floorspace in west London also reflected the shift in the function of the area. Between 1966 and 1968 the square footage of industrial floorspace lying vacant in Hounslow alone increased by over 50 per cent as a result of manufacturers' moves, and it continued to rise in the early 1970s. Overall, an additional 822,000 square feet of industrial floorspace became vacant between 1967 and 1972 while vacant commercial land was rapidly redeveloped. The trend was a general one, and as an officer in one of the outer west London boroughs commented:

Obviously a large number of the premises are not on the market but of the remaining properties on the market the vast majority are old, obsolete buildings frequently with poor vehicular access and parking facilities, a number having been purpose-built for a specific occupier and not readily adaptable to the needs of other prospective tenants. A lot of the properties are in a poor state of repair and are not suitable for modern requirements and techniques.

In these circumstances the west London surburban boroughs found themselves presiding over a shift towards warehousing developments. In many cases the empty factories were taken over for warehousing purposes and local planners found this trend difficult to resist. The proximity of Heathrow and motorway links to expanding consumer areas to the west and south-west of London ensured a very strong demand for warehousing, and refusals of permission ran the risk of being overturned on appeal. While industrial land lay derelict, the take-up of warehousing permissions was rapid and largely speculative. Moreover, warehouse development was increasingly being permitted on land originally allocated for industry. As a planner in one of these boroughs pointed out, there had been a recent 'sinister development' involving 'the actual demolition of existing factories and their intended replacement by warehouse complexes with predictable consequences for employment'.

From the mid-1960s onward, then, it became apparent that industrial west Middlesex was undergoing an underlying and progressive change of function. The change in the employment structure was readily apparent, and the exodus of industrial firms could scarcely escape notice, for its effects were highly visible. That these were the twin manifestations of a deep-seated structural change in the local economy was perhaps less easily appreciated. It was experienced primarily in terms of pressures for land use change, for this was the only point in the transformation of the local economy at which the local policy-makers possessed a responsive decision role. How they coped with those pressures is the theme of a later chapter; before turning to it we review the rather different patterns of change occurring in the older inner city areas of London.

Decline in inner London

Some structural factors in inner London

The significance of manufacturing industry in Greater London is often overestimated. Nevertheless, as recently as 1966 there was a substantial manufacturing presence in the inner boroughs, varying from 22 per cent in Camden to a high of 40 per cent in Tower Hamlets. The figures for manufacturing contraction in particular boroughs have then to be seen against these variable baselines, which nowhere approach the high proportions previously employed in manufacturing in the outer west London boroughs.

It will be seen from these figures that while Hammersmith's manufacturing employment fell by more than a half over a nine-year period, it did so from a relatively low base, and the comparable percentage fall in Tower Hamlets is in real terms more dramatic. The gross figure of employment loss due to manufacturing closures in each borough shows more clearly the variations in magnitude as well as the greater apparent vulnerability of the docklands boroughs, where the very substantial declines in employment have attracted considerable attention.

It has been argued that the preponderance of small firms in the inner city increases the vulnerability of such areas, particularly in the light of changes in their competitive position which have followed from increasing scale and concentration. The Inner London Consultative Employment Group, a joint public-private promotional body, estimated in 1978 that over half of inner London's employment was concentrated in small firms, that is, those employing fewer than 200 workers. This is a rather broad definition of the small firm; indeed, among the smaller firms – those with less than 100 workers – there is a large number of *very* small firms employing less than a dozen, or less

Figure 5.6   Percentage employed in manufacturing, 1966, and decline 1966–1975: Inner London

	Percentage employed in manufacturing 1966	Percentage decline in manufacturing employment 1966–1975
Camden	22	33
(Greenwich)	33	46
Hackney	n/a	n/a
Haringey	37	32
Hammersmith	24	52
(Lambeth)	n/a	n/a
Lewisham	25	41
Newham	33	30
Southwark	29	44
Tower Hamlets	40	54
Wandsworth	37	35

Note: Inner London is taken to be the Group A boroughs for the purpose of this table. Greenwich is, however, included on grounds of its similar industrial experience. The West End boroughs of Kensington and Chelsea and Westminster are excluded.

Source: Estimated figures given in Proof of Evidence submitted to Parliament in respect of the GLC General Powers Bill, 1978.

Figure 5.7   Estimated employment loss attributable to factory closures, 1966–1974

Camden	10,700
(Greenwich)	14,100
Haringey	6,800
Hammersmith	5,700
Lambeth	7,100
Lewisham	5,000
Newham	12,100
Southwark	19,300
Tower Hamlets	14,400
Wandsworth	4,700

Source: R. Dennis, in A. Evans and D. Eversley, *The Inner City: Industry and Employment* (Heinemann, London, 1980).

than five persons. However, there are fairly marked differences between the boroughs in the size of firms, especially in the manufacturing sector. Figures 5.8 and 5.9 illustrate some of the variation among a selection of boroughs for which data are available.

While the size structure of inner city industry may be seen as an indicator of the vulnerability of the individual enterprise, the representation of larger firms (and particularly large branches of multi-plant manufacturing firms) may be a source of vulnerability for the inner city workforce. This is most obviously the case where the larger firms are located within declining sectors of the economy; such is the classic problem of the development areas. Overall, however, London's industrial problem has not been one of structural disadvantage in this sense. Rather, while Greater London's industrial structure has been favourable throughout the post-war years, this innate advantage has been more than offset by poor performance, a situation which is common to the older conurbations. Industry in London has done relatively badly, recording low levels of growth and with high levels of job loss

Figure 5.8   Size distribution of small firms in some inner London boroughs (all industries)

Borough	Number of firms employing:					All firms
	5	6–25	26–50	51–100	1–100	
Camden	5698 (55%)	3241 (31%)	710 (7%)	394 (4%)	10,043 (97%)	10,386 (100%)
Tower Hamlets	2445 (53%)	1569 (34%)	323 (7%)	138 (3%)	4502 (97%)	4615 (100%)
Lambeth	2989	1636	296	180	5101	n/a
Newham	1974 (48%)	1506 (37%)	263 (6%)	171 (4%)	3914 (95%)	4071 (100%)

Source: Estimated figures given in Proof of Evidence submitted to Parliament in respect of the GLC General Powers Bill, 1978.

Figure 5.9   Size distribution of small manufacturing firms in some inner London boroughs

Borough	Number of firms employing:					All firms
	5	6–25	26–50	51–100	1–100	
Greenwich	169 (45%)	118 (31%)	27 (7%)	24 (6%)	338 (89%)	375 (100%)
Southwark	307 (34%)	385 (43%)	88 (10%)	55 (6%)	835 (93%)	884 (100%)
Hammersmith	288 (57%)	162 (31%)	19 (4%)	22 (4%)	491 (96%)	509 (100%)

Source: Estimated figures given in Proof of Evidence submitted to Parliament in respect of the GLC General Powers Bill, 1978.

even in industries which were static nationally.[25] This poor performance to some extent reflects the trend discussed in the previous chapter of a drift of new investment away from traditional urban locations. While rationalisation or modernisation has taken place, the benefits have been enjoyed elsewhere since the usually older inner London plants have been the ones to contract or close.

Looking first north of the Thames, to the Canning Town area of Newham, between 1966 and 1972 dock employment there fell by 42 per cent, employment in ship repair by 70 per cent, in food manufacture by 30 per cent, and in chemicals by 68 per cent. The introduction of North Sea gas led to the loss of 5000 jobs in coal gas manufacture at the Beckton gas works. The contraction of employment in the docks and in ship repair arose during the early stages of the modernisation of the port in response to containerisation and was exacerbated by competition from the deep water ports. As the CDP team concluded of Canning Town, 'because two-thirds of its industries had survived successfully for so long, decline came very rapidly at the end. Since 1966, when 67 per cent of jobs were still in traditional industries, 24,000 jobs have disappeared'.[26]

Across the Thames at Greenwich we find evidence of a similarly severe contraction, despite the presence in that borough of a number of more modern industries. The industrial areas of Greenwich – largely on the riverside belt from Deptford to Woolwich – grew up around shipbuilding and there evolved a concentration in metal casting and in mechanical and electrical engineering. The riverside location also encouraged the development of those food processing industries which relied on the river for the transport of materials in bulk, particularly in those connected with flour milling and sugar refining. Decline has been steady and prolonged.[27] In 1950, plants on Greenwich riverside employed 50,000 workers. By 1971 employment had fallen to around 20,000. Among the major closures was that of the AEI factory in Woolwich, which closed following merger with GEC with the loss of 5000 jobs, the largest single closure experienced in Britain by that date.[28] Other closures followed soon afterwards, at Parsons Engineering Works and at Norton Villiers, where the Woolwich closure was but one in the series of mergers and rationalisations which ended in the virtual extinction of the British motorcycle industry.

In neighbouring Southwark the pattern is repeated. Here, 52,000 manufacturing jobs were lost between 1961 and 1971 and a further 11,500 during the next three years. In paper, printing and publishing – the largest single specialism – the numbers employed fell by 3000 during the period 1971–1974. In food and drink manufacture, the second largest category, employment fell by 29 per cent in two years. Food and drink production had been concentrated in large, elderly and mainly local firms. Take-overs of Courage breweries by Imperial Tobacco, of Peak Frean by United Biscuits and of Shuttleworth by Mackintosh preceded local closures and the transfer of production to more spacious sites elsewhere.[29]

The effects of corporate changes, technical changes and change in the urban structure worked together in Southwark to undercut the borough's particular status as a metropolitan centre of distribution. As a local trades council report observed:

The factors making Southwark an advantageous location for the food and drink industries have weakened. The docks have moved away and the import market has changed in such a way as to reduce the importance of the Central London produce markets . . . New containerisation techniques, with palletisation and bulk carriers, lend themselves to direct lorry load deliveries to customers and to new depots well placed for access to the national motorway network. Like most industries, food products are more frequently transported from factories in large lorries along the motorway network than by rail. In this way, Southwark's advantages in terms of its own network of railways and its access to the rest of the country have been reduced.[30]

The sugar refining industry provides an apt illustration of the complex of structural forces, exogenous to the inner city locations, which have led to substantial employment losses in several of the riverside boroughs. When Britain joined the EEC in 1973 an obligation to bring sugar production into line with the requirements of the Common Agricultural Policy was accepted, subject to a transitional period. The EEC aim was to work towards self-sufficiency using home-grown sugar beet, and Europe's powerful beet producing lobby maintained considerable pressure to exclude sugar cane imports from the African, Caribbean and Pacific countries. The 1975 Lomé sugar protocol provided certain guarantees to these cane producing countries, and between 1973 and 1980 Tate and Lyle, as the largest refiners of cane sugar and as the importers of 75 per cent of the cane sugar entering the country, encountered major problems of adaptation in a climate of extreme uncertainty.[31]

Before 1973 Tate and Lyle's processing of sugar cane accounted for about two-thirds of UK sugar production. Under the new sugar regime, Tate and Lyle clearly had considerable over-capacity. Such initial rationalisation as was attempted was negated by over-production of sugar within the EEC, and by a rise in UK beet production. Profits slumped drastically, and Tate and Lyle's export tonnage fell from 210,000 tonnes in 1977 to 94,000 tonnes in 1978.[32]

By 1979 the overall implication of EEC membership for Tate and Lyle was a reduction in capacity of 650,000 tonnes and a loss of 7000 jobs at the various refineries. The fall in capacity had a major impact on refineries in Newham and Hammersmith, as well as those in Liverpool and Scotland. In 1966, Tate and Lyle employed 5600 workers at the Thames refinery in Newham, where 1700 jobs were lost between that date and EEC entry. In 1976 Tate and Lyle acquired Manbre and Garton, one of their major competitors, with refineries further up river at Hammersmith and Battersea. In 1977 the Hammersmith plant was closed and a modernisation programme implemented at Battersea. In 1978, one of the Merseyside plants was closed and capacity reduced at another. In 1979 one of the refineries at Greenock, Scotland was closed. In 1980, with profits running at £5.6 million on a turnover of £375 million, Tate and Lyle moved to resolve finally their over-capacity crisis by closing the remaining Liverpool plant. By 1981 Tate and Lyle were left with just two refining plants, the Newham refinery remaining in operation only as a result of substantial modernisation and reduced manning levels.[33]

Sugar substitutes were also adversely affected by the EEC sugar regime. One of Tate and Lyle's associates, Tunnel Refineries, had developed the capacity for isoglucose production in a new plant in Greenwich. The EEC sugar beet lobby secured a levy on isoglucose production to render it uncompetitive. Within months of opening, Tunnel Refineries were running at just one-fifth of their capacity, to the dismay of local policy-makers and trade unionists. In 1978, however, the European Court quashed the levy, and the Greenwich plant was able to recover, despite the generally unfavourable market conditions prevailing.[34]

The case of Tate and Lyle is in no sense typical of large manufacturing firms, but its particular vulnerability to changes in world commodity prices and international agreements serves to illustrate ways in which exogenous factors can operate, via corporate economic strategies, upon the inner city economy. As Department of Industry figures indicate, however, excessive concern with the larger enterprise may be misplaced; substantial proportions of inner London job losses are attributable to the problems facing the smaller firm.[35] Moreover, the heavy emphasis placed upon corporate considerations by the CDP teams can lead to underestimation of factors specific to the inner urban areas or likely to be of special significance there; the structuralist argument can account for most, but not all of urban economic change. The inner city as an unfavourable milieu is a further factor reinforcing and interacting with broader, non-localised trends.

The inner London milieu
The aspects of the inner city milieu which constrain its attractiveness for industrial investment have been discussed in Chapter 4. Some aspects may be singled out here to illustrate the kinds of local factors which have contributed to the further de-industrialisation of the inner

areas of London. They include physical obsolescence and constraints on movement, skill shortages, fiscal stress, and public sector policies.

Physical obsolescence of premises and physical unsuitability of sites are widely quoted problems of manufacturing industry located in those areas of London which date from the nineteenth century. These reasons predominate among those given by firms vacating their premises to locate elsewhere and are closely linked to the desire to expand output. While firms generally prefer to expand *in situ*, the density of sites, congestion and the often complex pattern of landownership, coupled with the desire to escape from the constraints of multi-storey buildings, ensure that expansion on site is often not feasible.[36] Not only do firms bear costs specific to the inner city; those firms which choose to avoid such costs by movement are, by and large, those which will experience growth in their new locations. Firms remaining in the inner city on the other hand are likely to be less competitive (except in relation to particular local markets) due to the lack of space in which to achieve the necessary productivity gains. Space is also needed for car parking and goods handling. Inner city industrial premises often cover the whole of the available site, leaving loading, offloading and employees' parking to take place on the streets. As the Southwark Trades Council report eloquently puts it,

the increasing use of large heavy lorries for road transport has made access difficult to many of the industrial premises in Southwark on account of the narrow busy streets and sharp corners. The increasing use of containers requires not only large vehicles but also space for manoeuvring, storage and handling equipment which is not easily available on sites originally designed to be served by horsecarts or barges.[37]

The outward movement of many successful firms and the migration of skilled manual workers have led to shrinkage in the pool of inner London's skilled workers. High rates of unemployment in inner areas may then co-exist with skill shortages for those remaining manufacturing firms. Indeed, skill shortages often come a close second to unsatisfactory premises in firms' responses to questions about the problems of inner urban locations. Contrary to popular expectations, the decline of manufacturing in London has done little to ease the situation as skilled workers have proved more mobile, and it is the unskilled – and in particular those formerly employed in construction, distribution or transport – who remain behind. As the South-East Joint Planning Team observed,

this is in line with trends in industry generally, where the nature of the demand for labour is changing and jobs for the unskilled are becoming less readily available . . . [moreover] when firms move from London there is a tendency for their skilled workers to go with them and for the unskilled workforce to be left behind. Other things being equal, if firms continue to leave London there is clearly a danger of a pool of unskilled labour being left in the capital.[38]

The association of unskilled unemployment and of youth unemployment with problems of housing stress, race relations and police-community relations is beyond the scope of this chapter. It is none the less evident that black workers are more likely to be in low skill jobs and on lower earnings if in employment and, overall, are more likely to experience unemployment.[39] The recent volatility of the inner cities, with major disturbances in Brixton and elsewhere in the summer of 1981, can hardly enhance the image of the inner city as a milieu for enterprise. Nor do workers in these areas have much prospect of mobility. The job search horizons of unskilled workers tend to be narrower, in part because of their more limited access to transport, and in part because of their housing tenure.[40] In the case of black workers, discrimination in the housing system and labour markets compound this situational immobility.

The fiscal crisis of inner London has been well recognised since Eversley's seminal discussion of rising costs and static incomes in the metropolis.[41] The allocation of funds to particular authorities under the enhanced urban programme notwithstanding, London as a whole has suffered from massive withdrawals of central government grants, particularly in 1981–1982. If corresponding cuts in services are not made (and such services may include direct and indirect benefits to industry), then expenditure has to be met by increased local taxation. Rising rate demands are a source of loud complaint from industrialists, and have figured in the reasons given for closures and moves in respect of many inner London firms.[42] It is not possible to be precise as to how far rate bills do undercut the viability of inner city firms; nevertheless, they are perceived as an important – and increasing – disincentive to inner urban location. Moreover, closures and moves themselves, by reducing the fiscal base of inner urban authorities, necessarily increase the tax levy on those that remain. While it is difficult to disentangle real costs from the rhetorical claims of industrialists, the fact remains that the image of the inner city as providing an inhospitable fiscal climate for industry is potent and long-standing; the claimed association between high rates and industrial exodus in London pre-dates the Great War.[43]

The two major short-term determinants of rate levels – central government grant and the local rateable value – are beyond the direct control of local authorities, except at the margin. Other points of influence upon the locational preferences of firms lie more directly within their control through the application of planning policies. There can be no doubt that, historically, local decisions on land use have had a negative effect on industrial growth, on the retention of local industry, and in some cases on the survival capability of individual firms. The handling of routine planning applications has frequently been cited as a source of frustration for industrialists, arising from excessive delay and frequent conflict with the local authority priorities for non-industrial uses on particular sites.[44] The relocation of nonconforming industry expresses this conflict with particular acuteness.

Since the mid-1970s local practices have shifted sharply towards a more facilitating or even promotional approach to local industry in both inner city and suburban settings.[45] This aspect of the urban milieu has undoubtedly changed, if the transformation in intentions is any guide to current practice. Many London authorities, including the GLC are now attempting, by direct or indirect means, to reverse the deterioration in the urban industrial milieu and to restore the standing of London as an industrial city. How, why and to what purpose this aim was pursued in two London boroughs is the concern of Chapters 6 and 7 of this book.

The inner/outer contrasts

If we confine our interest to the sheer *scale* of manufacturing employment losses, we have to agree that 'the difference between inner and outer London is not great. . . . industrial decline is clearly a feature of the whole conurbation and is not confined to the inner city'.[46] The crucial differences between inner and outer London lie not in the scale of manufacturing job losses, but in three other areas: the relative success of the two zones in adapting to change; in their rather different industrial structures; and in the greater propensity of outer London industry to make successful moves out of the metropolis.

In outer London, manufacturing losses have been compensated for in large part by a steady increase in service employment. Although the overall changes, with gains in finance, insurance, banking, professional and technical services and public administration have been important – and to some extent underpin the shift from blue-collar to white-collar employment – they could hardly be assimilated by a static workforce. Much of outer London's adaptation has been achieved by journey-to-work changes, or by migration of skilled workers to the industrial growth areas in the Outer Metropolitan Area (OMA) or beyond.[47] For various reasons these options have been less readily available to the inner London population.

A further factor serving to differentiate inner and outer London is the contrast in the industrial structure of the two areas. While a substantial proportion of Greater London's employment is located in small firms, inner London firms are generally smaller still, and the inner boroughs are characterised by an increasing scarcity of large private sector manufacturing employers. In 1968 72 per cent of those inner London manufacturing establishments which employed more than 25 persons employed less than 100, and only 23 per cent between 100 and 500; in outer London the corresponding figures were 56 and 35 per cent.[48] Larger establishments have a greater effect on the local economy when they close, and for this reason a very substantial proportion of outer London's employment losses during the period 1966 to 1974 was attributable to the closure of a relatively small proportion of relatively large firms. In inner London in contrast, small rather than large firms accounted for more than one-third of the overall job loss.[49] Moreover, these figures do not include the smallest firms, those employing less than 25 workers, where the differentials between inner and outer London in both industrial structure and contributions to job loss are likely to be considerable.

The contrasts between the inner and outer zones in terms of size of firm are the legacy of different stages in the metropolitan life-cycle; they reflect the short-distance, space-seeking moves by firms which relocated in the expanding areas of the outer industrial suburbs in the inter-war and post-war years. Successful firms initially encountered their ceilings to growth in the cramped conditions of the Victorian inner city areas. The few that remained to grow *in situ* were those fortunate enough to have secured sites of sufficient size. Many of these are the very firms whose premises are inadequate for present-day needs and whose sites represent opportunities for profitable commercial redevelopment. To some extent, the size disparities also reflect the continued existence of small specialised enterprises supplying particular and highly localised inner London markets, or manufacturing nonstandard short-run products to special order, the small firms regarded as particularly characteristic of the inner city.

Thus, the initial impression given by the broad comparability in the magnitude of job loss in inner and outer London is misleading, since the size of firm figures as an important differentiating factor. There are further differences in the sources of job loss in the two zones. Complete closures are more characteristic of inner London, while relocation to a more favourable environment is of proportionately greater importance in explaining the contraction of manufacturing employment in the suburbs. As Dennis concludes:

A larger proportion of the decline in inner London can be attributed to the differences between openings and complete closures of manufacturing establishments than is the case in outer London (66 per cent as against 58 per cent). The role of industrial movement in inner London's decline is correspondingly smaller, accounting for only 34 per cent, with most of that being shorter distance movement either to London overspill towns (11 per cent) or to other locations primarily in the South East or East Anglia (15 per cent). In outer London, on the other hand, industrial movement is much more important, accounting for 42 per cent of the total job loss. In so far as firms move to expand this is an indication, perhaps, of the more dynamic nature of manufacturing in the outer areas.[50]

Finally, it will be apparent that the spatial pattern of adaptation in Greater London cannot be adequately described by such simple inner-/outer dichotomies, for of equal significance is the marked east/west skew in employment change. The most successful areas in outer London have been those to the west of the metropolis, conveniently based between the business and financial centre of central London and the airport at Heathrow, yet increasingly vulnerable to the counter-attractions of the growing towns strung out west along the M4 motorway, particularly Reading, Swindon and Bristol.[51] Today, the presence of Heathrow airport is a vital factor in west London's relative prosperity. Heathrow directly employs more than 52,000 workers, and the growth of the airport complex as a passenger and freight centre has exercised a dominant (and not entirely beneficial) influence over the outer west London labour market.[52] In contrast, the least successful areas in inner London are those of the East End and south-east boroughs, and particularly the dockland and industrial areas of the lower Thames.

The impact of change: two case-studies

The two London boroughs which we chose for more detailed study exemplify these several contrasts. 'Westborough' is an outer west London borough, subject to the sectoral and occupational changes which we noted in the first part of this chapter, and incurring the costs and the benefits of proximity to Heathrow. 'Southborough' is situated in inner London and shares with the south-east London boroughs many of the problems of rapid industrial decline, particularly along the industrialised stretch of the River Thames. At the same time, Southborough profits from easy access to both the City and Heathrow, and is regarded favourably as a prestige commercial and headquarters location.

There are, then, both parallels and contrasts between the circumstances of the two boroughs. It should be borne in mind that each authority covers a substantial area of London, and that neither is homogenous, economically or socially. Their boundaries are of purely historical significance; neither has much claim to correspondence with the realities of London's complex labour market structure.

Westborough and Southborough are also characterised by marked contrasts in what we termed, in Chapter 2, the organisational and appreciative contexts of policy-making. The style, structure and culture of the two authorities considered as organisations are quite different and we shall examine these differences more closely in Chapter 8. In the next two chapters we present a narrative of the early moves towards intervention in local economic affairs. In each case, the powerful and general forces for urban de-industrialisation which we have sketched out in these last three chapters are experienced in very local and particular ways. The closure of a factory, a gradual contraction of apprenticeships, or the persistent pressure of planning applications for the redevelopment of industrial sites for commercial or warehousing purposes are the immediate manifestations of change and the ones to which local officials are required to respond.

In the two case-studies which follow we see two different groups of actors, operating within two contrasting organisational and apprecia-tive contexts yet engaged in a similar process: that of establishing a claim to attention on behalf of economic factors. The crucial role of the 'policy entrepreneur' in securing a place for industry and employment issues upon the policy agenda will be apparent. So too will be the fluid and interactive nature of the internal politics of the two authorities in which claims as to the identification and 'ownership' of problems are made, contested, elaborated or abandoned over time. It is worth at this stage recalling Bossard's neat summary of the evolution of a social problem as following this course:

(1) recognition of the problem; (2) discussion of its seriousness; (3) attempts at reform, usually intuitively arrived at, often ill-advised, promoted by the 'Well, let's do *something* folks'; (4) suggestions that more careful study is needed – 'What we need is a survey'; (5) here follows some change in personnel of people interested; (6) emphasis upon broad basic factors; (7) dealing with individual cases; (8) another change in personnel; (9) program inductively arrived at; (10) refinements of technique of study and treatment; (11) refinements of concepts; (12) another change in personnel.[53]

It would be surprising if this precise sequence of events were followed in any particular case, yet, as we shall see, Bossard's portrayal of the process is powerfully suggestive.

6 Westborough: A Strategy Against the Tide

THE London boroughs came into existence on 1 April 1965 when, under the devolution of power effected by the 1963 London Government Act, they became land use authorities in their own right. In the early years of the new system of London government there was considerable uncertainty about the respective roles of the Greater London Council (GLC) – the 'metropolitan' authority – and the boroughs as local planning authorities.[1] As an interim measure, the development plans of the nine former county and county borough authorities were synthesised by the GLC in the Initial Development Plan, pending the preparation of a new strategic statement, the Greater London Development Plan. Planning in west Middlesex was thus set firmly in the context of policies established by the former Middlesex County Council, and the outer west London boroughs had to set the formulation of statements for the interpretation and implementation of planning decisions within these overall guidelines.

Coping with the pressures

The London borough of Westborough approved an interim industrial policy in September 1966. This policy statement reflected the wider Initial Development Plan in several respects: undeveloped land was to be reserved for the relocation of badly-sited nonconforming industry; developed industrial land would remain in the existing use; and schemes for the overspill of industry and population would be used to encourage the decongestion of London. In order to provide for the relocation of nonconforming industry from residential or amenity areas, warehouse development, in particular, would not normally be permitted on vacant industrial land.

This then was the policy framework within which specific decisions were to be taken over the next five years.[2] After its acceptance, applications to convert and extend manufacturing premises for storage were repeatedly turned down as 'contrary to the provisions of the Initial Development Plan'. When the developer appealed against the decision, as happened on several occasions, the minister upheld the ruling 'on the grounds that he accepted the Council's view that vacant industrial land should be reserved to satisfy the comparatively long-term objective of relocating nonconforming industry and to provide room for the expansion of those industrial firms which can justify remaining in the Greater

London area'. As this policy continued to be maintained, a surplus of vacant industrial land became apparent, and this surplus coincided with a growing demand for warehousing arising in part from the further development of Heathrow airport.

By the early 1970s prospects for maintaining a manufacturing base were being called into question. Departures from the approved policy became more common, and the borough planning department was increasingly seen to be at some disadvantage at inquiries into appeals resulting from refusals of planning consent for warehouses. There was a fear that in future such refusals would be difficult to sustain. Moreover, the industrial relocation policy was not being fully implemented. It is generally the case that planning departments prefer to avoid vulnerable positions in the exercise of development control, and in March 1971 the borough planning officer (BPO) advised a change of policy on the grounds that 'it would now seem desirable to permit, in principle, warehouse development on industrially allocated land . . . to accommodate the present demand for warehousing'. The planning committee would not give this change unqualified acceptance, and agreed to amend the existing policy to permit warehouse development only 'where special circumstances justify it'. These were broad guidelines, and open to varied interpretation. An internal 'practice note', giving policy guidance to development control officers, took the line that special circumstances had to be identified before warehouse development on industrial land was allowed, and that there was otherwise a *prima facie* case for refusal of planning permission. Despite this guidance, the next twelve months saw a flood of successful warehouse applications. In March 1972 one of the planning officers questioned the new policy, saying that 'we should at least be very selective in our approvals and try to insist that a real need to be in this area should be clearly demonstrated by applicants'.

During this period industrial policy was discussed at a series of joint meetings of the west Middlesex boroughs, all of which were facing similar pressures. A number of councillors held the view that

> although local authorities may prefer industrial use rather than warehouses, there was some obligation to ratepayers for accommodation to be in use and rated rather than standing unused with consequent loss of revenue. In some areas of south-west Middlesex there was a high level of unusual industrial buildings and any type of use was to be welcomed.

This thinking was reflected in some of Westborough's planning decisions at this time. Five approvals for change of use from industrial production to a mix of storage and office use between January 1969 and May 1972 represented a loss of over 80,000 square feet of production floorspace and of more than 100 jobs. Straight switches from production to storage use were involved in a further seven decisions in which more than 600 manufacturing jobs were lost but more than 1000 warehouse jobs gained. Where consent had been granted for *industrial* development, on the other hand, the implementation of the permission and the associated generation of new jobs seemed to lag far behind the expected benefits. It was also apparent that the overall employment level was affected by a small number of large warehouse developments, and that the lag in industrial developments largely turned upon a greater number of rather small projected developments. This implementation problem was crucial to the way in which existing policy was to be read: while the pattern of *consents* produced a positive balance of employment generation, the pattern of *development* indicated a fairly substantial employment loss.

Employment loss became an issue for the first time. The GLC itself, preoccupied with the preparation of the GDLP, was confronted with a fierce debate as to the long-term economic effects of decentralisation policies. The control of industrial location in particular was seen by some not as an essential tool for relief of metropolitan congestion but as a serious threat to the employment and welfare of the metropolitan population. As an *Evening Standard* leader in February 1972 put it: 'It is time to think closely about what variety of employment London should be providing if it is to halt the trend towards economic decline and avoid the kind of social polarisation that is now the blight of urban North America'.[3]

For the most part, officers of Westborough's planning department defended their policy line, maintaining that the switch of function to warehousing would continue to generate employment. The planners argued that any employment generation was preferable to empty sites, and that the changes, although undesirable in policy terms, were apparently inevitable. However, they were confronted with the increasing scepticism of a number of their colleagues. A local employment office manager estimated that the shift from manufacturing to warehousing could cut employment on any site to a tenth of the previous level, while other estimates suggested a 50 per cent cut was more realistic. The planning department officers tended to this latter view, regarding the employment potential of warehousing as 'by no means as unfavourable' as had been suggested, arguing instead that while warehouse estates had 'a somewhat deserted appearance' this was due to a long 'tail' of outworkers – for example delivery men – who routinely work off-site.

By the spring of 1973 the planners were able to argue that employment opportunities were growing and that the problem of the area, at least of the western end of the borough, was not unemployment but labour shortages in skilled trades. The shift to warehousing had indeed

been defended on this very ground. It was argued that its lower employment demands would relieve the problem of insufficient labour
supply. While the anxieties about warehouse substitution mounted
elsewhere, Westborough's planners continued to argue that, of the
several distinct types of warehouse development, theirs were mainly
relatively high users of labour – air freight and wholesale distribution
rather than long-term storage. Significantly, however, it was admitted
that the local authority could not control the mix of the warehouse
types: 'all the storage uses mentioned above fall into the same "Use
Class Category" as far as development control is concerned, and a
planning authority cannot control changes between warehousing which
is labour intensive and that which is not'.

The pressure to pursue employment objectives rather than permit
indiscriminate development came internally, and originated in the
borough's education department. During the spring of 1972 the careers
sub-committee had expressed concern 'at the number of manufacturing
firms which had closed down or moved out of the borough, particularly
in the London airport area, and the number of warehouses which had
been established. The warehouses offered fewer employment opportunities than manufacturing'. The education committee decided to
support this position, and called upon the planning and development
committee to 'investigate ways of limiting warehouse establishments
and development and of attracting manufacturing business to the area
instead'. The planning department line was still that warehouse employment generation was 'far from negligible', but the BPO now admitted that 'the change that is occurring is certainly . . . a reduction of
employment opportunities and the reduction seems to be weighted
against the production workers . . . Whether this change is inevitable is
a matter for consideration. That it has certain undesirable features also
seems clear'.

There were, however, no clear policy options which the planners
would have accepted as feasible. A return to the earlier policy of
resisting warehousing pressures was ruled out. Yet the internal pressures remained. The youth employment sub-committee (a body
advised by the borough careers officer) complained in November 1972
that no progress had been made in attracting manufacturing industry
and limiting warehouses, pointing out in addition that the planning
department had not pressed forward with joint meetings with neighbouring boroughs. Again, the education committee endorsed these
concerns, calling once more upon the planning and development committee to stem 'the continuing loss of employment opportunities in the
borough' and asking 'if ways have been found of improving the situation'. The planning department's position was still that the *overall* level
of employment gave no cause for concern, and that 'workers made

redundant by closures are very soon re-employed because of the overall labour shortage in the area'.

By this stage the terms of the debate were beginning to shift away from the level of unemployment towards the *structure* of it. When the BPO reported on the employment implications of industrial change the director of education succeeded in inserting a passage which achieved just such a shift:

For young people leaving school, there has been a reduction in the number of skilled apprenticeships available in the borough. The move in the margin from manufacturing industry to warehousing/services/offices has paradoxically done little to provide more vacancies in unskilled and semi-skilled work for school leavers. New warehouses often operate with advanced technical equipment which reduces the amount of manual labour employed. The increased demand for drivers, transport staff and other jobs off-site doesn't greatly help the job opportunities for young school leavers as most of these support jobs can be more suitably filled by applicants over the age of 18.

There was now some common ground between the several departments.

Armed with a consensual definition of the area's problem, the borough's leaders were more inclined to act. In June 1973 they joined the representatives of the neighbouring boroughs in a joint delegation to the Minister of Industrial Development. At this meeting they expressed their 'concern at the loss of manufacturing industry and jobs from West Middlesex and losses of job opportunities for skilled workers. Although in some cases alternative employment was available, there was a danger of skills being lost permanently . . . and a smaller range of opportunities for young people who might face prospects of early redundancy'.

Their favoured solution to the problem was the relaxation of controls over industrial locations, and in particular of the Industrial Development Certificate (IDC) controls which were intended to steer development to the assisted areas. The government's view was not sympathetic. The minister pointed out that IDC controls had already been relaxed and that the overall employment and earnings levels in Greater London were higher than elsewhere: west London, in the government's view, was an 'over-heated' area.

This meeting and others that followed prompted a re-evaluation of Westborough's position, and in particular of the borough's dependence on the warehousing spin-off from Heathrow: one planner complained that 'if London Airport ever became second to Maplin – which is what the government seems to intend – we should have no factories, a lot of warehouses, and all serving what? We need diversity of employment. But the government does not seem to realise this'. As a result, the planning department were less sanguine than before when the education committee made the by now annual demand for assurances that the need for manufacturing employment 'will be borne in mind when consideration is given to applicants for a change of use'. Indeed, the demand caused some irritation, for, as one planner remarked, the education officers 'didn't have to defend their policies at inquiries and see them constantly ignored by ministry inspectors'.

The most acute pressures took the form of applications for *in situ* changes of use from manufacturing to office premises. When one major manufacturer proposed to convert nearly 100,000 square feet of their Arterial Road factory to offices the planning officers were alarmed, noting that the implications were serious, 'not only for the Arterial Road but for similar industrial enclaves in other parts of West London . . . the central issue here seems to us to be whether it is expedient – it can hardly be desirable – to permit the use of this recently erected, purpose-built factory for office purposes. The application is of course contrary to policy on virtually every conceivable count'. On the other hand, it was recognised that a refusal might prompt the firm to move *all* their operations elsewhere, closing their *other* local factories. Moreover, it was recognised that the unusual 'tower' design of the factory building was unlikely to appeal to any other firms as a factory alone; mindful of the risks of having another refusal quashed on appeal, the planners reluctantly supported the application.

To some extent the considerable pressure for office development which began to mount after 1975 deflected the debate about warehousing to new territory. The borough valuer noted in October of that year that 'institutions are now returning to investment in the property market', and that their need for high rental values dictated a high proportion of offices. The newly-appointed chief executive pressed for office development on land held by the borough itself, but the Department of the Environment and the GLC were both hostile to any speculative office development. The GLC itself sought to steer new offices into those parts of London where the ratio of office jobs to redundant office workers was lowest, and on this basis Westborough would receive a low priority. The valuer was thus particularly keen to match prospective tenants with possible development opportunities and, providing Office Development Permits (ODPs) could be obtained, 'the development of any site should be pressed immediately without consideration of any possible order of priorities'.

Here, then, was a form of development that promised further employment generation. Pressure for commercial development was more welcome than pressure for warehousing, at least to those who were concerned with the fiscal health of the borough or its employment diversity. Only those members of the planning department who saw the exodus of manufacturing as primarily driven by labour shortage were worried. As one planner noted,

no one seems to have examined the possible consequences of nearly one million square feet of new office space in the borough . . . this would provide employment for some 6000 persons, but where would they come from? There is already a shortage of office workers. Aggravation of the shortage would probably further encourage commerce and industry to move out of the borough at an even further rate.

By mid-1976 the discussion of industry and employment issues had developed from a basically responsive posture, that of bowing to the development pressures, to a recognition of a need for selectivity in responding to the pressures for change. Warehousing was to be contained where possible, while office development was to be encouraged. Small industrial units to be constructed by the council itself, perhaps in partnership with developers, were being planned. Moreover, IDC controls had been further relaxed, permitting the speculative redevelopment and modernisation of obsolete industrial buildings.

Towards an industrial strategy

While Westborough's planners were struggling to define effective policies towards industry, warehousing and offices, the policy-making process itself was becoming more open to change. The council's organisation in the mid-1970s was characterised by a Labour group which was generally more interested in matters of routine and detail than in 'policy'. The council had a strong leader, operating departments with considerable autonomy, an unassertive chief executive, and a small planning department led by a somewhat remote and soon-to-retire chief officer. Said by some to be 'almost running the council single-handed', the leader chaired the one-party 'policy group' and took a close interest in planning matters. The chief executive was neither strongly placed with regard to the councillors nor accustomed to leading his departmental colleagues. The organisation was later described by a well-placed observer as 'a federal system with strong professionally oriented departments' in which policy group meetings were largely devoted to resolution of the conflicts that arose from this departmentalism.

Within the planning department the borough planning officer, a surveyor by initial training, concentrated a great deal of the department's work into his own hands. There was little that could be described as 'departmental policy', and prior to its abolition the development control division complained bitterly of the lack of guidance on industry and employment issues. Moreover, the borough planning officer and his deputy tended to take their leads from *ad hoc* pressures from the politicians while some of the planners, at least, felt that the BPO's proper role was to 'educate the councillors'.

In this situation the arrival of a new chief executive in 1975 was naturally seen as a catalyst for policy. This chief executive had a strong commitment to corporate policy-making, and he immediately began to institute inter-departmental 'topic' groups to deal with difficult or neglected issues. The more restless planners saw an intelligence and strategy role for themselves under this new regime and welcomed the implied counterbalance to their own neutral and detached departmental chief.

One area in which the chief executive sought to make an impact was industrial and commercial policy. Initially, however, his activities were more apparent in the *inter-corporate* rather than the corporate arena – wooing the management of large multi-nationals seeking operating bases in the UK, or negotiating with the Department of the Environment in a bid to gain more freedom to initiate commercial development on publicly-owned land. In 1976 the borough planning officer retired and was replaced by a younger, more professionally-oriented planner who shared the chief executive's desire for a more policy-oriented system of decision-making.

An immediate review of the borough's planning system revealed 'a major deficiency in the provision of explicit policy documents and guidance on which decisions affecting future planning are taken'. Topic papers – covering a wider area than the 'neutral' issues reviewed hitherto, and specifically directed at councillors – were to be prepared within the planning department, and it was suggested that other departments might like to follow this example. It was hoped that 'a substantial political input' would be made through 'free and open discussion'. Accordingly, the proposals aimed to pull the councillors into the planning decision process and to confront them with land use policy issues. The key proposal – accepted by the council – was for a new, small, policy-oriented sub-committee which would report to the large and unwieldy environmental planning committee on policy issues, consider topic papers, prepare work programmes and commission research studies from the planning department.

By the end of 1977, then, three developments had occurred which could potentially reshape the policy process. A new chief executive of strong corporate inclination had been appointed, a new borough planning officer had arrived and was seeking explicit policy guidelines, and a new small planning policy forum had been created. It was the natural inclination of young, incoming chief officers to put new policy-making structures into effect. The BPO needed to rehabilitate a highly vulnerable department, the chief executive sought cross-cutting or corporate issues to give reality to his notional power. An *industrial strategy* could meet their common need.

In July 1977 the Departments of the Environment and Transport published a joint circular – *Local Government and the Industrial Strategy* – in which they sought to persuade local authorities to 'develop and maintain a close awareness of the problems and difficulties that industrial undertakings face, to give help whenever it is practicable to do so, to deal speedily with applications *and to ensure that full account is taken of industrial needs in reaching decisions*'.[4] Circular 71/77 contained novel features of considerable importance for local authorities. In the first place, it defined their local industrial situations as components of the national economic problem – it sought to redefine the local issues as macro-issues, particularly as regards *manufacturing* industry. Second, it stressed the significance of a broad range of local powers – in planning, transport and housing – for industrial well-being, and implied that coordinated policies were essential. It advocated the appointment of identifiable liaison officers for industry.

This was an appropriate moment for Westborough's chief executive to press for action. Two weeks after Circular 71/77 was received, he formally urged the departmental directors 'to examine the operations' of their departments 'to ensure that the maximum assistance is given to industry'. The borough valuer and director of planning were quick to respond, for the Circular came at a useful time for them. The valuer's department had been preparing schemes for the development of small industrial units and the Circular's emphasis on small firms and 'seedbed' factories gave the schemes fresh impetus. Moreover, the valuer's and planning departments were already skirmishing with the housing department over a number of industrial sites on which eventual residential development was scheduled. The Circular, then, provided a counterbalance to the momentum of Westborough's housing programme, which depended in part on the relocation of existing small industrial firms from proposed housing sites. These gradual and *ad hoc* moves were presented as 'a significant anticipation of what is sought in the DoE's Industrial Strategy', but, as the BPO pointed out, top level political endorsement was necessary to codify them as a policy.

The chief executive, valuer and BPO now effectively had the initiative and were able to provide an impetus towards a jointly agreed position for all departments in the nominally corporate chief officers' meetings. In this respect they went far beyond the education department's recurrent demands for action on industrial employment. In particular, they were able to resurrect a suggestion made by the representatives of industry and the trade unions that a seminar on employment problems be sponsored by the council as a follow-up to a meeting convened two years before. The prime purpose of the seminar would be 'to give local employers the opportunity to explain what kind of assistance they would seek from the authority and for the council to explain its policies regarding assistance to industry'.

Those proposed policies were agreed by the chief officers' meeting and subsequently endorsed by the environmental planning committee. Within four months of the publication of Circular 71/77, Westborough had formally adopted its suggestions *largely verbatim* to provide the explicit policy base that the BPO had sought for the planning department. The new policy was undeniably consistent with national guidelines; its implications however sat less easily with the more subtle approach to development pressures that had arisen over the previous four years, for the key policy declaration was that 'every effort will be made to encourage the maintenance of existing firms and the establishment of new industries through development control measures. *Change of use from industrial purposes will be resisted*'.

Moreover, vacant industrial floorspace would be developed, developers would be supported by the council in applying for Industrial Development Certificates, and wider contact and consultation with industry was promised. Two new internal arrangements were proposed: the appointment of an industrial liaison officer (ILO) and the establishment of an interdepartmental officer group 'to discuss the problems of local industry and formulate detailed proposals for their solution'.

Industrial liaison, in its more general sense, was not new to Westborough. Indeed the borough was unusual in sponsoring an Industrial and Commercial Consultative Committee which was first established at the request of the Confederation of British Industry in 1969, and had met on average three times a year since then. Under the industrial strategy proposals this rather formal body was to remain in being, and the new specific liaison remit was intended to improve contacts with individual firms, particularly by providing a single point of contact for inquirers. This was entirely in accordance with the DoE's advice, and although the first moves towards the preparation of a policy paper had come from the chief executive's office, the BPO had successfully nominated one of his own senior staff as industrial liaison officer, apparently establishing the primacy of the planning department in the industrial field.

Formally, then, planning now appeared to have the major responsibility for industrial matters. However, this was deceptive. In the first place, the chief executive continued to develop and expand his own contacts with industrialists, engaging in a continuing series of meetings with local managing directors. Thus he continued to meet local firms – and in particular the *larger* local firms – at the top level, lending a sympathetic ear to their problems and prospects, and frequently following up his visits with instructions to the ILO to pick up the threads by visiting the firms. The chief executive performed a liaison role mid-way between the polite rituals of the consultative committee and the detailed negotiations into which the ILO would be drawn. He continued to intervene personally whenever relations with other major agencies or higher levels of government were involved. More significant still was his insistence that while detailed matters might be taken up with the ILO, '*policy issues relating to industrial matters will continue to be addressed to the chief executive*'.

Clearly, the chief executive had a strong personal commitment to the new economic policy. However, the decision that Westborough was to have an 'industrial strategy' of its own with the (self-perceived) needs of manufacturing industry as its cornerstone obscured a considerable degree of scepticism among the council's officers. The test of the strategy would be the way in which actual decisions affecting industrial concerns were taken, and in early 1978 this was still a matter of conjecture. That the strategy itself was regarded cynically in some quarters is illustrated by a remark of one senior planner that 'the council is trying to adopt an approach like the inner boroughs . . . we must be being laughed at . . . it's a waste of time and money'.

It was also well-known that the ILO himself, being a more traditional 'local plans man', with a strong orientation to the physical rather than the economic environment, shared this scepticism. He was one of the industrial strategy's many critics within the planning department. He did not subscribe to the reasoning behind it, and accepted the ILO responsibility almost under duress, seeking written agreement as to its temporary nature. He left the post with relief when the planning department underwent a long-awaited reorganisation in the autumn of 1978. The officer who replaced him was recruited especially for the post and brought rather more conviction to it. The new commitment of the council, represented by the creation of the ILO post, had however failed to impress local industrialists. One commented that 'what's being presented is a very big change indeed and we'll take some convincing'. Local CBI members claimed they 'would rather have someone with business experience' as ILO, for it was important 'to be able to talk the language and understand the problems'.

Despite the internal and external scepticism and the apparent implausibility of the initial corporate commitment to an industrial strategy, this commitment established for the first time a definite planning policy context in Westborough. The ILO was now able to define the borough's position for potential developers:

The Council's policy towards industry is, in principle, one of support for expansion and renewal of the manufacturing base and it aims to support industrialists and developers wishing to build within the area. Industries which would be most welcome are those providing jobs for men and school leavers across a wide skill band. Generally speaking, the attitude to speculative industrial development is conditioned by the supply of space, and developments which could be readily let for industrial use and in small units are likely to be viewed favourably.

The initial priorities of the new Industrial Strategy Working Group (ISWG), set up to report to the environmental planning committee and comprising officers of the planning, valuer's, finance, education and engineer's departments, precisely reflected this concern. The topics agreed as demanding attention at the first meeting of ISWG in February 1978 included the shortages and training of skilled workers; the lack of vacancies for unskilled workers; the amount of obsolescence of vacant industrial premises; the extent of demand for industrial sites for expansion; the problems of small firms, the problem of industrial movement, the constraints posed by IDC and nonconforming use controls and the labour market aspects of housing and education.

While discussions on some of these topics were to continue through the next two years, the immediate need was seen to be the provision of a factual statement on the current employment position. The ISWG agreed that: 'once the necessary information had been obtained it would be possible to analyse how any recurrent difficulties might be met and determine whether or not it was a realistic objective to halt the decline in manufacturing industry and if so, whether this should be by trying to create more industry or just consolidating existing'.

It was not clear, however, how far the type of readily available factual material could help in making such a judgement. Figures on employment vacancies and summary figures on the registered unemployed were not difficult to obtain, but there were no obvious inferences to be drawn from them. Information on firms' self-defined problems and future investment intentions was not routinely available, although a limited survey had been carried out in Brentford, the eastern extreme of the borough. The ISWG planned and eventually launched a questionnaire to employers on their recruitment of school leavers but the necessary information for making a judgement as to the future of the manufacturing base could only be obtained from a broader-based survey. Such a survey was *rarely* suggested. Reluctance to back research on industrial change was a considerable handicap to this group who had no independent budget of their own over and above a slim allocation for publicity. Accordingly, their attention came to focus on those tangible projects that were within their competence: a guide to borough services aimed at prospective developers; a register of vacant industrial and commercial sites, available to inquirers; and a survey of the preferences of employers recruiting from among school leavers. The first of these was almost two years in preparation and generated a series of discussions about how best to communicate the council's services to developers; the final product stressed the need for a joint public and private sector approach to the industrial welfare of the borough.

The survey of employers saw the re-emergence of Westborough's education department in developing corporate policy. The establishment of the 'industrial strategy' had enabled the planning and valuation departments to seize the initiative in Westborough, and there had been fears that the seminar for industrialists would exclude education from any role. However, with their long record of concern about the changing employment structure, education were able to claim reinstatement easily enough. Moreover, they continued to be heavily represented on the ISWG, and their particular interests, far from being subsidiary to the group's main work, gradually came to the forefront of collective concern. The ILO, as chairman, tended to give them their head in the group's early discussions, frequently deferring to their knowledge.

In terms of 'giving a factual account' of the borough's employment problems there was indeed no one better placed than the principal careers officer in the education department; he worked closely with local Employment Service Division managers and regularly fed lengthy tabulations of local employment figures to the group. For example, he held information on major employers' staffing practices and on the training schemes operating in the borough. His primary responsibility was to the careers sub-committee, a body on which industrial and commercial co-optees were a majority of the membership, and which (through the education committee) had been the source of pressure on the planning department for some years. As long as the focus of concern was on the employment consequences of industrial change the education department officials had a virtual monopoly of intelligence.[5] Thus, during the initial planning of the questionnaire to employers, the ILO was asked how many firms operated in the borough; claiming no precise knowledge he hazarded a guess at 25,000 and suggested a sample of 500 for the survey. The principal careers officer gently intervened: 'We reckon there are about 700 in Westborough central, 300 in [the east end] and 300 at [the west end]'.

With such intelligence gaps and with no common concern with the causes of industrial change the ISWG as such were unlikely to produce the definitive account of change in the local economy. Apart from the planning department, who were represented by the openly sceptical first ILO, and the education representatives, who were in effect gaining corporate endorsement for their pre-existing concerns, there were few obvious issues at stake for the members. An officer from another department recollecting the early days of the group openly wondered why he had bothered to attend. The work of the group tended to be *ad hoc*, considering a thin stream of issues the substance of which derived largely from the enthusiasm of the diverse individuals who promoted them. Thus an education department official brought considerable energy to the employers' survey. A member of the social services department occupied the group for most of two meetings with pleas for support in a campaign to establish crêche facilities at major employment centres. At the behest of the council leader, prolonged consideration was given to the possibility of establishing workers' co-operatives in the borough.

The discussions in the ISWG seemed to neutralise rather than extend the issues of change in the local economy. One influential officer repeatedly claimed to be 'mystified' by the processes of change in the local industrial base, but there was no attempt to develop an analysis of its causes. The industrial strategy group was becoming little more than a forum in which particular departmental concerns could receive an airing and gain a more general status and, thereby, a more direct access to the corporate processes – the chief officers' meeting and the councillors' policy group. The ISWG was at risk of losing its notional role as the definer of local problems, for it remained open to any other department to bid independently for that role by providing a cogent account of 'what was going on' in Westborough. The challenge came at the end of 1978 from the planning department as the fruition of one of the BPO's first departmental initiatives: an employment topic paper reviewing the state of the local economy and assessing its policy implications.

Coming to terms with change
The new BPO had brought to his department a commitment to exploring policy issues through the medium of the 'topic papers', a device which would serve not only to focus the department's own work, but to place strategic issues directly before the councillors. The preparation of these papers was assigned to the younger members of the planning department. The junior planner who was charged with the preparation of the employment topic paper had earlier written the script of the industrial seminar's tape/slide show and was now working as the research arm of the industrial development interest in his department. His work ran in parallel with that of the ISWG, but he did not attend meetings of the group. His topic paper was seen as an important restatement of the planning department's authority in the industrial field.

Something more specific than the council's anodyne 'industrial strategy' was required if definite policies were to be realised through development control decisions, and if planning appeals were not to be lost for the want of a well-argued policy base. Moreover, the internal standing of the department was itself at stake. Not only had the education committee been consistently critical over the years, but members of the chief executive's department were suspected of harbouring ambitions to wrest the formulation of local plans away from planning and into their own hands on the grounds of its centrality to corporate and community planning needs. The planning department had been, as one member put it, 'very much on the defensive'; their launch of a closely-argued topic paper, supported by appropriate data, strengthened their own position and regained the initiative that an uninterested ILO had let slip.

The thrust of the paper was the portrayal of the problem for the council as one of 'coming to terms with an enormous structural change in the economy'. The problem for the local economy was not to be found in the overall employment consequences of the 'transformation' – indeed, it was argued that the growth of the service sector accounted for the buoyancy of the local labour market. The problem was rather one of 'imbalances' – mismatches within the pattern and conditions of employment and between the opportunities available in the eastern end of the borough and those available in the western end. The position of 'vulnerable groups' – women, the disabled, young people and unskilled workers – should feature in the development of a new *strategy for employment* the objectives of which were no longer linked to the future of manufacturing industry.

Meanwhile, the ISWG had independently prepared its own 'progress report' on the industrial strategy. This was ready for consideration in October 1978. The report began with the premise that Westborough was not 'a crisis area' although 'the problems of maintaining a healthy industrial climate are considerable'. It sought to identify areas where 'a corporate approach to industrial problems would be helpful'. Its only substantive recommendation, beyond that of continuing its investigation of schools-industry links, the provision of information to firms and other projects in hand, was that the council should consider a deputation to London Transport to press for improved bus facilities in the borough.

As several members of the ISWG recognised, the planning department's topic paper upstaged their own efforts, and raised the issue of whether industry and employment matters were really a key corporate concern, or simply part of the proper remit of the planning department. The question was one of who could claim the proper authority for policy initiatives. The chief executive's policy coordinator immediately saw the issue and challenged the status of the topic paper, questioning whether it was 'a statement of *this* group's view'. If the paper were taken on board, he wondered, what would be left for the corporate group to do? Anxious to maintain their position, the ISWG simply adopted this latest expression of view; the ISWG report was rewritten so as to reflect the new appreciation of Westborough's situation which the topic paper had revealed.

The main points of departure from the ISWG's first draft report came in their conclusions where it was conceded that:

Whilst the group recognises the importance of maintaining an industrial presence in the borough of the smaller and successful larger firms, the transition of employment trends towards the service sector is recognised. It is considered that in future, the group should, therefore, be addressing itself to employment in the broader perspective and include consideration of the special problems of certain groups.

Accordingly, the environmental planning committee was asked to extend the group's terms of reference 'to cover the problems of employment in the borough as a whole, not just industrial problems' and rename the group the *Employment* Strategy Working Group (ESWG) 'to reflect this transition'.

The revision of the ISWG's terms of reference was approved with no difficulty, but the director of planning continued to press for firm policy guidelines in the industrial field. To this end, the topic paper was rewritten in more decisive terms and similarly submitted for approval to the new planning policy sub-committee. Yet in the event the sub-commitee's discussion ran on familiar lines, focusing in particular on recent closures, and emphasising the physical and fiscal effects of industrial dereliction.

More generally, the sub-committee's discussion exemplified the difficulties of achieving any firm strategic commitment in Westborough. Intervening to close the debate on the dilemma of whether or not to refuse warehouse development on industrial sites, the chairman commented that 'We are talking here about very broad policy. But individual cases are handled on their merits, as they always are'. No one disagreed; this was indeed the familiar decision style of Westborough. The test of the 'industrial strategy' therefore could not lie in the terms of the topic paper or any similar report. It would be found in the ways in which particular decisions were handled over time, in the light of the ambiguities as to Westborough's industrial character, and the inevitable conflicts with other policy objectives, conflicts which were embodied in the different committees, departments and professional interests.

These ambiguities were crucial. Even if a clear policy line on permitting and easing the transition to a service-based economy were read into the reports, it had to be carried forward within a political context in which manufacturing industry was seen as having real and continuing importance. This became immediately apparent during the public consultations on the local plan prepared for the eastern part of the borough, the rapidly declining area centred on the Arterial Road itself. This area was served by an advisory committee consisting of councillors, local tenants' associations, the community association and the

Chamber of Commerce, and at a meeting in January 1979 the advisory committee called for 'the establishment of industries with high manpower requirements' and the maintenance of the current balance between service and manufacturing industries. When these resolutions were reported back to the ESWG (as it now was) the chairman claimed that 'their choices are in line with our thinking' and deprecated the apparent clash of policy advice going to the planning committee. Other colleagues dissented, however, recalling that 'we decided not to swim against the tide on manufacturing'. While the group acknowledged that the loss of one of the Arterial Road's major factories 'would leave a mark' on the area, 'in the very long term one sees manufacturing industry moving out' and this 'in the long term affects the kind of place Westborough is'. Despite the local pressures it was agreed that 'we can't put the clock back' on a decade of industrial change.

The spirit of the industrial strategy had enjoyed only a brief heyday. The planners had long wrestled with the dilemma posed by land use and employment change, and the council's rhetorical support for manufacturing did little in their eyes to tip the balance against industrial job loss. The industrial and employment strategies assisted the chief executive's attempts to play a more central role in the policy direction of the council's departments, and helped the borough planning officer to revive a somewhat demoralised department. Yet the strategies had little impact on the way in which actual case decisions were handled, at least in the first few years.[6] Decisions continued to be taken 'on their merits', and the perception of merit was largely shaped by past practice and the immediate concerns of the elected members. This last was probably the most important factor. Many of the majority party members had close connections with the rapidly declining manufacturing sector. The image of Westborough as a manufacturing location – indeed, as a centre of engineering production – long outlasted the reality.

7 Southborough: Lobbying for Industry

In Chapter 2 we argued that policy change is better understood as a series of episodes in the political life of the organisation than as a mechanistic response to changing environmental conditions. In Chapter 6 we gave an account of the initial moves in the development of economic strategy in the London Borough of Westborough. There, the organisational dynamics were relatively simple, the stakes of the various participants distinct, and the divisions amongst them clear-cut. The restricted number of participants, the insulation of the policy debates from elected members, and the structure and working of the small planning department made the Westborough case amenable to a simple and generally linear account of policy development.

Southborough provides a sharp contrast. Here, the organisational dynamics were complex, the stakes elusive, the actors more numerous, and the interdependence of issues striking. Several separate strands of purpose and action intertwine, appearing distinctly only at key junctures in the story. This is a more complex organisation, more specialised, more interactive, more competitive. It would take a full-scale study to do justice to bureaucratic politics in Southborough. The brief account which follows is necessarily an abstraction and a condensation of a rich pattern of events, one moreover where the narrative form inevitably imposes an unreal linearity upon a non-sequential network of influence. The limitation is one we must accept. Our purpose is neither to write a purely analytic account nor to present an administrative history, but to indicate that, for all its complexity, Southborough's story is but a more elaborate version of Westborough's: the responses of both authorities to the experience of economic decline reflected the internal competition for control of the policy agenda and was by no means a mechanistic adjustment to the stimulus of decline.

Southborough is an inner London borough and, as such, shares many of the problems of poor amenities, physical obsolescence, deprivation and economic decline which we noted in Chapter 5. Southborough formed part of a typical nineteenth-century zone of industrial concentration and the diverse industrial base of the area contained few specialisms other than chemicals, food manufacture and light engineering. Today, it is predominantly an area of service activity with a substantial proportion of its population working in the public sector. Recent population loss has been particularly marked, falling from

220,000 in 1961 to 148,000 in 1981; in the 1970s Southborough declined faster than any other London borough with the exception of neighbouring Kensington and Chelsea. Equally striking has been the decline in the economically active population, which fell by almost 20 per cent in the six years from 1971 to 1977. Most indicators of deprivation increased sharply during the 1970s: the borough had a sizeable ethnic minority population, high levels of social dislocation and mental illness, and a substantial number of unfit houses. At the same time the borough's proximity to central London, its access to the River Thames, and its large stock of sound and sometimes elegant houses have led to a modest degree of gentrification.

The apparent social polarisation of the borough became a cause of concern to planners there during the early 1970s, when the replacement of manufacturing employment by service activity, the considerable growth in white-collar residence, and the decline of skilled manual jobs began to make their effects felt. These signs of change were dramatically underlined in the mid-1970s by accelerating job loss and rising unemployment. However, before the mid-1970s the policy positions of successive council majorities paid no regard to economic factors.

Commercial redevelopment was actively sought as a means of improving the physical environment and strengthening the fiscal base. Housing development was a major priority, the only partisan difference being one of emphasis as between the public, private and housing association sectors. The enhancement of amenity by parking control and by opening up river frontages as pedestrian walkways was strongly supported by leading members of the council, irrespective of party.

This was the situation that a small group of relatively junior officials sought to change. Their initial analyses and arguments were not well received. The passage of time and changes in personnel strengthened their position by drawing new and more powerful officials into the economic debate. Eventually, the employment lobby within the council's organisation was able to secure political support for a radically different appraisal of the local situation, one which recognised that the council's past policies had contributed to the borough's economic decline, the effects of which were becoming more severe.[1]

Initial policies and priorities

The basic assumptions of urban planning policy in the 1960s were well entrenched amongst the elected and professional policy-makers of Southborough. Decentralisation of industry and population to new and expanded towns and to the development areas was accepted as the solution to the problems of urban congestion and overcrowding. The senior officials of the department had been transferred from the now defunct LCC. Their preoccupations were those of the Abercrombie plan and the subsequent development plan for the County of London. They had little interest in the economic factors which underpinned urban change. Rather, the predominant vision of Southborough's future was of a cleaner, freer and more attractive area in which nonconforming industrial uses had been successfully extinguished.

Housing policies were central to this vision of reconstruction within a regional planning context. The decentralisation of industry was seen not only as providing for the enhancement of the environment, but as releasing sites for housing redevelopment. Industrial movement would alleviate housing problems and create opportunities to build to high standards of design. The planning department of the late 1960s was strongly design oriented, the positions of borough architect and director of planning being combined until 1974. The housing committee was powerful and successful and the successive directors of housing were able to sustain a substantial housing programme. The director of housing in the mid-1970s was regarded as powerful enough to by-pass any attempts at corporate decision in the directors' board and to brief his own chairman, who could usually count on support from the Labour Party group.

Amenity considerations had a similar prominence in the council's policies. Foremost in importance for the achievement of both housing and environmental gains was the future use of the river frontage, an area which had been in industrial use since the nineteenth century. By 1872 Southborough Distillery and the Manbre Sugar Company had established themselves on the riverside and the area rapidly became developed, largely for brewing and chemical operations. By 1914 the South Reach area was wholly in industrial use, in which it survived through to the late 1960s. The firms on site made extensive use of the river for transport, with considerable import, export and coastal traffic. With increasing controls on industrial pollution, processes involving chemical discharges into the river ceased, although in at least one case a chemical manufacturer retained a research laboratory on his former production site.

Southborough's two predecessor authorities had aspirations to see the river frontage become gradually opened up for amenity uses. Subsequent council documents did not shrink from quoting the romantic and anti-urban sentiments of William Morris's view of an idyllic future for this stretch of Thameside:

Both shores had a line of very pretty houses, low and not large, standing back a little way from the river . . . There was a continuous garden in front of them, going down to the water's edge in which the flowers were now blooming luxuriant, and sending delicious waves of summer scent over the eddying stream. Behind the houses, I could see great trees rising, mostly planes, and looking down the water there were the reaches toward Putney almost as if they were a lake with a forest shore, so thick were the big trees.[2]

Although no action was taken to secure such changes prior to 1965, the Greater London Council's GLDP written statement of 1969 definitely foresaw the provision of river walks, new green spaces and a high quality of riverside landscaping. In areas like South Reach, where space restrictions precluded future riverside industrial growth, the GLDP concluded that 'planning policy . . . should be to phase out riverside commercial and industrial uses when opportunities occur'.

In 1971 the then council leader announced that:

It was the policy of . . . our predecessors in office and it is certainly the policy of this council, to encourage the retention and expansion of riverside amenities and ensure that the opportunity is taken whenever it arises, to open up the River Thames frontage. It is our aim to provide and secure the provision of riverside walks and open space amenities wherever possible and to preserve the character of the river frontage where it is already open.

In that same year, a large asbestos producer was refused permission to redevelop its site and increase the workshop and warehouse area, on the grounds that such a consolidation of existing development would prejudice the implementation of the riverside policy. Later that same year, the application for the expansion of another manufacturing firm onto a nearby vacant wharf was refused on similar grounds. The council also moved quickly to acquire the wharf by compulsory purchase under its housing powers.

To refuse planning permission for such developments as contrary to policy requires local authorities to have some positive policy to which appeal may be made in the event of the refusal being contested. To that date, the implementation of the riverside policy had proceeded in a random way, phasing out industrial use as opportunities arose. At this point work began on a draft plan for South Reach which aimed at the revival of the area and the resolution of environmental and traffic problems. The goals of the plan were distinctively cast in urban design terms and were portrayed 'as leading to an opening up of the riverfront, an increase in the housing stock, a phasing out of large industrial riverside users, better shopping and other social amenities and improved pedestrian routes to the river'. The plan envisaged the eventual development of the entire river frontage for residential purposes, retaining a belt of land adjacent to the river for pedestrian use. Industrial users were not to be forced to leave, but the next application for development – for warehousing and offices – was refused on the now firmer ground of the riverside plan's recent adoption by the council.

During the next few years, Southborough sought to implement their riverside plan by the purchase of such sites as fell vacant. Several wharves were acquired for public housing, and luxury flat development by the private sector was permitted on two others. Moreover, the new developments were at very high densities, a factor which greatly increased site values, and encouraged the remaining firms to realise their enhanced assets by relocating elsewhere. This some of them did. However, the subsequent decline in the residential property market curtailed this option, leaving some of the remaining firms in a position where they could neither expand *in situ* nor find buyers for their sites.

Elsewhere in the borough, where housing and amenity considerations had less force, rather more attention came to be paid to employment questions. Eight thousand manufacturing jobs were lost between 1966 and 1971. A number of major industrial employers left the borough in the early 1970s causing a further loss of 6000 jobs. Between 1971 and 1976, at least 40 firms employing more than 50 workers ceased operation on their Southborough sites and moved elsewhere. During that period, only ten such firms commenced operations there. Moreover, the consequence of the movement of firms into and out of the borough was to increase the already marked dominance of the service sector, for most of the 'new' firms were not involved in manufacturing. The relative attractiveness of the area for non-industrial uses underlay the loss of 20 hectares of land from industrial use between 1965 and 1973.

A survey of local industrial and commercial enterprises carried out in 1977 indicated that the majority of larger manufacturing firms were not strongly linked to the area for either inputs or outputs. Moreover, half of the larger firms in the borough were part of a larger group of companies and hence vulnerable to higher level decisions on future investment. At the same time, the disadvantages of an inner urban location described in Chapter 5 were apparent in the number of firms citing high rates, space shortages, problems of goods access and staff parking, and recruitment difficulties as the major drawbacks of their present locations.

Of these several issues, physical obsolescence, and in particular obsolete premises, were of obvious relevance to the increasingly noticeable industrial exodus. Seventy per cent of small firms, 57 per cent of medium-sized firms and 39 per cent of larger firms occupied premises built before 1918. About a third of all firms regarded their present premises as unsuitable for their activity. Within the manufacturing sector 85 per cent of all firms were in pre-1918 premises and a substantial proportion of these were in multi-storey premises.

The exodus of industry in search of more suitable locations was demonstrated in 1972 when the management of a large food manufacturing group announced their intention to decentralise operations from their site in Southborough. The group's experience typified the problems which large inner urban manufacturers were facing, and the move served as a catalyst to a change of approach among the borough's planners.

The group employed around 5800 staff at a 10-acre site in the centre of the borough, on which the most notable feature was the massive multi-storey factory building. The food manufacturing companies located there cited persistent problems of labour recruitment and high turnover which, they claimed, impeded production. It was also claimed that the firms could not attain maximum output at their existing location. The cramped site hindered the delivery and dispatch of raw materials and manufactured goods. The premises themselves were old and the multi-storey layout prevented the adoption of modern production techniques. Long, low, single-storey buildings were required if the advantages of the latest technology were to be gained.

An immediate run-down of activity was therefore proposed. In 1973/4 one of the firms would move to Northampton where suitable premises were available, and where a minimum of 400 houses had been offered to accommodate their relocating staff. The other would move its production activities to a development area factory, probably within two to three years. In Southborough the group headquarters was to be retained on site, and additional office accommodation would be needed. The group proposed the redevelopment of the site to create 270,000 square feet of offices, a 1000-bed hotel, a convention centre, a supermarket and some 275 units of residential accommodation.

Planning officials initially reacted quite positively to these proposals, within the framework of which they hoped to negotiate significant planning gains in the form of highways and environmental improvements. Unexpectedly, however, the recommendation to approve the application was reversed in the Labour group and the council objected to the plans for the site on design grounds, claiming it would cause traffic problems and have a detrimental effect on the neighbouring conservation area. Their major objection was, however, on the grounds of the employment consequences of the change. The council claimed that it would be to 'abrogate their responsibility' to permit such a substantial loss of employment.

The proposed redevelopment would itself be an employment generator, and the company argued its case on appeal by pointing to local environmental improvements and the 'substantial' employment created by the development. For the council's planners, the most significant loss would be not the quantity but the type of employment. The head of the planning department's research section argued at the appeal that:

The claim . . . that an equivalent amount of employment will be replaced by the hotel, convention centre and offices is not disputed, but it is irrelevant to the local employment issue. The sort of workers attracted to hotel employment tend to be of a very special nature, and the routine tasks are often undertaken largely by migrant workers, who are relatively poorly paid. The menial nature of the tasks is unlikely to attract many of the existing manual workers in the area, even the unskilled workers. The office floorspace would obviously attract clerical and other office workers, but the major element of the unemployment problem is not concerned with this group, but with manual workers.

This argument about skill-level mismatch was difficult to sustain, for the planning department was unable to claim any precise understanding of the employment consequences of such major land use changes. Their own understandably half-hearted case was not well substantiated; the firm's, in contrast, was backed by detailed figures. Significantly, they were able to claim that of the 'residual' staff – those for whom no provision had been made in the form of continued employment, transfer or early retirement – only 738 were residents of that borough. The minister overruled the council's refusal.

The loss of the food manufacturing complex precipitated a re-evaluation of policy at the very point at which the riverside plan was being pushed toward implementation. Past assumptions were now to be questioned. A report drafted just two years later commented that:

It is becoming clear that many firms at present in Inner London would be better located in Outer London, or well away from London, in Development Areas or in the South West. The only firms now likely to establish themselves or expand their operations, are those closely tied to London, either by their market, or similar cogent reasons. Even so, the example of (the now-departed) producers of food goods with a very large market in London, shows that an industry that was previously considered to be tied to London can sensibly relocate at a great distance.

The predominant problems of the borough were henceforth seen not in terms of congestion and poor environment, but in terms of job loss and the deterioration of opportunities for the borough's resident workforce.

Achieving that redefinition of the issues demanded considerable effort on the part of a group of 'policy entrepreneurs' who found claiming attention for economic factors an uphill task. Their activities were closely entwined with a series of developments within the council's own organisational structures. The post-1975 shifts in the appreciative context of policy could not have been achieved without prior changes in the organisational context.

The changing organisational context
The single feature most closely associated with the rise to prominence of economic issues on Southborough's policy agenda was the transformation of the planning department over a period of five years. This

transformation affected its size and strength, working arrangements, personnel and expertise. It facilitated the growth of an employment lobby within the department which played a significant part in swinging the attention of the leading councillors away from amenity and housing issues towards employment. This transformation was not entirely independent of the prevailing opinions within the council itself; rather, political change permitted the growth of a more outward-looking and policy-oriented department, which in turn led to some planners gaining greater influence in the framing of policy issues.

From 1968 to 1971 the council was controlled by the Conservative Party. Just as the planning department was mainly concerned with development control, so too was the corresponding committee concerned less with policy than with matters of detail. No immediate changes followed Labour's gain of control in 1971; late in that year one planner complained that the 'lack of demand for policies on the part of the committee members' precluded his colleagues from dealing with anything other than routine work. Another later recollected that it was none the less possible to push through some minor innovations in this policy vacuum. A third criticised the prevalent assumptions of the ex-LCC officials as based on 'old policies, old plans, the [GLC's] Interim Development Plan, parts of the Greater London Development Plan, subjective judgements, hunches and personal whims'. Whether or not his was a fair appraisal, it was one with which many of the department's staff concurred.

The planning side of the department was, until 1974, organised into five groups: development control, development planning, research services, urban design and administration. Each group leader reported to the assistant director (development) and the entire department was the responsibility of the borough architect and director of development. The department was also rather small – the total professional and administrative staff numbered around 82. The development plan section consisted of its section head, one planning officer and a draughtsman. The subsequent transformation of the department brought the total number to 144 during which time architectural work had been hived off, and 33 transportation planning posts added from the engineer's department. Originally one of London's smallest planning departments, Southborough became one of the largest. Equally significant was the rapid growth of intelligence and policy posts; by 1975 the research section numbered ten staff, while the borough plans section was of similar size. Their responsibilities, moreover, included substantial areas of overlap.

The increased size of the department from the mid-1970s testified to the prevailing climate in local government finance in which establishment increases were relatively easily secured. In this instance it also reflected the determination of an incoming chief officer to compensate for the loss of the architectural function by rebuilding his department on a scale which was not entirely authorised by the council. The increase in size brought with it a greater degree of specialisation and facilitated the development of expertise.

Equally important, however, was the transformation of working relations, climate and morale. Complaints of poor working relations and morale were evidently widespread around 1970. One newcomer reflecting ruefully on his arrival in the department commented, 'one came, one met the chaos'. The accommodation of the department – at some distance from the main complex – was widely described as appalling. Dissatisfied officers alleged – and, when challenged, partially demonstrated – that the department suffered from high levels of sickness and absenteeism, which they attributed to very low morale. A group of younger planners publicised their deep concern and their 'feeling of isolation and futility in . . . day to day work', in which they saw themselves as 'under-used'. The absence of ordinary office equipment and the extensive delays in handling correspondence during this period testify to the difficult conditions in which the planning department operated.

Grievances formally set out during this time centred on the ineffectiveness of the department, claiming 'angry confrontations between staff and management', 'much time spent on maintaining the status of groups', 'abysmally slow production of work' which was 'inadequately conceived . . . and improperly vetted . . . ignored or quietly forgotten'. Some of the junior and middle-ranking staff attributed these problems to management style. As one of them argued, 'the senior management above group officer level must know what the department is seeking to achieve and indeed must have a predominant say in what emphasis is placed upon any given work topic. It is arguable that at the present time the senior management operate largely in ignorance and have little control over what is produced and, conversely, what is not produced'.

These bitterly dissatisfied planners urged a new style of operation, with topic-based project teams cutting across the existing group boundaries and relieving what was seen as an excessively hierarchical and compartmentalised style of working. Above all, the dissidents sought 'a sense of purpose or common objectives' to be found in a *borough plan*.

The absence of any single and authoritative policy base was a troubling factor for the department's top management. In March 1971 the planning committee had been advised of the need for a policy plan to enable the council to operate positively as a land use planning authority. Uncertainties over the Greater London Development Plan inhibited work on the complementary borough plans, and in Southborough no planning staff had been assigned to its production.

During 1971 considerable upward pressure for change was exerted to coincide with the appointment of a new director of planning. Early in the year a number of junior officers from different groups in the department began a series of meetings, chaired in turn by the group leaders. Papers were prepared and presentations made on such topics as the objectives of planning and the nature of planning in a London borough. Over as short a period as three weeks, discussion began to crystallise around the need for a defined policy base and for inter-disciplinary team working. Alternative management structures were proposed, and a series of papers compiled on new approaches to planning. The incoming director of planning was thus well placed to capitalise on this groundswell of critical thinking. He welcomed the papers which had been prepared, and held a series of meetings with group leaders and junior staff. He emphasised that he 'supported new thinking', agreed that 'planning could not and should not operate in a vacuum', and that 'the whole department must have a meaningful direction'.

The subsequent growth in the planning establishment was extremely rapid and produced new problems of overlap and competition for responsibility. There was a brief flowering of topic groups and a reorganisation into four divisions (development, planning and land use, transportation and administration) and considerable informal joint working developed within the planning and land use group. Work on local plans and action area plans was begun, and led to close and informal involvement with the corresponding ward councillors. A great deal of anecdotal evidence testifies to the close and friendly relations that grew up between junior planners and those participatory Labour councillors who wanted to involve themselves in the department's work. The contrast between the situation in 1975 and that just four years previously was striking. 'Enthusiastic' was a frequently used term and, as one of the earlier critics reflected, the business of plan-making was now 'all very informal and fun'.

These changes brought their own contradictions. The new emphasis on a defined policy base had led to the riverside plan of 1973, but this was no sooner cited as an achievement than it was attacked as leading to cumulative (and unintended) industrial decline there. The new director of planning was, despite his enthusiasm, primarily interested in architectural design issues. Very strong inter-sectional rivalries remained, and there were several attempts to minimise the potential role of the research section. The new and close relationship with councillors had its own drawback; the planning committee members were not, by and large, influential figures within the Labour group.

Other organisational changes during this period were to prove important in the coming contest for influence. A new chief executive brought to Southborough a commitment to ambitious and far-reaching corporate planning procedures. His attempts to produce a corporate plan soon ran into difficulties, and the emerging borough plan promised for a while to assume a new significance as a *de facto* corporate plan. This gave the planning department and committee a potential significance that belied their political weakness. The new chief executive had established a policy analysis unit within his own department, recruiting a group of officers (including the former head of planning research) with a very wide-ranging remit. This, then, was the organisational context when, from around 1974, a growing 'industry lobby' began a campaign to put the issue of economic decline onto Southborough's policy agenda.

Making industry an issue

Unlike Westborough's relatively straightforward experience of inter-departmental coalition and competition, Southborough's eventual adoption of an inter-departmental strategy arose from a more complex, diverse and conflictual process, the eventual solution of which owed much to the confluence of separate forces. The organisational changes of the mid-1970s were important in establishing several distinct nodes of policy initiation; the chief executive's policy analysis and research unit (PARU), the planning research group, the borough plans group and, late in 1976, an industrial and commercial development officer. Moreover, a handful of Southborough's council members played crucial roles in the policy shifts which marked the second half of the decade. Resistance to change was at the same time more strongly entrenched than in Westborough. Southborough's planning department had a strong civic design tradition; there was long-standing political commitment to enhancement of the physical environment; and renewal of the nineteenth-century housing stock was the prime objective of the controlling Labour group between 1971 and 1977.

The first important shifts in the balance of forces perhaps began not with the formal restructuring of the planning department in 1974, but with the informal realignment secured by pressure from below during the previous year. Two specific changes flowed from this realignment. The first was an increased emphasis on research and intelligence; the second a shift towards a more analytic and interdisciplinary style of working, with the identification of broad strategic policy choices for the council, commonly in the form of strategic options papers. With these developments the younger policy-oriented planners gained some redress for their earlier grievances about the *ad hoc* and directionless style of their department.

Research had formerly served the purpose of information gathering for development control decisions. The limits of this conception were unambiguously demonstrated by the reversal of the food manufacturing company decision on appeal, and the weak and perhaps reluctant performance of the planning department officials at the appeal inquiry. That the department was unable to identify the employment consequences of the group's relocation plans was understandable; it served, however, to point up the absence of a general and informed appraisal of the patterns of change in the industrial and employment structure of the borough. The catalyst for expanding the role of the planning research section was then the organisational imperative of a firm knowledge base from which to defend decisions and make reasoned objections to major change of use proposals. As the research staff thereafter underwent a significant growth in numbers and strength, their preoccupations moved away from *ad hoc* information gathering towards generalisable survey investigations.

As the research group's involvement in questions of industrial employment developed, its members naturally gained a closer relationship with the borough plans group, which was itself undergoing a rapid expansion due to the influx into the department of a younger, more policy-oriented cadre of planners. These newly-qualified officials tended to share the perspectives of the researchers and in some cases had a strong prior commitment to employment issues. Despite tensions between them (which arose in part from their competitive positions), the interests of the two groups converged in a commitment to policy analysis. Their object was to secure a place for economic issues on the policy agenda of the council, a difficult undertaking in the light of the pre-existing commitments of elected members and the delocalisation of the inner west London labour market, which tended to reinforce the insulation of councillors from the far-reaching economic changes taking place in the very wards which they represented.

The other important link was between these two groups and the chief executive's policy analysis unit. The senior planner who had formerly headed the research section joined PARU in 1975. He was soon followed by one of his more employment-oriented staff, who in effect became (in the words of a colleague) 'a policy analyst with an employment brief', thus giving economic issues something of a secure foothold in the central policy forums of the council. The apparent emphasis was perhaps accidental; the then chief executive was seeking to extend his own action space via corporate policy analysis and had no particular concern for employment issues as such. In a similar fashion, the establishment of an inter-departmental economic development programme group (EDG) in 1975 as part of the corporate planning machinery testified less to the early recognition of employment questions than to the very broad aspirations of the corporate planning system in the form in which it was originally introduced.

The rise in the salience of employment issues followed rather than led these developments, and arose initially from the progress made towards area-based planning at the borough and local levels. From 1975 the borough plans staff were working towards the specification of options in an economic activity topic paper; both they and PARU were also seeking to call attention to the need to determine the future of South Reach, the once densely industrialised stretch of Southborough's riverside.

The basis of the 1973 South Reach plan was gradually to replace the existing industry with residential development without placing undue pressure upon firms to vacate their existing sites. By 1977 more than 300 housing units had been built on former industrial sites and planning permission for a further 400 had been granted. The decline of industry in South Reach had begun in the late 1960s. The previous use of compulsory purchase powers to block the expansion of one firm onto an adjacent wharf in 1971 has already been mentioned; at around the same time another major oil company was approached by a property developer with a view to the residential development of their site. The company, which planned to retain the site, sought clarification from the council, only to be told that council officers 'regretted' their intention to remain on South Reach, and offered talks on 'the possibilities of removal and relocation and a change of use of the site in accordance with the council's objectives'. The promulgation of the plan in 1973 had done little to assuage the anxieties of remaining firms, for while it provided for a limited medium-term industrial presence on the riverside, it also reiterated the long-term goal of creating a riverside walk.

The first doubts as to the effectiveness of the plan were voiced by individual members of the borough plans group, who, aware that the housing plans and the active land acquisition programme had increased land values and encouraged firms to move, sought to highlight a possible domino effect whereby the remaining industry would fall under increasing pressure leading to its eventual extinction.

Despite their lack of standing in the policy process, these officers argued that bringing a residential use to the riverside area resulted in 'considerable pressure for further residential development which would be difficult to resist', and that 'activities on a single, or small number of sites appear to encourage a similar activity on adjoining sites'. Isolated changes of use had such severe repercussions on adjoining industry that 'the speed of change in South Reach was overwhelming'. They urged that 'the lesson to be learnt . . . is that the consideration of a change of use of a single site must be seen in its context, and that whilst benefits in one area (e.g. housing) may accrue, there may be considerable disbenefits in other fields (e.g. employment)'. While it had formerly been assumed that displaced industrial uses could be accommodated on more suitable sites elsewhere in the borough, it was now argued that 'the case for the relocation of local nonconforming industrial uses is likely to fail because the cost of new premises would be far beyond the means of most nonconforming users. They tend to be on very tight cost margins, usually in low cost accommodation, and relocation often destroys them'.

The opportunity to re-open consideration of the riverside's future came fortuitously in 1975. A large flour milling company were considering closing their Chelsea Flour Mills and consolidating their production on a riverside site in Southborough; at the same time the GLC were also in the market for a riverside site for a new bulk refuse transfer station. The advice to permit the firm to expand on South Reach and actively to seek further employment gains was a challenge to established policy, but had insufficient backing to persuade the council to do other than equivocate; after many months of delay and uncertainty as to whether the site would be purchased for housing or allowed to remain in industrial use, the firm withdrew its application.

No single decision was likely to transform the prospects for industry on South Reach. The plans of several firms had to be taken into account, and action to encourage industrial retention on an *ad hoc* basis was bedevilled by the perceived problems of housing provision on a mixed site with fairly severe pollution problems and by continuing uncertainty as to future land values. Several other skirmishes in the campaign to retain industry had to be fought – some successfully, some not so – before the council could be persuaded to pass, in 1977, a resolution assuring existing firms of their security on South Reach and lifting the threat of implementation of the walkway scheme in the foreseeable future.

During the two years or so that elapsed before this point was reached a recognisable employment lobby had first to develop from the links between the borough's plans and research groups and the recently strengthened PARU. The preparation of the borough plan enabled employment work – research and policy analysis – to be set in hand, but the more astute planners recognised that the borough plan was an insufficient vehicle to carry a policy reversal through the council. The employment lobby had at this stage two possible routes to a place on the policy agenda, for the processes for dealing with economic issues had yet to crystallise. The first was to go in the conventional manner through the planning committee, the second to ensure that the issues were raised in the strategic resources committee. Had they taken the first route they would have risked favourable policy decisions there being overturned in a higher political forum such as the strategic resources committee itself or the Labour group. Planning was unlikely to be able to win in any direct confrontation either at chief officer level or at the inter-committee level. PARU however was a key position from which the reshaping of the policy agenda could be attempted, and the generality of councillors confronted directly with the issues.

Accordingly, two documents were independently prepared. The first was the economic activity topic paper, an analytic document written by planning staff and submitted to the development plan and application review committee. The topic paper outlined three areas where the council could take action. The first was active advocacy, recognising that 'to the extent that remedies lie with other agencies, the council can make representations and direct its political energies to influence these agencies into directing resources and adopting policies favourable to Southborough'. The second was management: the appraisal of all land use decisions in relation to employment needs and the establishment of a coordinating office within the council's organisation to deal with employment issues. The third was resource use: the allocation of funds to direct intervention in the industrial development market.

The second paper, fairly described as 'a short and punchy document', was the outline interim strategy produced by PARU. Less discursive, it assumed the existence of an economic problem and concentrated on enumerating possible ameliorative actions. The council had recently experienced a *further* change of chief executive, the new appointee bringing to the council's administrative leadership a greater emphasis on achieving definite policy positions with less concern for formal structures. Accordingly, the new chief executive introduced the outline strategy at the strategic resources committee. It then progressed through the Labour group with the backing of the leadership and to council for approval before being referred *down* to the planning committee for further elaboration.

The most significant stage in this process was the presentation of the essentials of the strategy at a specially convened 'teach-in' for members of the council. The object of the teach-in was not to secure decisions, but to enable the employment-minded planners to set out the full statistical picture of what was happening to Southborough and thereby to 'face the councillors with the employment consequences of their own decisions'. Specific policies had yet to be proposed and the presentation was confined to identifying issues. It was suggested that the council should take steps to help local firms; that it should aim to attract new employment to the borough; and that it should identify and seek to meet the employment needs of the most vulnerable groups within the borough's population. More critically, the teach-in presentation not only analysed the land and physical constraints upon industrial growth, but pointed out that 'council policies have often aided the development' of the very forces which were inimical to the well-being of firms. Thus, 'in planning, for example, the negative attitude to industry embodied in the interim development plan persists despite the changed economic environment'. In a similar fashion, existing policies on housing, amenity and traffic were identified as inhibiting or undermining business growth.

By these several routes – in particular, the outline strategy and the teach-in – the employment lobby was able to establish industrial decline as an issue for the chief executive and leading members and not something to be confined to the departmental preserve of the planners and their relatively weak committee. The significance of the outline strategy was its concentration upon industrial land as a vital resource for the borough. The housing department had been extremely active in land assembly with little reference to the planners. Redefining employment and industry questions as a land utilisation issue effectively transferred the locus of decision-making to the strategic resources committee where overall priorities for land could be asserted against the normal claims of individual service committees. It was evident at this stage that the housing committee – itself the largest consumer of the land resource – could easily win battles against planning over the use of particular sites; two important industrial sites were acquired for housing purposes during this period. The prospects for the success of an economic strategy therefore depended on winning the wider argument about land in the corporate arena.

Few took the outline strategy or the more developed interim strategy which followed to be much more than a gesture in the direction of the employment lobby. They gave the chief executive the opportunity to raise issues with members and perhaps served to focus the attention of the political leadership. But the strategy was not as yet the policy base within which decisions on industrial support could be taken. By far the most substantial outcome of the discussions engendered by the topic paper and the strategy was the decision to establish an employment adviser, hastily renamed industrial and commercial development officer (IDO). Due to the new chief executive's strength and evident interest in the area, the IDO was to be located outside the planning department, thus minimising the risks of linkage to a weak committee and emphasising the corporate nature of the implied commitment to industry. Located instead within the chief executive's department, the post represented a remarkable consolidation of the employment lobby's influence. The IDO was to head the proposed Industrial and Commercial Development Office and 'to spearhead . . . this new initiative by the borough in promoting a positive and interventionist role in industrial and commercial development and the expansion of job opportunities'.

The officer appointed as IDO in December 1976 became one of

Southborough's most significant policy entrepreneurs over the next few years, not least because of his virtual freelance status under the ultimate protection of the chief executive. He became closely involved in attempts to retain individual firms. His appointment had been preceded by those of the chief executive and a new assistant director of planning who was identified with urban economic issues. It was followed in 1977 by the appointment of a new director of development planning who was himself evidently less ambivalent than his predecessor. Taken together, the four were crucial to the success of the more junior employment lobby. Of them all, the IDO post represented the most visible shift in the terms of policy-making, for it institutionalised the place of industrial employment issues on the policy agenda. The remit to 'coordinate the activities of the council's departments in relation to employment' and to 'develop the image of the council in its efforts to encourage local employment' was a licence to intervene on a wide front in departmental affairs. Moreover, the interim economic strategy, itself no more than a suggestive framework, none the less provided the IDO with a rationale and a text to cite when challenging colleagues. Thus, as the IDO took up his post in time to participate in discussions on the borough plan, he was able 'to reinforce the "employment argument" and . . . [he] sought to afford it equal weight with the more rehearsed arguments of housing, open space, or social services provision'.

The most dramatic example of the IDO's involvement in internal policy advocacy concerned the council's commitment to a more restrictive parking policy designed to restrain traffic in the interests of environmental improvement. The effects of parking restraint on local firms, whose employees faced the prospect of a £200 annual permit fee with additional Saturday charges, were frequently cited in the IDO's meetings with local firms, many of whom already experienced shortages of skilled staff. For example, one major firm employed 250 car users, half of whom were dependent on on-street parking. These key workers, who travelled from outside the borough to work on a shift basis, could hardly be serviced by public transport. When Southborough sought to extend parking restraints on neighbouring streets at the end of 1976, the firm protested to the GLC arguing that

the inevitable result will be that a number of our key workers will leave and seek employment nearer home . . . Our ability to expand, or even remain at our present size, will inevitably be affected as we cannot recruit new workers for training if our key supervisory and skilled staff leave our employment . . . These proposed parking and traffic restrictions will inevitably compel companies such as ourselves to examine their positions very carefully and, if the scheme is implemented, it will almost certainly result in the long term in a further drift of industry out of the area.

The complaint was without doubt a common one, and was readily made to the IDO as he travelled extensively in the borough to meet local managements and discuss their problems.

The IDO had only been in his post for a few weeks when he gave notice of his opposition to the proposed parking scheme, advising the transportation planning section that 'if the council is really keen to retain employment in the borough, then clearly restrictions of this kind may need to be reconsidered, however attractive they may appear from an environmental/transportation viewpoint. I look forward to discussing the scope for concession'. *Ad hoc* concessions were unlikely within the context of a broad strategic commitment to enhance the physical amenities of the area; the parking policy was open to amendment only at the margin. In March 1977, the IDO circulated a note urging that 'some aspects of the council's proposed policy of traffic restraint are directly at odds with its stated intention to attract and retain industrial and commercial employment and job opportunities' – a scarcely veiled reference to his own responsibilities. He strongly advised that the parking policy be reconsidered 'as a practicable means of alleviating one of the many constraints felt by employers but also as a positive statement of intent in support of [the council's] purported concern for local employment'.

Within a month of this report the IDO felt strong enough to make his criticisms public; the parking scheme was already under bitter attack by the District Manpower Committee and the National Federation of Self-Employed, as well as by many of the local residents who would also be required to hold permits. The IDO's statement to the press that the parking controls were 'potentially dangerous' to future employment brought an angry response from the chairman of the transportation sub-committee, who was at that time attempting to steer the proposals through the council. The chairman's attack on 'this fairly new officer of the council' for publicly criticising council policy 'without first discussing it with the relevant committee chairman' received some publicity, and the IDO needed the dual protection of his unusually wide remit and the chief executive's moral support. His opposition not surprisingly failed to halt the parking proposals, which were passed by the council. However, three months later they were rejected by the Conservative-controlled GLC and with the reference back of the proposals the council's enthusiasm declined.

The IDO's uncomfortably public dispute over parking policy was seen as a useful trial of strength for the industry lobby. It served to establish that a new factor – the views of local industrialists – had been introduced into policy consideration, not by external pressure but by providing a single internal advocate for their interests. During this same period – the first six months of the IDO's operations – a number of parallel initiatives were under way which would eventually serve to strengthen his position. Following the approval of the outline strategy, a major survey of manufacturing, construction, warehousing and commercial firms had been launched. Information was collected on all firms with over 50 employees and on a sample of smaller firms, with an interview programme designed to broaden the council's knowledge base, to better inform policy options, to ascertain the future locational intentions of the firms, and to build up a closer relationship with them. At another level the survey was intended to revive the momentum of what was increasingly seen as a faltering interim economic strategy; it also helped to underpin the arguments which the IDO was conducting within the council's organisation.

The corporate nature of the concern for industry and employment was also symbolised in this period by the revival of the economic development programme group (EDG), one of the few remnants of the earlier corporate planning structure. Now chaired by the recently arrived assistant director of planning, the EDG had played an overseer role in the drafting of the economic activity topic paper, and from the spring of 1977 it assumed formal responsibility for the council's work programme in the industrial development sphere and sought to operate as a major inter-departmental forum. While some observers saw the EDG as 'planners talking to each other', it provided a forum for discussion between rival sections within the planning department. While it is likely that the successful initiation of issues and the garnering of support for them took place before their emergence in the EDG, the group gained in significance as the employment lobby role of PARU declined. From mid-1977 the PARU role in employment discussions was to act as a link with the chief executive.

The major battles between the increasingly numerous employment lobbyists and the traditional power blocs of amenity and housing remained to be fought. South Reach was inevitably the territory within which some at least of these contests would be settled. By mid-1977 the IDO was deeply involved in discussion with management and unions of some of the riverside firms, taking care meanwhile to keep the chief executive (and, indirectly, the leader of the council) informed of his movements. The rationalisation of the sugar refining industry, described in Chapter 5, resulted in an important closure on South Reach: a sugar refining company, one of the first manufacturing firms to locate there, found its Southborough plant scheduled for shut-down within months of the company's acquisition by Tate and Lyle. The proposed closure of the company in May 1977 persuaded the leader of the council to convene a series of urgent meetings to consider the impact on neighbouring firms. Local trade unionists, alarmed by the loss of more than 350 jobs, claimed that the company's attachment to the site in the years preceding the take-over had in any case been weakened by the long-term housing plans of the council, and that relocation had long been anticipated. A statement by the IDO which recalled that the council's 1973 plan for South Reach envisaged the phasing out of industry there 'only over a period of many years so that the borough's economy could be safeguarded' was approved. A chink in the formal commitment to a residential riverside was now apparent.

The refining plant's closure was to become an important catalyst for a general reappraisal of the policies for South Reach, policies which had been repeatedly questioned in their detailed application since 1975. Employment lobbyists in the planning department had continued to criticise the provisions of the plan as unrelated to the prevailing economic circumstances, pointing up the deleterious effects both of the council's housing policies ('with the council providing a ready buyer of industrial sites at inflated housing values . . . [it] is in a weak position to argue for the retention of existing industry or to seek alternative tenants of vacated premises') and of the amenity policies ('past commitments may make the future of a substantial proportion of the employment insecure . . . and councillor commitment to provision of the almost sacrosanct riverside walk may make a reversal of existing policies difficult'). Their ability to challenge existing policies outright even after the refining plant's closure was nevertheless constrained by the ambivalence of the outgoing director of planning, who, while ready to confront councillors with the emerging divisions – the advice of his own staff was 'definitely in conflict with the established history of policy in the area' – none the less supported the earlier use of CPO powers to block industrial development as averting a situation which 'would have wrecked the riverside walk'.

Any earlier move to seek definitive decisions of policy (as distinct from cases) at member level would probably have been premature, but after the sugar refining case there were some indications of support for employment concerns on the part of the leader of the council and the chief executive. When the notionally corporate directors' board failed to settle the future of the riverside, its discussions ending inconclusively, the chief executive pushed the issue towards members, putting his own weight behind the strategic options paper for South Reach which the planning department had prepared. The aim of the paper was to state the employment policy alternative and thereby reopen issues which some still insisted were closed. The new planning chairman, now firmly on the side of the employment lobby, responded to this opportunity, but unexpectedly went further and overturned the existing commitments on riverside. At a specially convened meeting of the planning committee, the chairman abandoned all of the proposed options for South Reach save that of industrial retention. The riverside walk would remain an aspiration only where it would not prejudice the prospects for industry, and the chairman conveyed to the press the hope that 'firms in the area will be encouraged by the clear shift of thinking in my committee'.

The about-face by the planning committee, while significant, was in itself insufficient to settle the issue and the policy for riverside remained uncertain for several months until the planning chairman was able – rather against the betting – to carry the Labour group and thus pave the way to the council revoking the former riverside policy in October 1977. As one planner gleefully remarked, 'for the first time we had a land use policy clearly favouring employment'. Moreover, the intention was to extend the same principle and give priority to employment-maximising land uses throughout the borough. Suddenly the employment lobby found themselves, as one planner put it, 'winning all the debates'.

But not winning all the decisions. The strategic resources committee that autumn saw intense and bitter arguments between the emerging majority for industry and the now defensive supporters of a continued large-scale housing programme. There were highly publicised rifts and hostile criticism for the chief executive from the housing chairman. Despite the reservations of a substantial number of Labour councillors, the leader and the chief executive became increasingly open in their support for industry. Disappointed that the South Reach reversal had failed to carry over into subsequent site decisions, and unconvinced that the borough plan could provide a sustainable framework of land allocation, the chief executive pressed for work to begin on an explicit economic strategy to serve as a framework for future site decisions. The completion of the industrial and commercial survey conveniently coincided with the decision to prepare a formal strategy statement and a condensed version of the survey report was published in a glossy format with a foreword by the planning committee chairman. The cover sketch of industrial premises in South Reach neatly symbolised the recent policy reversals. Finally, tangible commitment had been made in the form of the council's first capital allocation for industrial development, £250,000 being allocated for 1977/8.

At this advanced stage, the old rivalries between industry and housing came to be eclipsed by a new competition for 'ownership' of the economic issues, a clear indicator that the basic argument as to the primacy of industrial needs had been won. The planning chairman pushed hard both for early production of the economic strategy and for the eventual incorporation of the industrial development office within the planning department. The initial moves in the preparation of the strategy itself were similarly characterised by protracted competition for its drafting between the IDO (supported by the chief executive) and the borough plan and research groups (supported by the new director of planning). The PARU staff, authors of the original outline strategy of two years before, were effectively excluded from this competition. Some months passed before the planning director won the argument and it was conceded that the planning department should assume authorship. Few were satisfied with the initial product and, to the planning chairman's chagrin, it was held back from publication until after the 1978 borough elections at which Labour narrowly lost control of Southborough.

The change of party control in favour of the Conservatives, who took office in 1978 (and again in 1982) with Liberal support, finally resolved the question of land use. Whatever divisions existed in the Conservative group concerning the propriety of different modes of involvement with industry and commerce, they had frequently opposed the use of 'windfall' sites for housing, and had been openly hostile to the highly successful attempts by the housing directorate to achieve a comprehensive housing service. The era of large-scale housing development was over.

The gradual realisation of the employment lobby's goals had been aptly crowned at the end of 1977 by Southborough's designation as a programme authority under the Inner Urban Areas Act.[3] Confidence in Southborough's prospects for growth helped secure the extra resources of programme status, some £2 million annually, although it fell short of the council's rather long-shot bid for designation as a partnership authority. The partnership bid had placed considerable emphasis on site assembly and improvements to publicly-owned industrial land in the borough, focusing on a handful of sites which were to occupy prominent positions in the Southborough Inner Area Programme (SIAP) of the following years.

The operation of the programme arrangements, like the substance of Southborough's multi-faceted economic strategy since 1978, lies outside the scope of this study. So too does any assessment of the prospects of such policies for the successful management of what we have suggested, in Chapters 3 to 5, is an inexorable process of urban decentralisation. But in attempting to reverse or contain this decline Southborough's policy entrepreneurs demonstrated a considerable capacity to define, analyse and operate upon the problems of industrial decline in an inner city setting. That capacity cannot be imposed by the expedient of a declarative strategy, nor can it be purchased overnight with IAP money. In this case at least it was painstakingly developed as a by-product of a long-run exercise in bureaucratic politics, the initial and more modest aim of which had been to win a place for employment issues on the council's policy agenda.

8 The Management of Change

THE account which we have so far presented falls into two parts. In Chapters 3, 4 and 5 we sketched out the essentials of that complex of forces which is bringing about the rapid de-industrialisation of the older manufacturing city. We sought to identify structural factors, local factors, the points at which they interact, and their implications for urban management. In Chapters 6 and 7 we presented an account of how policy-makers in two London boroughs experienced these changes, interpreted their significance, and resolved to intervene in the hope of ameliorating their impact.

As the protracted disputes over policy and practice in each borough show, there is nothing automatic about adjustment to the situation of urban deconcentration which emerged in the 1970s. Far from seeing 'the local state' at work, we see something more modest and more familiar: groups of officials voicing their uncertainties, demonstrating their perplexities and becoming collectively more aware of the widening gulf between expectation and experience. Among them, a smaller number of policy entrepreneurs who seek to impose a new cognitive order through the redefinition of local problems and the elaboration of accounts of events which bear a closer relation to identifiable realities; doing so, moreover, in such a way as to enhance their own action spaces and link policy outcomes to career outcomes. There is no reason to suppose that the internal politics of organisations serve any external function; environmental change, manifested in this instance as industrial decline, merely provides fresh cues for plausible accounts and alibis for entrepreneurial action.

The underlying force for policy change, if it must be so described, is internal, not external. It arises less from a remorseless logic of organisational processes than from the inherent activism – some will say hyperactivism – of modern public administration, that simple urgency expressed by Bossard's 'Well, let's do *something*, folks.' The need to intervene, to act and to be seen to be acting underpins the recent growth of local authority economic management which is apparent not just in London but in all the major British conurbations. This need is endorsed by the belief, only recently formulated with clarity, that local government is in the business of environmental management and should assume responsibility for orchestrating the processes of urban change.

In the economic field at least, intervention embodies a paradox that is by no means lost on the policy entrepreneurs themselves and which is displayed in their characteristic alternation between a determination to stem or reverse the tide of change and a despairing acknowledgment of the marginality of their actions. 'Regeneration' and 'retention' alternate as objectives for industrial employment and it is today still unclear what the limits of a feasible local economic strategy might be. The most common tendency, and one which was widely supported until recently, has been simply to attempt to facilitate *in situ* growth, rather than to obstruct it. Hence the abandonment of earlier policies to extinguish nonconforming uses, the accelerated (and more sympathetic) treatment of industrial planning applications, the playing down of such environmental goals as traffic restraint in industrial areas, and the useful moves to assemble and service industrial land. Here, however, the consensus ends. Should local authorities intervene to support market forces or to secure the welfare of the local population? Should the emphasis lie in small business development, promoted by advisory services and underwritten with financial support, or in such labour market ventures as skill centres to train the untrained, support for vulnerable groups and the encouragement of co-operative enterprise?

These in a sense are national issues, debated, decided, challenged and redebated locally in the absence of a national urban policy. Central government policy-makers are overwhelmingly concerned with sectoral and not spatial issues, with promoting industrial efficiency, international competitiveness and, thereby, the welfare of a spatially undifferentiated population. The older conurbations bear the consequential costs of modernisation.[1]

As a nation, we have so far evaded the question of how best to *manage* the consequential transition to a post-industrial city and in the absence of national policy, decision-making is effectively decentralised to the local authorities themselves, who intervene in ways that may be both mutually inconsistent and inconsistent with national – or even metropolitan – goals.[2] In this book we have not been concerned with the substance of those interventions but with their origins, the stumbling and often conflict-generating moves towards the establishment of a claim to attention on behalf of industrial decline.

This is an appropriate moment to return to our starting-point, an inquiry into what might be termed the springs of policy intervention. We argued in Chapter 2 that neither the materialist nor the idealist view can account convincingly for policy change, the first because it denies the significance of human agency (so apparent in the account presented in Chapters 6 and 7), the second because it overlooks the pressures of rapidly changing circumstances (as manifest in Chapters 3 to 5). A simple materialist viewpoint would imply the acceptance of urban deindustrialisation as sufficient in itself to account for intervention.

How then might the divergences between the two cases presented here be explained? Westborough experienced an astonishing transformation in its industrial base within a short space of time, with unemployment remaining low until very recently, and responded with symbolic action. Southborough launched a more sophisticated, inventive and comprehensive economic strategy in response to a proportionately larger, but in real terms far less significant, contraction in *its* manufacturing sector. Where then is the common driving force? In manufacturing employment? in unemployment? or in youth unemployment?

Our own approach is to attend instead to the symbolisation of these changes and their signification as problems. The main line of our analysis, already signalled in Chapter 2, is to draw together both changing circumstances and their subjective (or intersubjective) interpretations in accounting for intervention. In this, two distinct issues may be identified for further discussion: the initial *conditions* of intervention as they arise in the form of perceived stress, and *interventiveness*, or the variable propensity to intervene. But we need first to consider the concept of intervention itself.

The nature of intervention

For no justifiable reason, some concepts in the social sciences attract considerable attention and generate a substantial body of literature before attention wanes and the opportunity to mine an untapped seam is exhausted. 'Conflict', 'decisions', integration' and, latterly, 'implementation' are examples of such favoured concepts. In other cases intellectual curiosity and fashion alike will pass a concept by, leaving it neglected and underdeveloped, irrespective of its prevalence within the social order or its role in maintaining that order. Such is the case of intervention.

In a survey of the literature dealing with the interventions of states in the affairs of other states Rosenau concludes that: 'scholarly writings on the subject of intervention . . . are singularly devoid of efforts to develop systematic knowledge of the conditions under which interventionary behaviour is initiated, sustained, and abandoned'.[3] These strictures are apparently equally applicable to intervention in its broader sense. As Little, in virtually the sole general exploration of the concept, comments:

Intervention is a ubiquitous social phenomenon. Actions varying from the donation of foreign aid to the use of military force are described as intervention in the international system, while intervention in the domestic system extends from financial support to private industry to measures introducing wage restraint. At the individual level social workers intervene in family relationships, policemen intervene in brawls and parents intervene in the lives of their children . . . The pervasive character of intervention places it in the same category as conflict, its diversity challenging social scientists who wish to identify order in the social world.[4]

Little's own attempt to meet this challenge fails, however, to secure for intervention an analytic status comparable with that of conflict or integration, where a body of knowledge may be drawn upon in the analysis of interactions over so wide a span as international, inter-local, inter-organisational, inter-group and interpersonal relations.

In the absence of a general intellectual concern with the springs of interventive action, few studies take intervention itself as problematic, that is, as requiring explanation in other than obvious terms. That most writers implicitly subscribe to evocative theories in which changing societal conditions precipitate intervention indicates how far material-ist assumptions are embedded in the deep structures of our social thought. The dissenters, the less numerous historical and sociological idealists, see intervention as requiring no further explanation than the demonstrable existence of a belief, current among policy-makers, that action should be taken and the public welfare (or that of the agency) thereby promoted. As we argued in Chapter 2, neither the materialist nor the idealist conception can provide a satisfactory account of policy intervention, for such an account would have to centre on the *relation-ships between* circumstance and belief, between the knower and the known, in short on that central problem in the social sciences: the foundation of consciousness.

The assumptive world approach provides one way of conceptualising those relationships and thereby understanding the purposive actions of policy-makers. The interplay amongst the cognitive, affective, cathec-tic and directive elements of consciousness establishes man as an active agent, interpreting, adapting to, but ultimately *acting upon* the world of everyday experience. More than a synonym for 'ideology' or 'world view', the concept of the assumptive world credits the agent with the power to intervene and with the self-confidence to choose intervention; to make, as well as to experience, history.

The nature of the interventive choice can therefore be understood as action taken to avert the unacceptable. It follows directly from the central place which we accord to anticipation in the assumptive world: the past is condensed and projected so as to order the future and create an expectable environment. Stress arises when changing conditions seem to flow against expectations, or when they threaten to bring about the consummation of some dreaded future state of the lifeworld. Thus, in intervening, the agent acts diagnostically, for 'what predicates action is an agent's understanding of his own situation as in some respect unacceptable to himself . . . the spring of conduct is a situation [which is] recognised to contain a specific unacceptability'.[5] Interventions are then innovative acts of which 'crises are the crucibles'.[6]

Here then is the paradox of conservative innovation. The entrepreneur engaged in 'disruptive social change' is essentially trying to 'restore the continuity of expectation'.[7] Intervention will be embarked upon, despite its costs, if the stress engendered by the gulf between expectation and experience is too great to be borne. Those who are moved to act as policy entrepreneurs 'foresee some more profound threat to the realisation of their essential purposes, which impels them to withstand the anxieties of breaking out. They repudiate the security of a structure of relationships they understand, so as not to lose the more fundamental attachments which make their lives meaningful.'[8] As Marris puts it: 'We are driven to innovate by the incompatibility of present life with our self-conception, rather than by its intrinsic disadvantages.'[9] Intervention is then a response to stress. The stress arises from the felt incompatibility between aspects of the lifeworld and our images and expectations of it. The goal of intervention is the harmonisation of image and experience by manipulation of the experience itself.

When we shift our attention from the individual agent to the agency the analysis is inevitably complicated by the organisational context of action. For the agency, intervention to arrest economic decline commonly takes the form of a package of policies for land use, industrial support, co-operative development, and so on. Yet, while the agency may be said to be intervening (in the sense of attempting to manage change within its policy space), the officials who administer those policies are not. Individual interventions occur when concerned officials turn policy entrepreneur and intervene in the agenda-setting process of the agency itself. This is an important distinction. The agency might appear to be acting mechanistically in responding to the obvious pressure of circumstances: however, as our two case-studies illustrate, there is nothing mechanistic about the processes by which the choice of intervention came to be posed, still less endorsed.

It would be a mistake to draw too rigid a distinction between the agency and the individuals who act on its behalf in accordance with the roles which it confers on them. It is true that problems of industrial decline or rising unemployment arise within the policy space of the organisation, not within the lifespace of the individual. Yet in playing the role of policy entrepreneur the individual agent takes upon himself the broader responsibilities of the agency itself. His arguments are framed and his energies committed within the limits of those responsibilities; to campaign for intervention as a policy entrepreneur is to act 'as if' one were the omnipotent agent; 'as if' the organisation's problems were one's own. And, to the extent that the policy agenda can indeed fall under the sway of tactically skilful bureaucratic lobbies, the stance of the entrepreneur is both rational and justified.

All intervention incurs costs. First there are the disruption costs, which are likely to loom large for the individual agent who intervenes in the agenda-setting process, not on behalf of his own lifespace management needs, but on behalf of the wider responsibilities and needs of his agency. Second there are the opportunity costs of any course of action, which, in the routinised life of an organisation, are likely to be perceived as prohibitively high. For the policy entrepreneur, however, opportunity costs will be negligible; he may lobby in favour of industry and against housing, for example, and he will not normally be called upon to make the choices or to bear the costs of diverting resources from one to the other.

Moreover, time is on the side of the agent as entrepreneur. In the first place the passage of time reduces the disruption costs of intervention. It is less disruptive to intervene in the forward planning process then to contest the here-and-now decisions. The second point is that changing circumstances have a powerful cumulative effect which may be used to advantage by the policy entrepreneur; every 'crisis' is but an episode in a current of change, but it is in the entrepreneur's interest to dramatise the discontinuities. Our two case-studies throw light upon the ways in which changing circumstances come to be construed as crises.

The conditions of intervention

The precondition for intervention is the felt discontinuity of experience, and in particular the threat to expectation posed by unanticipated change. In the context with which we are concerned here, significant change is that which occurs only within the immediate operating environment of the local authority. It is in the nature of local government to define issues in ways which are bounded by the territorial limits of a local jurisdiction. The powers of local authorities apply, with few and specific exceptions, within precisely defined territorial limits. Their duties are invariably just so circumscribed. In attempting to operate upon the local economy they are forced to impose these spatial boundaries, however incongruously, upon the problem in hand. As Westborough's Employment Topic Paper put it:

> Essentially the Westborough strategy is based on the problems and needs of its own residents . . . [its] obvious links with the rest of Greater London make it difficult to define a 'local economy' which could be studied in isolation. The borough is both an employment centre and a dormitory area. However, the existing administrative boundaries clearly define the immediate target area of Council policies and the residents who benefit from them. Thus while Westborough is not thought of as an 'island' by referring to policies and changes at the international, national and regional levels the problems still tend to be localised.

While the objective reality may then be that of partial and multiple boundedness, urban change is appreciated as something happening in the space defined by statute.[10] Yet such a bounded environment defines only *where* change occurs. To achieve significance change must bear upon the perceived *characteristics* of that environment. How are those characteristics determined?

A sense of place is a vital aspect of the assumptive world of the individual, for it provides the reference points that enable him to locate himself in physical and social space. Nowhere is this more evidently the case than in the large city. The scale and complexity of the city, the flux of its internal boundaries, the anonymity of its 'emporium of styles', all enable the individual to impose his own construction of the urban scene.[11] The images through which this is done serve to order the information generated by the experience of urban life. The city as a whole is incomprehensible and inaccessible to immediate knowledge; but the image mediates between the individual and the city, enabling him to simplify, interpret and make sense of it.[12]

However, images provide more than just a representation of spatial form and relationships; the individual's values, assumptions and cultural traditions assign a deeper significance to place.[13] Embedded in particular social milieux, shared and taken for granted, they enable him to encapsulate a fragment of continuous space and to affirm 'what kind of place this is'. Such a process of characterisation occurs for any individual within his social context, and the context itself plays a major role in the assignment of meaning. The social frame of reference serves to consolidate and sharpen the image.[14] This is especially the case within organisations and, above all, within local authorities, where the responsibility to act upon the environment argues for explicit definition of its nature.

To define, we have argued, is also to anticipate. The image imposes both order *and* hope through the creation of expectation. As we saw in our earlier discussion of the assumptive world, the expectable environment provides models both of the world as it is and as it might be: 'possible situations, ideal situations, or dreaded situations'.[15] Circumstance alone dictates which model will be brought to the foreground of consciousness. It was argued in an earlier study that the purpose of local policy-making is to give effect to such preferred images and so act as to avert unacceptable outcomes. The assumptive worlds of decision-makers provide the predicates of action in which:

the over-riding concern is to manage, maintain and enhance the social, physical and fiscal characteristics of the locality *as presently imagined*. The interplay of wider social and economic forces operating locally ensures that the image is continuously strained by changing realities. Policy-making is therefore a dynamic response and the impetus behind . . . policy is the mismatch of 'models of the world' as perceived by local policy-makers: specifically, between models of the local world as it is and was, and models of the local world *as it might become* in both preferred and dreaded situations. From these imagistic tensions derive the main lines of policy.[16]

Often such images will centre upon and symbolise a particular place which will then provide the iconography for a far larger entity. In Southborough's case this seemed to be the river: while the Thames provides the borough's southern boundary, only part of it has ever been in industrial use. Its significance lies not in what it is, but in what it stands for: an *industrial* place. Thus, South Reach became a major arena of symbolic conflict. The plans of the pre-1977 councils had sought to realise William Morris's vision of an idyllic riverside, free from industry and open to ramblers. The subsequent arguments about its future had symbolic as well as substantive importance. There is the sharpest of contrasts between the quotation from Morris used to preface the 1973 plan for this stretch of riverside – 'the soap works with their smoke-vomiting chimneys were gone; and the lead works gone; and no sound of riveting and hammering came down the west wind from Thorney-crofts' – and the cover picture of the 1977 industrial survey with its depiction of the barges, cranes, hoppers and factories of South Reach as emblematic of industry in Southborough *at large*. It takes effort to recall that in 1977 only eight firms actually used the river for the transport of materials.

If the Thames served such symbolic purposes in Southborough, the position of the Arterial Road in Westborough is surely analogous. The use of an aerial photograph of this, once the richest stretch of industrial ribbon development in England, as the cover picture for the borough's guide to industry has already been mentioned. Few of the factory buildings shown survived another two years in manufacturing use, and most had been vacated or converted at the time of publication. Yet the Arterial Road is the most tangible symbol of Westborough as a manufacturing place. In their different ways, the river and the road served as symbols of the nature of each of the two boroughs, focusing the hopes, disappointments and fears of the policy-makers; that each bore the brunt of the rapid change which overtook the respective boroughs is ironic.

Beyond the iconography of the river and the road lay more general assumptions about the kind of place each borough could claim to be. In Westborough's case acceptance of change sharply differentiated officers and councillors. The councillors included a significant group of industrial workers and trade union officials. Their natural propensity to identify with the manufacturing sector and to view office and retailing development with suspicion was undoubtedly sustained by their occupational roles. The tape/slide show prepared for the council's first industrial seminar caught the mood perfectly with its images of high street prosperity intercut with glum graphs of falling manufacturing employment. It was also reinforced by the unusual institution of a standing consultative committee of leading councillors and local CBI members. Notionally an industrial and *commercial* committee, its leading members were predominantly from the large firms in the manufacturing sector. When council officers attempted to broaden the representative base of the committee to include a local Chamber of Commerce, the councillors agreed the change subject to a restriction of membership to the *industrial* members of the Chamber.

The redefinition of Westborough's problems described in Chapter 6 was entirely an officer initiative. While education and careers officials continued to be preoccupied with manufacturing ('We need to bring the factory into the classroom', insisted the director of education) the planners were deeply sceptical of the borough's future manufacturing role: 'Decline isn't a problem but just something that's happened,' said one senior official: hence the employment topic paper which formally succeeded in the latent purpose of shifting concern away from manufacturing industry as such. Yet when the paper was presented to the committee which approved it, its various sections were received with either perplexed silence or the expression of continuing anxiety about the recent spate of closures in local manufacturing firms.

Thereafter, Westborough officers rapidly adjusted their own expectations while councillors continued to feel deeply committed to manufacturing industry. The surface changes, the underlying continuities and the delicate balance of responsibilities posed dilemmas for the officers. Here is a group of them discussing the policy options at a meeting of the ISWG:

A. The council's policy has been perfectly clear – they're against the loss of manufacturing. I wonder more and more whether they're right . . . Some opinion says the UK economy should be service-based, no point in competing with Third World manufacturing . . . the local authority is swimming against the tide . . . Is it desirable to preserve jobs in manufacturing? It will be a brave officer who goes to the council to say that the industrial strategy is wrong!

B. It is difficult to find a very good reason for trying to prop up manufacturing industry . . . the real problem is do we want to encourage manufacturing? Is it worth doing?

C. Maybe we would do the country more good by encouraging manufacturing to move elsewhere.

D. Are [we] trying to keep some manufacturing because we want to implement the government's industrial strategy of keeping a manufacturing base?

Industrial change was evidently a greater problem for Westborough's councillors than for their officials, for it threatened to precipitate a shift in the *character* of the area from an engineering centre to an office location, from blue-collar employment to white. Because there were few apparently adverse employment consequences most officers found it difficult to share the concern so repeatedly voiced by their elected members.

For their opposite numbers in Southborough, on the other hand, sectoral change was seen as leading to high unemployment and a worsening of the conditions of, and returns to, such employment as remained. Because these adverse welfare consequences were apparent long before they came to councillors' attention, those officers who recognised the magnitude of the changes which the locality was undergoing were apprehensive: 'Further erosion of Southborough's industrial base and the change of use of industrial sites to other uses will convert the current job recession into a permanent one, denying not only the current generation but future generations opportunities for industrial employment in the borough'.

The tape/slide show prepared for the Southborough members' teach-in in 1977 accordingly presented a compelling picture of population and economic decline linked to 'a severe loss' in manufacturing, the 'very sharp decline' of which was itself linked to the high levels of unemployment then current. Again, the elaboration of the outline strategy argued that 'there has been a loss of particular kinds of jobs catering for those who are either unskilled or who have manufacturing skills and who represented about 30 per cent of the resident workforce in 1971. Between 1971 and 1977 the number of manufacturing jobs in the borough fell by 50 per cent, and male unemployment is concentrated in the manufacturing and manual sectors'.

It was a neat argument and an easily assimilable one, important qualities in any case for policy change. Yet it was misleading in two senses. First, the frequently quoted high proportionate decline in Southborough's manufacturing was from a low initial base. Second, only a small proportion of those unemployed locally had previously worked in manufacturing. In 1978 most of Southborough's unemployed workers previously worked in the service sector in offices, shops, and public service establishments. Manufacturing supplied only 13 per cent of unemployed men and 11 per cent of unemployed women. This was true even in the lowest skill groups of manual labour; only 170 of the unskilled workers on the local register had previously worked in manufacturing industry. The evidence pointed strongly towards a process of adaptation on the part of local manufacturing workers either by migration, or, in the case of older workers, by exit from the labour force. It was however noticeably difficult to deploy such arguments effectively in Southborough once the manufacturing decline/unemployment link had gained, after 1978, the status of an idea in good currency.[17]

Three aspects of this preoccupation with manufacturing industry in the two boroughs are worth considering here: assumptions about occupational roles, beliefs about the transactional basis of the economy itself, and images of Britain as a manufacturing nation. The shift toward service employment may evoke deep-rooted assumptions about sex roles and the structure of occupational opportunity. In particular, office development may be seen as providing jobs for women at the expense of their menfolk. Thus, traditional role assumptions are invoked in the complaint voiced in Westborough that the service industries 'have been the traditional source of work for women whereas many men have effectively been forced to take them up due to lack of opportunities in manufacturing. This is not a desirable situation given that today men are still the main "breadwinners" in the family'. More typical, perhaps, is the recognition in Southborough that a shift towards service employment may represent a decline in earnings for the employed population. In this case, resistance to manufacturing decline is based in part on a concern for income maintenance.

In the second place there may be a belief, particularly among those whose occupational background is in manufacturing industry, that the services are inherently 'non-productive'. In such cases the transactional basis of the economy is seen as turning on the exchange of tangible 'goods' for money. The service sector as a whole is here conflated with certain *public* services and seen as 'parasitic' upon the wealth generated by manufacturing; hence the (unchallenged) familiar-sounding complaint of a local manufacturer at Westborough's first industrial seminar that 'we need manufacturing [here] to pay for services'.

In the third place, participants in the policy process often subscribe to an image of Britain as a manufacturing nation. This image is embodied in the wider culture and transmitted and reinforced by the media and by national government policy.[18] The image may itself be a potent influence within the local policy-making process, shaping the definitions of local problems by reference to national concerns. This assimilation of the preoccupations of national policy at the local level (which we noted in Westborough) may or may not be a justifiable and rational adjustment of local priorities to a wider interest. Equally, it may simply reflect the need of local policy-makers to order their experience of local economic change in terms of a *metaphor* from the national level. In so far as this is the case, it may be attributed to the sheer difficulty of conceptualising local level economic processes. The 'local economy' is an elusive phenomenon, and its problems, while experienced in a most immediate fashion, do not lend themselves to interpretation in local terms. The process of what we earlier termed 'bringing explanations to problems to give them order and hope' may lead local policy-makers to have recourse to pre-existing models of change in the wider economy. The DoE Circular 71/77 on the Industrial Strategy was readily adopted in Westborough not least for its translation of goals, problems and processes at the national level into metaphors for local economic problems. Under the Labour government of the day, the *economic* policy arguments for supporting manufacturing industry were eclipsed by an almost moral concern to 'regenerate' a manufacturing economy. Yet while national governments are primarily concerned with manufacturing output and productivity, local policy-makers' concerns can rationally extend only as far as the level of manufacturing *employment*.

In these several ways images of industrial society allowed the local policy-makers to account for changes in the occupational structure, to grasp the transactional basis of the economy, and to integrate local economic activity conceptually into the national and international systems. More important, the growing disjuncture between image and experience provided *the springs of action*. The definition of the local problem as one of sectoral mismatch served in the case of both Westborough and Southborough to justify the initial intervention into local economic affairs. In neither case did the simple manufacturing decline model survive the further research and examination which, as Bossard suggests, tend to follow intervention into new problem areas. Yet in both cases it was a necessary catalyst to a competitive process of claim-making; it thereby provided, for all its analytical insufficiencies, the primary condition of intervention.

Interventiveness: the propensity to intervene

While a perceived problem of manufacturing job loss was common to both authorities, there were marked differences between them in their responses to economic change, and few parallels in the actual activities or levels of resource commitment. Behind these differences in the substance of response lay evident variations in the *interventiveness* of the two organisations.

Before considering this further, it is worth noting the striking contrast of roles between the planning staffs of Westborough and Southborough. This contrast is important where, as in much of urban government in England, officials tend to be the architects of new programmes. In Westborough, declining manufacturing employment was identified by the *councillors* as the major problem facing the locality; with the exception of the education officials and the interventionist chief executive, few other officials construed this change as problematic. There was correspondingly little policy entrepreneurship amongst the officers, save for those who wished to steer attention *away* from manufacturing. In Southborough, on the other hand, officers, having made the running in the struggle to reconstruct the policy agenda, were the principal authors of the stream of innovations which followed. It was commonly the case that particular officers could be identified as having initiated particular programmes and the recurrent problem for the EDG and its members was to find ways of 'selling' successive projects to the planning committee and the leadership.

There is, however, far more here than a simple association between the officer origination of programmes on the one hand, and the degree of interventiveness on the other. In both boroughs, as in local government at large, there was for most of the period under review a vague but variable presumption in favour of intervention, conventionally expressed in terms of 'managing change'. Local authorities in the 1970s have gradually come to assume the role of environmental managers. Professor J. D. Stewart writes of *the assertive authority* as being required to 'develop a lead role in environmental and community governance':

> if the local authority is to take seriously the statement of the Bains report that local government 'has within its purview the overall economic, cultural and physical well-being' of the local community . . . those responsibilities imply a *governmental* role. [Moreover] it is a mistake to see the local authority's capacity for action restricted to the formal duties laid upon it.[19]

In Stewart's view, the local authority is both *responsive* to change and *responsible* for affecting desirable outcomes:

> The local authority cannot evade its responsibilities for urban management. It has inherited them and it maintains them. True, it shares them with many other organisations. [But] the local authority, because it is a multi-purpose authority impinging on the environment at many points, has a special role in urban management. That role can be identified, recognised, and planned for. Or it can merely be allowed to happen. The local authority is playing a key role in urban management, even where it does not recognise it.[20]

Within such accepted notions of responsive and responsible urban management there is ample scope for variations in approach. These variations may be construed as a propensity to intervene and encompass both beliefs as to the inherent *tractability* of the external world and perceptions of the *resources* available for acting upon it.

The tractable environment

Belief as to the inherent tractability of man's environment and its responsiveness to manipulation is a basic variable in both culture and personality. What might be termed the 'managerialist view' is sometimes portrayed as a model of man/nature relations which is distinctive to modern industrial societies.[21] Less-developed societies, unfamiliar with technology, are supposedly more inclined to fatalism, in which the individual believes that 'the events affecting his own life are largely determined by external forces rather than by his own efforts' and will therefore 'tend not to engage in behaviour designed to positively reshape [his] environment'.[22] Any single culture – or more localised sub-culture – displays variation on this dimension within broad limits, from the traditional conservative to whom it is a truism that events are the outcomes of decisions which lie beyond the reach of government, through the disillusioned social democrat, who is acutely aware of policy failure and unintended consequences, to the strict managerialist who sees the operating environment of government as essentially plastic and tractable.[23] The prevailing assumptions about intervention in the two boroughs showed distinct and consistent differences in this respect.

Southborough officials did not debate the nature and limits of intervention in our presence. Preoccupied with actual programmes, they initially took feasibility for granted. They acted out their belief that economic forces are inherently manageable and that the urban economy could respond, at least at the margin, to interventions which were appropriately designed and deployed. The recognition that local policies had in the past exercised negative effects on industrial well-being sustained the eventually successful campaign by the employment lobby to reverse the direction of policy in the expectation of positive effects. They were flexible enough to continue to revise and extend their programmes as they ascended the learning curve, re-evaluating their earlier initiatives. Their activism was accompanied by extensive and sophisticated data gathering and analysis, with current interpretations of local circumstances tested out in periodic employment seminars with officials of other agencies and interested research workers.

This rather intense spirit of inquiry and assessment led eventually to serious questioning of the rationale of the council's economic strategy by some officers. The earlier expectation that unemployment could be reduced by facilitating industrial development was eroded by the accumulation of research evidence; by 1980 facile assumptions about the isolation and tractability of the local environment were under attack:

the primary achievement of the programme of industrial and also of office development in the borough will be to boost the amount of economic activity taking place in the borough. This will benefit London's economy, as long as developments are not simply taking place there instead of elsewhere. These industrial and office developments will have a very marginal impact on local unemployment . . . conventional office and industrial development is not a cost-effective method for reducing unemployment in this borough. If these policies are pursued, they should be pursued primarily for other reasons.

Thus, complexity, interdependence and structural shifts in the economy suggested that 'it would be more realistic for this council . . . to accept that they have a population which will remain vulnerable to unemployment'.

Westborough's officers and councillors appeared to share a deep pessimism as to the tractability of economic forces throughout the period of our presence there. As one officer bluntly put it (without dissent from his companions), 'I don't think there's any role for the council in physically entering the scene and they don't have the resources and they always fail anyway'. The expression of similar views seemed commonplace.

The author of Westborough's economic activity topic paper repeatedly disavowed intervention: he advised the ISWG that 'broadening our involvement in the local economy is playing our worst hand because here we don't have enough influence'; moreover, he was 'repelled' by the policy papers produced by other authorities with 'their grandiose plans'. Elsewhere, he confessed himself unsympathetic to any intervention designed to 'prop up' the capitalist order and for that reason would not consider it. Other key officials were, for quite different reasons, reluctant to countenance any extension of the council's role, for example when asked to clarify ambiguous passages in reports. Committee members were, on the occasions when we observed their deliberations, unresponsive to suggestions that they should extend the scope of council action *in pursuit of the very goals to which they frequently alluded*. Both groups made frequent reference to the wider forces operating in the national or even the international economy. Their initial industrial strategy was of almost consciously symbolic value; it was hardly expected to arrest the changes which the councillors deplored.

Knowledge gathering is a prerequisite of sustained intervention and vital to the management of environmental change. In this respect Southborough were unusually data-rich, at least in the period following the industrial and commercial survey launched in 1976. While the interpretation of research results was often hotly disputed there, serious and professional attempts were constantly made to generate new data on, for example, firms' plans and their implications for the labour market. Among the more significant of these exercises was the development of links with local ESA office managers which enabled Southborough's planners to obtain invaluable data on the composition of the locally unemployed labour and thereby greatly to refine their policy in the direction of a 'skill mismatch/training failure model' of the local problem.

The contrast with Westborough is almost total. There both the chief executive and the borough planning officer tried with limited success to increase the policy analysis and intelligence capabilities available to them. A report prepared for the chief executive noted that no department has a clear research policy or programme. Research in departments is carried out on an *ad hoc* basis, frequently in response to particular problems or pressures from outside rather than as a planned activity as part of the policy formation or management process . . . few departments allocated money in the budget for research . . . the number of officers who are designated research officers or have a specific responsibility for research is very small.

The same Westborough report noted that the local authority required 'a wide perspective on the needs and problems of its environment', citing the examples of demographic and industrial change. Consider, on the other hand, the following exchange in a meeting of the ISWG, which took place after nearly twelve months' explicit discussion of the council's industrial strategy:

A. We must not exaggerate the rot [but] there are problems of lack of labour and poor premises.
B. But there are rumours of impending doom.
A. Yes, but sites don't stay vacant for long periods.
C. That's right!
A. (reflectively) We don't know why firms leave, do we?
B. Perhaps we could do some research; that *would* concern this group.
A. Yes, I think it's essential, even though I don't think there's much we could do. (later) But we need to know why [firms] go.
D. Should we recommend research in this report?
B. No, but we should be sure that it's going to happen.

It didn't. Westborough had a very weak research capability, a fact which arose from and helped sustain the widespread scepticism concerning the authority's role as a manager of change.

Resources for intervention
When planning extensions to their managerial role in local economic affairs, officials are customarily mindful of the resources needed to mount any intervention.[24] The primary resource is statutory authority, for local authorities must act within their explicit powers. In this Southborough had the benefit, after 1978, of the additional powers conferred on designated authorities under the Inner Urban Areas Act. However, such powers – and their further enhancement elsewhere in the partnership authorities – are variously viewed as either somewhat marginal or as highly significant. The important point is how powers are interpreted, and how far their enhancement serves to provoke new thinking about possible means of achieving the ends that are implicit in the powers themselves. The same may be said of the ambiguous general powers under s.111 and s.137 of the Local Government Act 1972, which may be interpreted in a restrictive fashion or more generously.[25] The uncertainties inherent in general powers may be resolved by testing their limits or deciding to forgo their use; while all authorities

must operate *intra vires* in a legal sense, the behavioural correlates are extremely elastic.

In one instance, a meeting of the EDG in Southborough, while pondering the limits to Industrial Improvement Area powers, identified a possible opportunity for their more extensive use, and called in a member of the council's legal department to give such reassurance that they would be *intra vires* as a generous construction of the Inner Urban Areas Act would allow. The most closely comparable example from Westborough concerns a request from the council leader for a report on the scope for co-operative industrial development. When the draft was presented to the ISWG, it evoked a remarkable convergence around the view that support could *not* be given to co-operatives. First, one officer repeatedly probed for evidence of the existence of a specific power to promote co-operative enterprise, concluding, when none could be produced, that this was beyond their powers. A second mentioned that Wandsworth had sponsored a co-op, but a third interjected that this would have been done under inner cities' powers which were not available to Westborough. Finally, any further discussion was discouraged by a series of dark references to the forthcoming rate support grant settlement which was expected to constrain them severely.[26]

It is, of course, true that the two authorities differed in their financial resources; but the direction of the difference favours Westborough with its greatly superior rateable value and lower incidence of needs.[27] More specifically, Southborough enjoyed the advantage of additional urban programme money earmarked for the council under the IAP arrangements. At a rare meeting of officers from the two authorities, it was readily agreed that IAP status was the crucial distinguishing feature, without which Southborough could not have developed what was seen by Westborough officers as their neighbour's elaborate and sophisticated economic strategy. However, the background to strategy, as recounted in Chapter 7, hardly supports that view. Southborough was firmly established in the economic field before the (unexpected) grant of programme status, and the initial capital allocation of £250,000 for industrial development had already been made. Moreover, during the late 1970s, Southborough officers readily drew comparisons between what they saw as their own council's rather modest operations in the economic field and the more ambitious and comprehensive programme operated by some other authorities. It cannot be denied that financial resources were vital to Southborough's economic strategy; the key variable is, however, the perceived willingness of the council to spend, which in Westborough's case was rated as extremely low by officers, leading them to anticipate the councillors' reactions to any expenditure-incurring proposal and to block it at source.

The significance of organisational culture

Interventions in the local economy are experiments in the management of change. On our argument they arise when the initial condition of unwelcome stress-inducing change is identified as such by policy entrepreneurs, when they are successful in gaining access to the policy agenda, when change is seen as manageable and when resources are seen as sufficient. Both problem definition and policy response are therefore to be understood as organisational processes on which the wider patterns of social and economic change have few direct effects. Instead, change constitutes an experience which is interpreted and accounted for within an organisational context of communication and power relations, and within an appreciative context of prevailing images and myths.

It follows from this that what might be termed the institutional capacity to analyse situations and to act upon them effectively varies between otherwise similar organisations (as the two case-studies suggest) and is affected as much by appreciative factors as by formal structures and processes. This is not however to make the common-sense mistake of reducing organisational performance to 'the quality of the people'. Rather, it calls our attention to the elusive complex of factors that bear upon the ways in which people work together in the roles ascribed to them: above all to organisational culture.

Culture is pervasive within organisations. It consists of a set of generalised orientations, shared by the members but specific to their organisational situation.[28] Shaping the ways in which organisational roles are played, culture provides a common assumptive world within which any particular individual may be more or less comfortable, more or less effective. Mobility and the recruitment process help to sustain organisational cultures through the processes of staff selection and self-selection, so lending a sometimes formidable resilience to shared dispositions and taken-for-granted assumptions.

Southborough and Westborough present us with a contrast of cultures. Indeed, perhaps the most startling feature of the two organisations is not their comparative 'performance' but the differing scope which they offered to those policy entrepreneurs *who moved from the one organisation to the other*. Westborough's chief executive was formerly the innovative director of operations at Southborough. On making the move he took with him two of the staff of Southborough's chief executive's department, one of whom had played a major role in reversing that council's policies towards industry in the mid-1970s. Movement was in both directions; Southborough's first industrial development officer had formerly played an inconspicuous role in Westborough. We distinguish, then, not between individuals on the basis of their relative creativity, but between organisations on the basis of their cultures; in particular, whether or not they value activism, innovation, responsiveness and the desire to shape the policy space of government.

Speculations on the constitution of cultures lie outside the scope of this book. We can only note that culture pervades the decision process and establishes the climate of interaction within the organisation to an extent that the outsider can hardly fail to sense. Seated amongst the rubber plants or lounging at the bar, the transient observer encounters the sights, sounds and sensations of other people's everyday worlds in a way which gives different authorities (and sometimes different departments within the same authority) a distinctive quality that is entirely theirs. Moreover, whatever their origins, there are strong indications that the subtle reference points of organisational culture operate with particular potency in the group discussion of policy options.

Because local economic management is a relatively recent area of local authority operation it tends to generate high levels of uncertainty amongst policy-makers. Accordingly, the policy process is often characterised by problem search of a quasi-theoretical nature and rationales for action which are required to be taken on trust.[29] Typically, the discussion of policy options will take place first in an inter-departmental working group of officers, of which Westborough's ISWG and Southborough's EDG are examples. The net effect of decision-making under such conditions and within such a forum is the development of a response style towards environmental change which typifies and expresses *in exaggerated form* the cultural norms of the organisation. Why might this be so?

It is not possible to answer this question with any certainty, pending a future analysis of the group discussion data generated in a far larger number of cases from three successive projects. The elements of an argument may nevertheless be sketched out here. First, it is well established among social psychologists that group discussion *per se* has a measurable impact upon learning, attitude change and decision-making.[30] Second, groups faced with choice dilemmas consistently show more extreme or polarised choices than the members would make individually. Third, while this *choice shift* was initially supposed to operate normally in the direction of higher risk decisions, subsequent work has demonstrated that cautious shifts may equally well occur.[31] Fourth, one important line of argument in the explanation of bi-directional choice shift (as distinct from uni-directional risky shift) has been to identify cultural values in the wider society as favourable to either risk or caution.[32] Finally, the phenomenon of discussion-induced shift is manifest in many group situations other than the laboratory-based preference-ordering experiments; discussion in the face-to-face group has a dynamic density that tends towards the amplification or intensification of the values held in common among group members.[33]

If we accept the concept of an organisational culture the relevance of these processes to the life histories of the two groups whose discussions we witnessed becomes apparent. The distinctive cultures of the two authorities bore upon the group discussion processes in ways which found intensified expression in the conclusions reached within the respective groups. Southborough's EDG members consistently expressed the interventionist norms of their organisation in group discussions which typically took the form of fast moving and intense dialogue on the scope and need for further programme developments. Westborough's ISWG tended to converge, through sequential and mutually sustaining contributions from the members, around conclusions that little could be done. There is no reason to suppose that Westborough's officers are significantly more fatalistic than their opposite numbers in the neighbouring borough.[34] The conclusion to be drawn is rather that while the small, focused strategy group or policy committee may be an effective way of developing new initiatives in an organisation with an activist culture, *they may have the contrary effect* in an organisation which historically has displayed a low propensity to intervene in its own environment. Further, it suggests that the broad drift of policy in any one authority is unlikely to be reversed by the import of more interventionist staff unless this is done on such a scale and over sufficient a period to bring about shifts in the culture of the organisation itself.[35]

*   *   *

Our primary concern in this book has been with the urban impacts of a socio-economic transformation which appear to some as a threat of deindustrialisation and to others as a promise of a post-industrial future. The perception of urban change, the desire to shape its course, and beliefs as to its manageability are organisational attributes which vary for reasons which are beyond our present understanding. Yet, as we enter the next stage of the metropolitan life-cycle, these variations might be crucial to the relative adaptability of urban communities and the life-chances of the inhabitants. We cannot say with any confidence that attempts to manage change can – even at best – do more than ease the transition at the margin. But that is perhaps a sufficient justification for making them. The emergence of the post-industrial city – in a sense a reversion to the pre-industrial functions of command, control, learning and exchange – entails welfare costs on a nineteenth-century scale. The attempt to bring order to that process will critically affect both the magnitude of those costs and the compensating gains to the national economy. As ever, a general gain is a particular loss and no formula for the management of change can defuse the conflicts or avoid the choices inherent within it.

Notes

Chapter 1

1 Department of the Environment, *Review of Local Authority Assistance to Industry and Commerce* (London, 1982); Joint Unit for Research on the Urban Environment, *Local Authority Employment Initiatives* (University of Aston, Birmingham, 1980); N. Johnson and A. Cochrane, *Economic Policy Making by Local Authorities in Britain and Western Germany* (Allen & Unwin, London, 1981); J. Mawson (ed.), 'Special Issue on Unemployment and Economic Development', *Local Government Studies* 7(4) (July–August 1981); F. Robinson, *Local Authority Economic Initiatives: a Review*, Centre for Environmental Studies Occasional Paper No. 10 (1979); K. Young and C. Mason, *Urban Economic Development. New Roles and Relationships* (Macmillan, London, 1983).

2 See also K. Young and J. Kramer, *Strategy and Conflict in Metropolitan Housing* (Heinemann, London, 1978); K. Young and N. Connelly, *Policy and Practice in the Multi-Racial City* (Policy Studies Institute, London 1981); K. Young and P. L. Garside, *Metropolitan London: Politics and Urban Change, 1837–1981* (Edward Arnold, London, 1982).

3 Our use of the term policy entrepreneur is somewhat wider than that adopted by A.J. Meltsner, in *Policy Analysts in the Bureaucracy* (University of California Press, Berkeley, 1976). Specifically, our 'entrepreneur' need not hold a formal policy analysis role in any of the senses discussed by Meltsner, still less possess the valuable mix of technical and political skills for which he reserves the term.

4 We have elaborated our position on this point in K. Young and L. Mills, 'The Decline of Urban Economies', in R. Rose and E. Page (eds), *Fiscal Stress in the Cities* (Cambridge University Press, London, 1982).

5 During the course of this project we reviewed a number of the methodological and technical issues specific to interpretative policy analysis, and that paper may be read as a methodological appendix to this book; see K. Young and L. Mills, *Public Policy Research: A Review of Qualitative Methods* (Social Science Research Council, London, 1980).

6 For a useful discussion of the problems of responsibility, see M. Bulmer (ed.), *Social Research Ethics* (Macmillan, London, 1982). The classic literature on participant observation is too extensive to cite here, but is pulled together in G. J. McCall and J. L. Simmons (eds), *Issues in Participant Observation*, (Addison-Wesley, Reading, Mass., 1969) More useful by far to the practitioner is R. Bogdan, *Participant Observation in Organisational Settings* (Syracuse University Press, Syracuse, NY, 1972); while we also found J. Lofland, *Analysing Social Settings* (Wadsworth, Belmont, Calif., 1971) to be a useful handbook. The role of the transient observer in short-term policy oriented studies is also discussed – along with the ethical and prudential issues that may arise – in J. Murphy, *Getting the Facts: A Fieldwork Guide for Evaluators and Policy Analysts* (Goodyear, Santa Monica, 1980).

7 Our position with regard to interviewing in this and other projects is broadly in line with the notion of the interview as an interpersonal encounter between co-participants, as elaborated by I. de Sola Pool, 'A Critique of the Twentieth Anniversary Issue', *Public Opinion Quarterly*, 21 (Spring 1957), pp. 190–8; C.R.F. Cannell and R.C. Kahn, 'Interviewing', in G. Lindsey and E. Aronson (eds), *The Handbook of Social Psychology: Vol. 2: Research Methods* (Addison-Wesley, Reading, Mass., 1968); I. Deutscher, 'Public and Private Opinions: Social Situations and Multiple Realities', in S.Z. Nagi and R. G. Corwin (eds), *The Social*

Context of Research (Wiley, New York, 1972); M. Brenner, 'Interviewing, the Social Phenomenology of a Research Instrument', in M. Brenner, P. Marsh and M. Brenner (eds), *The Social Context of Method* (Croom Helm, London, 1978). On the interviewer role we are sympathetic to the position taken by L. A. Dexter, in 'Role Relationships and Conceptions of Neutrality in Interviewing', *American Journal of Sociology*, 62 (1956), pp. 153–7, and elaborated in L. A. Dexter, *Elite and Specialised Interviewing* (Northwestern University Press, Evanston, 1970).

8 Productivity is enhanced when two researchers can attend meetings together, as the observational role can be divided up. Some two-hour meetings on this project produced up to 6000 words of notes. We hope to explore these issues in a future paper. A sensitive discussion of problems in group observation is given in T. M. Mills, *The Sociology of Small Groups* (Prentice-Hall, Englewood Cliffs, NJ, 1967), pp. 25–41.

9 E. J. Webb, 'Unconventionality, Triangulation and Inference', in N. K. Denzin (ed.), *Sociological Methods* (Butterworth, London, 1970). For further discussion of triangulation or 'multiple operationalisation' as a research strategy, see N. K. Denzin, *The Research Act* (Aldine, Chicago, 1970).

10 We admit to viewing the research act as a transaction which imposes certain obligations or reciprocity on the investigators. We became more explicit about this during the course of the project and have each grown more comfortable with the interactive role since then. For an important discussion which emphasises the research benefits of a more involved stance, see L. D. Brown, 'Research Action: Organizational Feedback, Understanding and Change', *Journal of Applied Behavioural Science*, 8 (1972) pp. 697–711. See also, more generally, P. Reason and J. Rowan (eds), *Human Inquiry: A Sourcebook of New Paradigm Research* (Wiley, New York, 1981).

Chapter 2

1 K. Deutsch, *The Nerves of Government* (Macmillan, New York, 1966).

2 See generally C. Russett, *The Concept of Equilibrium in American Social Thought* (Yale University Press, New Haven, 1966); D. Easton, *A Framework for Political Analysis*, (Prentice-Hall, Englewood Cliffs, NJ, 1965); W.J.M. Mackenzie, *Politics and Social Science*, (Penguin, Harmondsworth, 1967), pp. 96–110. The implausibility of much of equilibrium analysis stems from its simplistic homeostatic metaphors; for a dynamic conception of equilibrium seeking in a changing environment – homeorhetic equilibrium – see C.H. Waddington, 'Progressive Self-Stabilising Systems in Biology and Social Affairs', *Ekistics*, 22 (133) (1966), pp. 402–405.

3 Among the many US studies, see especially R.I. Hofferbert, 'The Relation Between Public Policy and Some Structural and Environmental Variables in the American States', *American Political Science Review* (March 1966), pp. 73–82; T.R. Dye, *Politics, Economics and the Public* (Rand McNally, Chicago, 1966); M. Hoffman and J. Prather, 'The Independent Effect of Region on State Government Expenditure', *Social Science Quarterly* (June 1972), pp. 52–65. The most directly comparable British study is N.T. Boaden, *Urban Policy Making: Influences on County Boroughs in England and Wales* (Cambridge University Press, Cambridge, 1971).

4 A. Koestler, *The Ghost in the Machine* (Hutchinson, London, 1967), Appendix 2.

5 S. Wolin, *Politics and Vision* (Little Brown, Boston, 1960), Chapter 10.

6 There are many such accounts, though none so encyclopedic as R.H.S. Crossman, *Diaries of a Cabinet Minister* (3 vols) (Hamish Hamilton and Jonathan Cape, London, 1975, 1976, 1977).

7 G.T. Allison, *Essence of Decision* (Little Brown, Boston, Mass. 1971); H.M. Sapolsky, *The Polaris System Development* (Harvard University Press, Cambridge, Mass., 1972); H. Heclo and A. Wildavsky, *The Private Government of Public Money* (2nd edn) (Macmillan, London, 1981).

8   W. H. Walsh, *An Introduction to the Philosophy of History* (Hutchinson, London, 1967), p. 102; E.H. Carr, *What is History?* (Penguin, Harmondsworth, 1964); B.A. Haddock, *An Introduction to Historical Thought* (Edward Arnold, London, 1980).

9   H. Arendt, *The Origins of Totalitarianism* (3rd edn) (Allen & Unwin, London, 1967), pp. 461–8. For a clearly argued discussion of Arendt's understanding of Marx, see B. Parekh, 'Hannah Arendt's Critique of Marx', in M.A. Hill (ed.), *Hannah Arendt: The Recovery of the Public World* (St Martin's Press, New York, 1979).

10 P. Geyl, *Debates with Historians* (Collins, London, 1962), pp. 279–80.

11 E. Nagel, 'Determinism in History', in P. Gardiner (ed.) *The Philosophy of History* (Oxford University Press, London, 1974), p. 187.

12 P. Gardiner, *The Nature of Historical Explanation* (Clarendon Press, Oxford, 1961), p. 138.

13 K. Marx, *Selected Writings in Sociology and Social Philosophy*, T. Bottomore and M. Rubel (eds) (C.A. Watts, London, 1961), p. 90.

14 I. Berlin, 'Historical Inevitability', in *Four Essays on Liberty*, (Oxford University Press, London, 1969), pp. 61–2.

15 J. Larrain, *The Concept of Ideology* (Hutchinson, London, 1979), p. 38.

16 E. Mandel, quoted in R. Mishra, *Society and Social Policy: Theoretical Perspectives on Welfare* (Macmillan, London, 1977), p. 74.

17 N. Ginsburg, *Class, Capital and Social Policy* (Macmillan, London, 1979).

18 I. Gough, *The Political Economy of the Welfare State* (Macmillan, London, 1979).

19 M. Swenarton, *Homes Fit for Heroes* (Heinemann, London, 1981).

20 P. Dunleavy, *Urban Political Analysis*, (Macmillan, London, 1980), p. 101.

21 C. Cockburn, *The Local State* (Pluto Press, London, 1977).

22 See V. George and P. Wilding, *Ideology and Social Welfare* (Routledge & Kegan Paul, London, 1976); J. Carrier and I. Kendall, 'The Development of Welfare States: the Production of Plausible Accounts', *Journal of Social Policy*, 6 (3) (1977), pp. 271–90.

23 J. Hart, 'Nineteenth-Century Social Reform: the Tory Interpretation of History', *Past and Present*, 31 (1965), pp. 39–61.

24 O. MacDonagh, 'The Nineteenth-Century Revolution in Government: A Re-appraisal', *Historical Journal*, 1 (1) (1958), pp. 52–67; see also H. Parris, 'The Nineteenth-Century Revolution in Government: a Re-appraisal Re-appraised', *Historical Journal*, 3 (1) (1960), pp. 17–37. For general reviews of this debate, see V. Cromwell, 'Interpretation of Nineteenth-century Administration: an Analysis', *Victorian Studies*, 9 (March 1966), pp. 245–55; H. Perkin, *The Structured Crowd: Essays in English Social History* (Harvester, Brighton, 1981).

25 MacDonagh, 'Nineteenth-Century Revolution', pp. 17–18.

26 R. Lambert, 'Central and Local Relations in Mid-Victorian England: the Local Government Act Office, 1858–71', *Victorian Studies* (December 1962), p. 149.

27 D. Roberts, *The Victorian Origins of the British Welfare State* (Yale University Press, New Haven, 1960).

28 G. Kitson Clark, *The Making of Victorian England* (Harvard University Press, Cambridge, Mass., 1962).

29 Lambert, 'Central and Local Relations'; R.M. Gutchen, 'Local Improvements and Centralisation in Nineteenth-Century England', *Historical Journal* (1961), pp. 85–96.

30 D. Fraser, *Power and Authority in the Victorian City* (Blackwell, Oxford, 1979), pp. 167–8, 172.

31 Ibid, pp. 2, 3.

32 MacDonagh, 'Nineteenth-Century Revolution', p. 53. See also O. MacDonagh, *A Pattern of Government Growth*, (Macgibbon and Kee, London, 1961).

33 Lambert, 'Central and Local Relations', p. 149.

34 See C. Perrow, 'Organizational Goals', *International Encyclopedia of the Social Services*, 11 (Macmillan, New York, 1968), pp. 305–16; E. Gross, 'The Definition

of Organizational Goals', *British Journal of Sociology*, 20 (1969), pp. 277–94.

35   E. Yuchtman and S.E. Seashore, 'A System Resource Approach to Organizational Effectiveness', *American Sociological Review*, 32 (1967), pp. 891–903.

36   P. Georgiou, 'The Goal Paradigm and Notes Toward a Counter-Paradigm', *Administrative Science Quarterly*, 18 (1973), p. 292.

37   D. Silverman, *The Theory of Organizations* (Heinemann, London, 1970), p. 9; see however L. Haworth, 'Do Organizations Act?', *Ethics* (1961), pp. 59–63.

38   L. Mohr, 'The Concept of Organizational Goal', *American Political Science Review*, 67 (1973), pp. 470–81.

39   P.M. Hirsch, 'Organizational Analysis and Industrial Sociology: an Instance of Cultural Lag', *American Sociologist*, 10 (1975), p. 10; see also J.K. Benson, 'The Inter-organizational Network as a Political Economy', *Administrative Science Quarterly*, 20 (1975), pp. 229–49.

40   W.M. Evan, 'An Organization-set Model of Interorganizational Relations', in M.F. Tuite, M. Radnor and R.K. Chisholm (eds), *Interorganizational Decision-Making* (Aldine-Atherton, Chicago, 1972). See also S. Elkin, 'Comparative Urban Politics and Interorganizational Behaviour', in K. Young (ed.), *Essays on the Study of Urban Politics* (Macmillan, London, 1975).

41   M. Aiken and J. Hage, 'Organizational Interdependence and Intra Organizational Structure', *American Sociological Review*, 33 (December 1968), pp. 912–930.

42   See, for example, H. Aldrich and Mindlin, 'Uncertainty and Dependence: two Perspectives on Environment', in L. Karpik (ed.), *Organization and Environment: Theory, Issues and Reality*, (Sage Publications, London, 1978); J.K. Benson, 'Innovation and Crisis in Organizational Analysis', *Sociological Quarterly*, 18 (Winter 1977), pp. 3–16; R.A.W. Rhodes, 'Research into Central-Local Relations in Britain: A Framework for Analysis' in Social Science Research Council, *Central-Local Government Relationships*, (SSRC, London, 1979); R.A.W. Rhodes, 'Analysing Intergovernmental Relations', *European Journal of Political Research*, 8 (1980), pp. 289–322.

43   J. Pfeffer and G.R. Salancik, *The External Control of Organizations* (Harper & Row, New York, 1978); Yuchtman and Seashore, 'Organizational Effectiveness', p. 898; S. Levine and P.G. White, 'Exchange as a Conceptual Framework for the Study of Interorganizational Relationships', *Administrative Science Quarterly*, 5 (1961), pp. 583–601.

44   R. Randall, 'Influence of Environmental Support and Policy Space on Organizational Behaviour, *Administrative Science Quarterly*, 18 (1973), pp. 236–47; J. D. Thompson, *Organizations in Action* (McGraw-Hill, New York, 1967); Levine and White, 'Exchange as a Conceptual Framework'.

45   J.D. Thompson and W. McEwen, 'Organizational Goals and Environment', *American Sociological Review*, 23 (1958), pp. 23–31; A. Gouldner, 'Reciprocity and Autonomy in Functional Theory', in L. Gross (ed), *Symposium in Sociological Theory* (Harper & Row, New York, 1959).

46   Q. Skinner, 'Some Problems in the Analysis of Political Thought and Action', *Political Theory* (August 1974), pp. 277–303.

47   R.G. Collingwood, *The Idea of History* (Clarendon Press, Oxford, 1946); see also H.P. Rickman (ed.), *Meaning in History: W. Dilthey's Thoughts on History and Society* (Allen & Unwin, London, 1961); Gardiner, *Nature of Historical Explanation*.

48   Gardiner, *Philosophy of History*, p. 4.

49   Collingwood, *Idea of History*, p. 215.

50   *Ibid*, p. 315.

51   *Ibid*, p. 317; see, for a more plausible formulation of the same point, G. Vickers, 'Values, Norms and Policies', *Policy Sciences*, 4 (1) (March 1973), pp. 103–11.

52   A.V. Dicey, *Lectures on the Relation between Law and Public Opinion in England during the Nineteenth Century* (Macmillan, London, 1905).

53   S.E. Finer, *Sir Edwin Chadwick* (Harper & Row, New York, 1952).

54 Hart, 'Nineteenth-Century Social Reform', p. 61.
55 *Ibid*, p. 45. For an opposing and subtle discussion of 'ideas' and 'emotions' as springs of action, see J. Brooke, 'Namier and Namierism', *History and Theory*, 3 (1964), pp. 331–47.
56 MacDonagh, 'Nineteenth-Century Revolution', and *Pattern of Government Growth*.
57 Hart, 'Nineteenth-Century Social Reform', pp. 48–57.
58 R.W. Cobb and C.D. Elder, *Participation in American Politics: the Dynamics of Agenda-Building* (Johns Hopkins University Press, Baltimore, 1972), p. 14.
59 R.C. Fuller and R.R. Myers, 'Some Aspects of a Theory of Social Problems', *American Sociological Review* (February 1941), p. 25.
60 W.I. Thomas, quoted in K. Weick, *The Social Psychology of Organizations*, (Addison-Wesley, Reading, Mass., 1969), p. 28.
61 For the significance of Dilthey, see H.A. Hodges, *Wilhelm Dilthey: An Introduction* (Howard Fertig, New York, 1969); M. Ermath, *Wilhelm Dilthey: the Critique of Historical Reason*, (Chicago University Press, Chicago, 1978).
62 M. Brinkerhoff and P. N. Kunz (eds), *Complex Organizations and Their Environments* (W.C. Brown & Co, Dubuque, Ia, 1972); P.R. Lawrence and J.W. Lorsch, *Organization and Environment* (Harvard University Press, Cambridge, Mass., 1967); J. Child, 'Organization Structure, Environment and Performance: the Role of Strategic Choice', *Sociology* (1972), pp. 1–22.
63 Child, 'Organization Structure'.
64 W.R. Dill, 'Environment as an Influence on Managerial Autonomy', *Administrative Science Quarterly*, 2 (1958), pp. 409–43; Duncan, 'Characteristics of Organizational Environments and Perceived Environmental Uncertainty', *Administrative Science Quarterly*, 17 (1972), p. 324. See also C. Eden, S. Jones and D. Sims, *Thinking in Organizations*, (Macmillan, London, 1978).
65 F. Emery and E.L. Trist, 'The Causal Texture of Organizational Environments', *Human Relations*, 18 (1965), pp. 21–31; S. Terreberry, 'The Evolution of Organizational Environments', *Administrative Science Quarterly*, 12 (1968), pp. 590–613; Duncan, 'Characteristics of Organizational Environments'.
66 Thompson, *Organizations in Action*. For a study of rumour as an uncertainty reduction device, see T. Shibutani, *Improvised News: a Sociological Study of Rumor* (Bobbs-Merrill, New York, 1966).
67 For a similar process in international politics, see R.C. Snyder, H.W. Bruck and B. Sapin, *Foreign Policy Decision-Making* (Free Press, New York, 1962), p. 67. See also J.K. Friend, J.M. Power and C.J. Yewlett, *Public Planning: the Intercorporate Dimension*, (Tavistock, London, 1974).
68 Child, 'Organization Structure'.
69 Pfeffer and Salancik, *External Control*, p. 78.
70 Weick, *Social Psychology*, p. 70.
71 *Ibid*, p. 28.
72 R.K. Merton, 'Social Knowledge and Public Policy', in R.K. Merton, *Sociological Ambivalence and Other Essays* (Free Press, New York, 1976), pp. 174–5. For an uncompromising defence of the famous Thomas dictum see D.W. Ball, ' "The Definition of the Situation": Some Theoretical and Methodological Consequences of Taking W.I. Thomas Seriously', *Journal for the Theory of Social Behaviour*, 2(1) (1972), pp. 61–82.
73 Weick, *Social Psychology*, p. 70.
74 Pfeffer and Salancik, *External Control*, p. 258.
75 Collingwood, *Idea of History*, p. 316.
76 Marx, quoted in Gough, *Political Economy*, p. 10. For a helpful discussion of the implications of such a position, see Nagel, 'Determinism in History'.
77 See D. Emmett, *Function, Purpose and Powers* (Macmillan, London, 1958); see also M. Hollis, *Models of Man* (Cambridge University Press, London, 1977), pp. 107ff.

78   D. Davidson, 'Action, Reasons and Causes', *Journal of Philosophy*, 23 (7 November 1963), pp. 685–700; see also Q. Skinner, 'On Performing and Explaining Linguistic Actions', *Philosophical Quarterly*, 21 (January 1971), esp. pp. 13–21; and 'Motives, Intentions and the Interpretation of Texts', *New Literary History*, 3 (1973), pp. 393–408. For an energetic portrayal of all action as purposive, see R. Taylor, *Action and Purpose* (Prentice-Hall, Englewood Cliffs, NJ, 1966), pp. 256ff.

79   A. MacIntyre, 'A Mistake About Causality in Social Science', in P. Laslett and W.G. Runciman (eds), *Philosophy, Politics and Society* (Social Services) (Blackwell, Oxford, 1962); but see Skinner, 'Explaining Linguistic Actions'.

80   C. Dickens, *Our Mutual Friend* (first published 1864/5) (Penguin, Harmondsworth 1971), p. 348; and see generally pp. 338–49. For unconscious 'intentional' actions, see C. Olsen, 'Knowledge of Our Own Intentional Action', *Philosophical Quarterly*, 19 (1969), pp. 324–36.

81   Except in the area of work and class consciousness, where an extensive literature grew up in the wake of D. Lockwood's 'Sources of Variation in Working Class Images of Society', *Sociological Review*, 14 (3) (November 1966), pp. 249–67; see especially H. Davis, *Beyond Class Images: Explorations in the Structure of Social Consciousness* (Croom Helm, London, 1979).

82   See the essays on cultural systems as 'conceptual structures that inform . . . acts', in C. Geertz, *The Interpretation of Cultures*, (Hutchinson, London, 1975).

83   R. Tagiuri and G.H. Litwin (eds), *Organizational Climate: Explorations of a Concept* (Graduate School of Business Administration, Harvard University, Cambridge, Mass., 1968).

84   B. Barry, *Economists, Sociologists and Democracy* (Collier-Macmillan, London, 1970).

85   W. Dray, 'The Historical Explanation of Actions Reconsidered', in Gardiner, *Philosophy of History*; K. Young, 'Discretion as an Implementation Problem: a Framework for Analysis' in M. Adler and S. Asquith (eds), *Discretion and Welfare* (Heinemann, London, 1981).

86   Collingwood's unsatisfactory treatment of this conundrum is brought out in Gardiner's discussion, in *Nature of Historical Explanation*; Gardiner's own account, however, is seriously flawed, especially in the closing pages of his book.

87   P. Berger and T. Luckmann, *The Social Construction of Reality* (Doubleday, Garden City, NY, 1966), p. 61.

88   M. Oakeshott, *On Human Conduct* (Clarendon Press, Oxford, 1975), p. 87 (our emphasis).

89   R. Harré, *Social Being: a Theory for Social Psychology* (Blackwell, Oxford, 1979).

90   The following pages summarise a conception of the assumptive worlds of actors which is more fully set out elsewhere: see K. Young, 'Values in the Policy Process', in C. Pollitt *et al.*, *Public Policy in Theory and Practice* (Hodder & Stoughton, Sevenoaks, 1979); K. Young, 'Discretion as an Implementation Problem'; K. Young and L. Mills, *Public Policy Research: a Review of Qualitative Methods* (SSRC, London, 1980).

91   K. Lewin, *Resolving Social Conflicts: Selected Papers on Group Dynamics* (ed. G.W. Lewin) (Harper & Row, New York, 1948).

92   E.T. Gendlin, *Experiencing and the Creation of Meaning* (Free Press, New York, 1962), p. 228.

93   G. Bateson, 'Cultural Determinants of Personality', in J. Hunt (ed.), *Personality and the Behaviour Disorders* (Ronald Press, New York, 1944); see also U. Neisser, *Cognitive Psychology* (Appleton-Century Crofts, New York, 1967); J. Frank, *Persuasion and Healing* (Johns Hopkins University Press, Baltimore, 1973).

94   Gendlin, *Creation of Meaning*; for the concept of condensation, see E. Bott, *Family and Social Networks* (Tavistock, London, 1957), p. 167; K. Young, C. Mason and L. Mills, *Urban Governments and Economic Change* (SSRC, London, 1980).

95   Geertz, *Interpretation of Cultures*, p. 220; see also the introduction to A. M. Rose,

Human Behaviour and Social Processes (Routledge & Kegan Paul, London, 1962). The metaphor of the map recurs in discussion of the symbolisation of meaning, not only in Geertz, but in Oakeshott's *Human Conduct* (at pp. 25–6) and, in a profound if elliptical manner, in Russell Hoban's novel, *The Lion of Boaz-Jachin and Jachin-Boaz*, (Picador, London, 1973).

96   R. Dahrendorf, *Class and Class Conflict in Industrial Society* (Routledge & Kegan Paul, London, 1959), p. 282.

97   J.P. Hewitt and P.M. Hall, 'Social Problems, Problematic Situations and Quasi-Theories', *American Sociological Review*, 38 (1973), pp. 367–74.

98   H. Cantril, *The 'Why' of Man's Experience* (Macmillan, New York, 1950).

99   C.M. Parkes, 'Psycho-Social Transitions: a Field for Study', *Social Science and Medicine*, 5 (1971), p. 104; G.A. Kelly, *The Psychology of Personal Constructs* (2 vols) (Norton, New York, 1955); D. Bannister and Fay Fransella, *Inquiring Man: the Theory of Personal Constructs* (Penguin, Harmondsworth, 1971).

100   G. Vickers, 'Motivation Theory: a Cybernetic Contribution', *Behavioural Science*, 18 (4) (July 1973), p. 245.

101   Parkes, 'Psycho-Social Transitions', p. 104.

102   Oakeshott, *Human Conduct*, pp. 52–3.

103   For support for this position, see P. Marris, *Loss and Change*, (Routledge & Kegan Paul, London, 1974), pp. 105–23; and D. Schon, *Beyond the Stable State* (Temple Smith, London, 1971), pp. 52–8.

104   McHugh, *Defining the Situation*; Gendlin, *Creation of Meaning*; A. Schutz, *The Phenomenology of the Social World* (Northwestern University Press, Evanston, 1967).

105   Gendlin, *Creation of Meaning*, p. 4. For further discussion of the fragility of meaning in the face of social change, see G. Gurvitch, *The Social Frameworks of Knowledge* (Harper & Row, New York, 1971), pp. 27–8; and the papers in R. Horton and R. Finnegan, *Modes of Thought: Essays on Thinking in Western and Non-Western Societies* (Faber & Faber, London, 1973).

106   Bannister and Fransella, *Inquiring Man*; we have discussed this quality of predictability further in Young and Mills, *Public Policy Research*.

107   See Marris's important account of entrepreneurship as an attempt 'to restore the continuity of expectations', in *Loss and Change*, pp. 105–13.

108   See especially L. Festinger, *A Theory of Cognitive Dissonance*, (Row, Peterson, New York, 1957); L. Festinger, *Conflict, Decision and Dissonance*, (Tavistock, London, 1964); L. Festinger, H.W. Riecken and S. Schachter, *When Prophecy Fails* (Harper & Row, New York, 1956).

109   M. Douglas, 'The World-View and the Core', in S.C. Brown (ed.), *Philosophical Disputes in the Social Sciences* (Harvester, Brighton, 1979).

110   R.P. Abelson, 'Modes of Resolution of Belief Dilemmas', *Journal of Conflict Resolution*, 3 (4) (1959), pp. 343–52.

111   K. Boulding, Preface, in R.M. Downs and D. Stea (eds), *Image and Environment* (Edward Arnold, London, 1974).

112   This possibility is recognised in Festinger's work, but its implications are not pursued.

113   Marris, *Loss and Change*; Schon, *Beyond the Stable State*.

114   R.C. Fuller and R.R. Myers, 'The Natural History of a Social Problem', *American Sociological Review*, 6 (June 1941), p. 321.

115   W. Solesbury, 'The Environmental Agenda', *Public Administration* (Winter 1976), p. 381.

116   Fuller and Myers, 'Natural History', p. 320.

117   For which see in particular H.S. Becker, Introduction, in Becker (ed.), *Social Problems: a Modern Approach*, (Wiley, New York, 1967); R.C. Fuller and R.R. Myers, 'Some Aspects of a Theory of Social Problems', *American Sociological Review*, 6 (February 1941), pp. 24–32; M. Spector and J. Kitsuse, *Constructing Social Problems* (Cummings, Menlo Park, Cal., 1977).

118 H. Blumer, 'Social Problems as Collective Behaviour', *Social Problems* (Winter 1971), p. 303.
119 The term is from Spector and Kitsuse, *Constructing Social Problems*, where, after a comprehensive review of the literature, the authors opt for a view of problem definition as a process of 'claim-making'.
120 K. Young and N. Connelly, *Policy and Practice in the Multi-racial City*, (Policy Studies Institute, London, 1981), Chapter 9.
121 J. Carrier and I. Kendall, 'Social Policy and Social Change: Explanations of the Development of Social Policy', *Journal of Social Policy*, 2 (3) (1973), p. 211.
122 Note the influence on Carrier and Kendall of Schutz, Berger and Luckmann and the phenomenological school of British sociologists; their criteria for an 'adequate account' of social policy development are spelt out in 'Social Policy and Social Change', p. 220 n. 69.
123 J. Edwards and R. Batley, *The Politics of Positive Discrimination* (Tavistock, London, 1978), p. 173.
124 Young and Connelly, *Policy and Practice*, p. 158.
125 See Douglas, 'World View and Core', p. 177.
126 See K. Young, 'The Problems of Economic Strategy', in K. Young and C. Mason (eds), *Urban Economic Development: New Roles and Relationships*, (Macmillan, London, 1982).
127 Festinger, *Conflict, Decision and Dominance*; Abelson, 'Belief Dilemmas'.
128 E. Hughes, 'Professions', *Daedalus* (Fall 1963), pp. 655-68.
129 Becker, *Social Problems*, p. 13.
130 The term is introduced in Young and Connelly, *Policy and Practice*, p. 163.
131 Young and Connelly, *Policy and Practice*.
132 J.H.S. Bossard, 'Comment' (on Fuller and Myers), *American Sociological Review*, 6 (June 1941), pp. 328-9.
133 We have given accounts of regime stability and change in the London County Council and Greater London Council in relation to housing and landuse policies in, respectively, K. Young and P.L. Garside, *Metropolitan London: Politics and Urban Change 1837-1981* (Edward Arnold, London, 1982); and K. Young and J. Kramer, *Strategy and Conflict in Metropolitan Housing* (Heinemann, London, 1978). For the relations between elected members and appointed officials generally, see K. Newton, *Second City Politics* (Cambridge University Press, London, 1975); and J. Gyford, *Local Politics in Britain* (Croom Helm, London, 1976).
134 Some aspects of the organisational context of information flows are discussed in H. Wilensky, *Organizational Intelligence: Knowledge and Policy in Government and Industry* (Basic Books, New York, 1967); and A. Pettigrew, 'Information Control as a Power Resource', *Sociology*, 6 (1972), pp. 187-204.
135 S. Barrett and C. Fudge (eds), *Policy and Action* (Methuen, London, 1982), Introduction; Young, 'Discretion as an Implementation Problem'.
136 For an extended discussion, see Young and Mills, *Public Policy Research*.
137 Our position on the familiar *Verstehen-Erklären* debate will be clear from these remarks, and is elaborated in Young and Mills, *Public Policy Research*; for further discussion, see J.D. Baldwin and J.I. Baldwin, 'Behaviourism on *Verstehen* and *Erklären*', *American Sociological Review*, 43 (June 1978), pp. 335-47; F.R. Dallmayer and T.A. McCarthy (eds), *Understanding and Social Inquiry* (University of Indiana Press, Notre Dame, 1977).
138 R.E. Money-Kyrle, *Man's Picture of His World* (International Universities Press, New York, 1961), pp. 17-18.

Chapter 3

1 Haggett has defined the space economy as the spatial organisation of 'the basic economic resources, labour and capital, and the flows that link them together'. P. Haggett, 'The Spatial Economy', *American Behavioral Scientist*, 22(1) (September/October 1978), p. 151.

2   The term is attributed to Brian Berry, to whom the end-product of counter-urbanisation is 'nothing less than an urban civilisation without cities'. B.J.L. Berry, 'The Counter-urbanisation Process: How General?', Paper prepared for a conference at the IIASA Schloss Laxenburg, Austria (December 1976).

3   K. Young and P.L. Garside, *Metropolitan London: Politics and Urban Change, 1837–1981* (Edward Arnold, London, 1982), pp. 107–8, 198–216.

4   J. Gottman, *Megalopolis: the Urbanized North-eastern Seaboard of the United States* (The Twentieth Century Fund, New York, 1961).

5   B.J.L. Berry, 'Transformations of the Nation's Urban System: Small City Growth as a Zero-sum Game', Paper for the 1976 Public Policy Forum of the Joint Center for Political Studies, Washington DC (December 1976), p. 25.

6   See, for example, C. Beale, 'The Recent Shift of US Population to Non-metropolitan Areas', *International Regional Science Review*, 2 (1977), pp. 113–22; B.J.L. Berry and Q. Gillard, *The Changing Shape of Metropolitan America: Commuting Patterns, Urban Fields and Decentralization Processes, 1960–1970* (Ballinger, Cambridge, Mass., 1977). L. Long and K. Hansen, 'Trends in Return Migration to the South', *Demography*, 12(4) (November 1975) pp. 601–14. For a useful summary of the US trends, see also P. Hall and D. Hay, *Growth Centres in the European Urban System* (Heinemann Educational Books, London, 1980).

7   B.L. Weinstein and R.E. Firestine, *Regional Growth and Decline in the United States: the Rise of the Sunbelt and the Decline of the Northeast* (Praeger, New York, 1978), p. 10.

8   G. Sternlieb and J.W. Hughes, 'New Regional and Metropolitan Realities of America', *Journal of the American Institute of Planners*, 43 (1977), p. 229.

9   Ibid, p. 228.

10 R.D. Norton and J. Rees, 'The Product Cycle and the Spatial Decentralisation of American Manufacturing', *Regional Studies*, 13(2) (1979) p. 144.

11 *Business Week*, No. 3432 (17 May 1976) p. 92. More detailed figures illustrating the dramatic inter-regional shift in manufacturing and other non-agricultural employment and in per capita income are supplied by Weinstein and Firestine, in *Regional Growth and Decline*, pp. 12–22.

12 C.E. Browning and W. Gesler, 'The Sunbelt-Snowbelt: A Case of Sloppy Regionalising', *Professional Geographer*, 31 (1979), pp. 66–74.

13 Ibid, p. 74.

14 P.T. Muller, *The Outer City: Geographical Consequences of the Urbanization of the Suburbs*, Association of American Geographers, Commission on College Geography, Resource paper No. 75/2 AAG, Washington, DC, 1976).

15 L.F. Schnore and V.Z. Klaff, 'Suburbanization in the Sixties: a Preliminary Analysis', *Land Economics*, 48 (1972), pp. 23–9.

16 Sternlieb and Hughes, 'New Regional and Metropolitan Realities', p. 238.

17 See P.E. King, 'Mobility of Manufacturing and the Intrastate Redistribution of Employment', *Professional Geographer*, 27(4) (1975), pp. 441–48. King's study of manufacturing mobility in Connecticut showed larger central cities to be 'losing manufacturing industries and a . . . substantial number of jobs', and he concluded that 'there are strong economic motives encouraging firms to move to smaller centres, even though this may create a greater separation between employers and their traditionally central-city employees. As institutional and economic boundaries to low and moderately priced housing in the suburbs are broken down, then perhaps labour will follow the firms.' Ibid, p. 448. For a recent and more general discussion, see D.N. Steinnes, 'Do "People Follow Jobs" or do "Jobs Follow People"? a Causality Issue in Urban Economics', *Urban Studies*, 19(1982), pp. 187–92.

18 A. Hecht, 'Industrial Decentralization and the Changing Residential Location of Employees', *East Lakes Geographer*, 10(1976), pp. 69–90.

19 Muller, *Outer City*, p. 3.

20 See B.J.L. Berry and Y.S. Cohen, 'Decentralization of Commerce and Industry:

the Restructuring of Metropolitan America', in L.M. Masotti and J.K. Hadden (eds) *The Urbanization of the Suburbs*, Urban Affairs Annual Review No. 7 (Sage Publications, Beverly Hills, Cal., 1973).

21   P.A. Wood, 'Urban Manufacturing: a View from the Fringe', in J.H. Johnston (ed.), *Suburban Growth* (Wiley, London, 1974), pp. 129–54.

22   Muller, *Outer City*, p. 30.

23   J.R. Logan, 'Industrialization and the Stratification of Cities in Suburban Regions', *American Journal of Sociology*, 82(2) (1976) pp. 333–48.

24   Muller, *Outer City*, p. 1.

25   D.E.C. Eversley, 'Rising Costs and Static Incomes: Some Economic Consequences of Regional Planning in London', in G.C. Cameron and L. Wingo (eds), *Cities, Regions and Public Policy* (Oliver & Boyd, Edinburgh, 1973).

26   G. Sternlieb, 'The City as Sandbox', *Public Interest*, 25 (Fall 1971), p. 15.

27   Sternlieb and Hughes, 'New Regional and Metropolitan Realities', p. 239.

28   R.P. Nathan and P.R. Dommel, 'Understanding the Urban Predicament', *The Brookings Bulletin*, 14(1 and 2) (Spring/Summer 1977), pp. 9–13.

29   G.C. Cameron, Introduction, in G.C. Cameron (ed.), *The Future of the British Conurbations: Policies and Prescriptions for Change* (Longman, London, 1980), p. 5.

30   Nathan and Dommel, 'Urban Predicament', p. 11; see also J.F. Kain, 'The Distribution and Movement of Jobs and Industry', in J.Q. Wilson (ed.), *The Metropolitan Enigma* (Harvard University Press, Cambridge, Mass., 1968), pp. 1–40. Kain considers that the racial dimension is critical to an understanding of trends in housing and employment in those inner city areas where the majority of the population was black.

31   See, for example, R.W. Bahl (ed.), *The Fiscal Outlook for Cities* (Syracuse University Press, Syracuse, NY, 1978); R. Kirwan, 'The Fiscal Context', in Cameron, *Future of the British Conurbations*; Kain, 'Distribution and Movement of Jobs'.

32   M. Yeates, *North American Urban Patterns* (Edward Arnold, London, 1980), pp. 96–7.

33   Hall and Hay, *Growth Centres*, p. 27.

34   Ibid, p. 14.

35   Yeates, *North American Urban Patterns*.

36   L.S. Bourne and M.I. Logan, 'Changing Urbanization Patterns at the Margin: The Examples of Australia and Canada', in B.J.L. Berry (ed.), *Urbanization and Counter-urbanization*, Urban Affairs Annual Review, 11 (Sage Publications, Beverley Hills, Cal., 1976) p. 136.

37   L.S. Bourne and J.W. Simmons, *Canadian Settlement Trends: an Examination of the Spatial Pattern of Growth, 1971–1976*, Major Report No. 15; Centre for Urban and Community Studies, University of Toronto (Toronto, 1979).

38   G. Hodge and M.A. Qadeer 'The Persistence of Canadian Towns and Villages: Small is Viable', *Urban Geographer*, 1(4) (October/December 1980).

39   Bourne and Logan, 'Changing Urbanization Patterns'.

40   Hall and Hay, *Growth Centres*, p. 17.

41   F.M. Little and R.A. Carter, *Urban Development, Economic Development and Growth*, Report to the Planning Branch, Melbourne and Metropolitan Board of Works (The Board, Melbourne, 1978) p.xii.

42   See N.J. Glickman, *The Growth and Management of the Japanese Urban System* (Academic Press, New York, 1978), and T. Kawashima, *Changes in the Spatial Population Structure of Japan*, Research Memorandum RM–77–25 (IIASA, Laxenberg, 1977).

43   D.R. Vining and T. Kontuly, 'Population Dispersal from Major Metropolitan Areas: an International Comparison', *International Regional Science Review*, 3 (1978) p. 52.

44   Hall and Hay, *Growth Centres*, pp. 19–20.

45   Vining and Kontuly, 'Population Dispersal'.

46   In a later paper the authors admit to several errors in their comparative analysis and

add New Zealand to the list of countries which have not experienced a reversal in the direction of the net flow of population. See Vining and Kontuly, 'Population Dispersal from Major Metropolitan Regions: a Correction Concerning New Zealand', *International Regional Science Review*, 4(2) (1979).

47 Vining and Kontuly, 'Population Dispersal', p. 51. The work of Vining and his colleagues has now progressed towards the search for explanation. See D.R. Vining and R. Palone, 'Migration between Peripheral and Core Regions: a Description and Tentative Explanation of the Patterns in 22 Countries', Center for Population Studies, University of Pennsylvania, Working Paper No. 61 (March 1982).

48 Hall and Hay, *Growth Centres*, p. 23. For a discussion of some of these problems, see M.G. Coombes, J.S. Dixon, J.B. Goddard, P.J. Taylor and S. Openshaw, *Functional Regions of the 1981 Census of Britain: A User's Guide to the CURDS Definitions*, (Centre for Urban and Regional Development Studies, University of Newcastle upon Tyne, Newcastle, 1980).

49 Hall and Hay, *Growth Centres*.

50 Ibid, p. 227.

51 Ibid, p. 228.

52 *New Society* (15 June 1978), p. 606.

53 A.J. Fielding, *Counter-urbanization in Western Europe*, Progress in Planning, 17 (Pergamon Press, Oxford, 1982), p. 9.

54 See P. Hall, R. Thomas, H. Gracey and R. Drewett, *The Containment of Urban England* (Allen & Unwin, London, 1973).

55 R. Drewett, J. Goddard and N.A. Spence, 'What's Happening to British Cities?', *Town and Country Planning*, 43 (December 1975), pp. 523–30. R. Drewett, J. Goddard and N.A. Spence, 'What's Happening in British Cities?', *Town and Country Planning*, 44(1) (January 1976) pp. 14–24; R. Drewett, J. Goddard and N.A. Spence, *Urban Change in Britain: 1961–1971*, Working Paper No. 21 (Department of Geography, London School of Economics) (April 1976); Department of the Environment, *British Cities: Urban Population and Employment Trends, 1951–1971* DoE Research Report No. 10 (Department of the Environment, London, 1976); N.A. Spence, 'Population and Employment Trends in British Cities', Paper to the Regional Studies Association Annual Conference on 'The Economic Crisis and Local Manufacturing Employment', University of Aston (8–9 July 1976); S. Kennett, *The Inner City in the Context of the Urban System*, SSRC Inner Cities in Context No. 11 (SSRC, London, 1980).

56 Drewett, Goddard and Spence, *Urban Change in Britain*, p. 51.

57 Hall and Hay, *Growth Centres*. See also Department of The Environment, *British Cities*, p. 29.

58 Drewett, Goddard and Spence, *Urban Change in Britain*, p. 51.

59 *New Society* (18 January 1979), p. 141.

60 OPCS, *Census 1981 Preliminary Report: England and Wales* (HMSO, London, 1981), p. 9.

61 P.H. Rees, *Migration and Settlement: I United Kingdom* (IIASA, Laxenburg, 1979), p. 125; J.D. McCallum, 'Statistical Trends of the British Conurbations', in G.C. Cameron, *Future of the British Conurbations*.

62 OPCS, 'The First Results of the Census of England and Wales', *Population Trends*, 25 (HMSO, 1981), p. 6.

63 Ibid, p. 8.

64 See Cameron, *Future of the British Conurbations*; D.A. Hart, *Urban Economic Development. Lessons for British Cities from Germany and America*, Occasional Paper No. 2, School of Planning Studies, University of Reading (Reading, 1980).

65 See D.E.C. Eversley, 'Old Cities, Falling Populations and Rising Costs', *Quarterly Bulletin of the GLC Intelligence Unit*, No. 18 (March 1972), pp. 5–16; and C. Jones, 'Population Decline in the Cities', in C. Jones (ed.), *Urban Deprivation and the Inner City* (Croom Helm, London, 1979).

66 McCallum, 'The Economics of the Conurbations', in Cameron, *Future of the British Conurbations* p. 59.

67 See R.M. Kirwan, 'The Fiscal Context', in Cameron, *Future of the British Conurbations*.

68 Eversley, 'Old Cities'.

69 Jones, 'Population Decline in Cities', p. 212.

70 McCallum 'Statistical Trends', p. 14.

71 W. Zelinsky, 'Coping with the Migration Turnaround: The Theoretical Challenge', *International Regional Science Review*, 2 (1977), pp. 171–8.

72 P. Gordon, 'Deconcentration Without a Clean Break', *Environment and Planning A*, 11 (1979) p. 281.

73 P. Hall, *Recent Urban Change in Europe*, SSRC Inner Cities Working Party Contractor's Report, University of Reading (1978), p. 2. For more on the perspective of this school, see W. Alonso, 'The Current Halt in the Metropolitan Phenomenon', in C. Leven (ed.), *The Mature Metropolis* (Lexington Books, Lexington, Mass., 1978); Berry, 'Transformation'; B.J.L. Berry, 'The Counter-urbanization Process: Urban America since 1970', in Berry, *Urbanization and Counter-urbanization*; D.R. Vining and A. Strauss, 'A Demonstration that the Current Deconcentration of Population in the United States is a Clean Break with the Past', *Environment and Planning*, A9 (1977) pp. 751–8.

74 See L.S. Bourne, 'Alternative Perspectives on Urban Decline and Population Decentralisation', *Urban Geographer*, 1(1) (January-March 1980), pp. 39–52; and R.L. Morrill, 'The Spread of Change in Metropolitan and Non-metropolitan Growth in the United States, 1940–1976', *Urban Geographer*, 1(2) (April-June 1980), pp. 118–29. We take the view that this debate cannot be resolved with the data at present available, and that the available data and methodology can in any event be manipulated to support a preferred point of view, especially when analyses of change are conducted at varying urban scales. For example, Vining and Strauss use the Hoover index of population concentration to support their view that the tendency for America's population to concentrate has been broken. Gordon, on the other hand, describing Vining and Strauss's interpretation of the Hoover index as 'novel', uses the same statistic to suggest that the counties he examined were experiencing 'more traditional outward expansion'. See Vining and Strauss, 'Demonstration', and Gordon, 'Deconcentration Without a Clean Break'.

75 Hall and Hay, in *Growth Centres*, p. 225, conclude that their data support the 'outward wave' interpretation of change in European cities, and that 'the drift to the remoter rural areas is not yet evident in Europe'. See also C. Hamnett, 'The British Continue to Head for the Country', *Geographical Magazine*, LIII (12) (September 1981), pp. 745–6. However Vining and his colleagues disagree with Hall and Hay. Their rather different approach leads them to identify a 'rapid and abrupt . . . discontinuity' in urban patterns in a number of European countries, including the United Kingdom. See D.R. Vining, R. Pallone and D. Plane, 'Recent Migration Patterns in the Developed World: a Clarification of some Differences between our and IIASA's Findings', *Environment and Planning*, A 13 (1981), pp. 243–50.

76 For a summary, see W. Alonso, 'Surprise and Rethinkings of Metropolitan Growth: a Comment', *International Regional Science Review*, 2(2)(1977) pp. 171–4.

77 Ibid, p. 173.

78 M. Clawson, 'Economic Implications of the Current Recent Population Shift Towards Rural Areas', *American Journal of Agricultural Economics*, 58(5) (December 1976) p. 963.

79 Hall and Hay, *Growth Centres*, p. 231.

80 Ibid, p. 14.

81 Alonso, 'Surprise and Rethinking', pp. 173–4.

82 Hall and Hay, *Growth Centres*, p. 12.

83 Ibid, p. 26. Note that very similar ideas have been expressed by Richard Morrill; see R.L. Morrill, 'Stages in Patterns of Population Concentration and Dispersion', *Professional Geographer*, 31 (1979), pp. 55–65, and Morrill, 'Spread of Change'.

84 Hall and Hay, *Growth Centres*, p. 26. For a discussion of the political and governmental aspects of such a growth cycle, see Young and Garside, *Metropolitan London*, pp. 1–8, 331–9; and J.J. Harrigan, *Political Change in the Metropolis* (Little Brown, Boston, 1976).

85 Fielding, *Counter-urbanization*, p. 31.

86 Ibid, p. 32.

Chapter 4

1 F. Blackaby (ed.) *De-industrialisation* (Heinemann for NIESR, London, 1980) See in particular the essay by Sir Alec Cairncross (pp. 5–17), and the summary contribution by the editor (pp. 263–8). Many commentators agree that 'if full employment is to be achieved again it will not be done by relying largely on the services sector but by reversing the process of de-industrialisation': M. Westlake, 'Economic Evolution – or Costly Decay? Perspective: De-industrialisation', *The Times* (18 March 1982). See also the call by the Governor of the Bank of England for the government to reverse 'the de-industrialisation of Britain' on similar grounds, reported in *Financial Times* (14 December 1981). It is important to bear in mind that 'de-industrialisation', as used in this and subsequent chapters, refers to falling manufacturing employment within a given locality. Such falls in themselves are not necessarily indicative of 'decline', and may be welcomed if they follow from productivity increases. Yet even in such a case aggregate benefits may impose local costs.

2 P.E. Lloyd and C.M. Mason, 'Manufacturing Industry in the Inner City: a Case Study of Greater Manchester', *Transactions of the Institute of British Geographers*, New Series, 3(1) (1978), pp. 66–90. A.M. Warnes, 'A Long-term View of Employment Decentralisation from the Larger English Cities', in A. Evans and D.E.C. Eversley (eds), *The Inner City: Employment and Industry* (Heinemann for CES, London, 1980).

3 D. Keeble, *Industrial Location and Planning in the United Kingdom* (Methuen, London, 1976) p. 201.

4 S. Fothergill and G. Gudgin *Unequal Growth: Urban and Regional Employment Change in Britain* (Heinemann, London, 1982); and see OPCS, 'The First Results of the 1981 Census of England and Wales', *Population Trends*, 25 (HMSO, 1981); Keeble, *Industrial Location*, pp. 286–8; and D. Keeble 'Industrial Decline in the Inner City and Conurbation', *Transactions of the Institute of British Geographers*, New Series, 3(1) (1978), pp. 101–14, 102.

5 Fothergill and Gudgin, *Unequal Growth*, Chapter 3.

6 For a discussion, see A. Evans, 'An Economist's Perspective', in Evans and Eversley, *Inner City*, pp. 445–59.

7 See G.C. Cameron, 'The Inner City: New Plant Incubator?', in Evans and Eversley, *Inner City*, pp. 351–66.

8 J.J. Fagg, 'An Examination of the Incubator Hypothesis: a Case Study of Greater Leicester', *Urban Studies*, 17 (1980), pp. 35–44.

9 E.M. Hoover and R. Vernon, *Anatomy of a Metropolis: the Changing Distribution of People and Jobs in the New York Metropolitan Region* (Harvard University Press, Cambridge, Mass., 1959); E.M. Hoover and R. Vernon, *The New York Regional Study Plan* (Harvard University Press, Cambridge, Mass., 1960).

10 Evidence for a number of British conurbations is reviewed in J.R. Firn and J.K. Swales, 'The Formation of New Manufacturing Establishments in the Central Clydeside and West Midlands Conurbations 1963–1972: a Comparative Analysis', *Regional Studies*, 12(2) (1978), pp. 199–213. The authors dispute the argument that new firms and innovation are synonymous, concluding instead that new enterprises are not necessarily concentrated in the fastest growing sectors of the economy, nor are they a major source of technological innovation, although it is conceded that there is some evidence that 'new firms provide regional economies with an important degree of industrial flexibility', p. 202. See also S. Fothergill and G. Gudgin,

The Job Generation Process in Britain, CES Research Series, 32 (November 1979). They conclude that 'from . . . evidence on job generation it would be wrong to ditch policies which work with large corporations in favour of new and small firms. The latter, on past form, do not by themselves offer a basis for the regeneration of British industry' (p. 24).

11   B.M. Nicholson, I. Brinkley and A.W. Evans, 'The Role of the Inner City in the Development of Manufacturing Industry', *Urban Studies*, 18 (1981), pp. 57–71.

12   See W. Thompson, 'Internal and External Factors in the Development of Urban Economies', in H.S. Perloff and L. Wingo (eds), *Issues in Urban Economics* (The Johns Hopkins Press for Resources for the Future Inc., Washington DC, 1968); R.A. Vernon, 'International Investment and International Trade in the Product Cycle', *Quarterly Journal of Economics*, 80 (1966), pp. 190–207; R.D. Norton and J. Rees, 'The Product Cycle and the Spatial Decentralisation of American Manufacturing', *Regional Studies*, 13(2) (1979), pp. 141–51; J. Rees, 'Technological Change and Regional Shifts in American Manufacturing', *Professional Geographer*, 31 (1) (1979), pp. 45–54. The incubator hypothesis has been described as a basic component of a major category of explanations of the phenomenon of industrial decentralisation which together make up the 'incubation, product cycle and hierarchical filtering theory'. This is based on 'a conception of the locational needs of small, new firms, second, an analysis of the evolutionary pattern of outputs as firms grow and mature, and third, a concomitant description of the diffusion of firms down the urban hierachy'. Its explanatory attraction lies in its concern with the long-run dynamics of growth and change. A.J. Scott, *Locational Patterns and Dynamics of Industrial Activity in the Modern Metropolis*, University of Toronto, Department of Geography Discussion Paper Series No. 27 (Toronto, 1980). A broad discussion is given in R.E. Lonsdale and H.L. Seyler, *Non-Metropolitan Industrialisation* (W.H. Winston & Sons, Washington DC, 1979), see in particular Chapter 4. This basic approach might be not unfairly described as a reduction to a domestic scale of theories from international economics. See, for example, S. Hirsch, *Location of Industry and International Competitiveness* (Clarendon Press, Oxford, 1967).

13   R.A. Leone and R. Struyk, 'The Incubator Hypothesis: Evidence from Five SMSAs', *Urban Studies*, 13 (1976), pp. 325–31; and see R. Struyk and F. James, *Intrametropolitan Industrial Location* (D.C. Heath, Lexington, Mass., 1975)

14   G.C. Cameron, 'Intra-urban Location and the New Plant', *Papers and Proceedings of the Regional Science Association*, 29 (1973), pp. 125–43.

15   Cameron, 'New Plant Incubator?', p. 366.

16   Nicholson, Brinkley and Evans, 'Role of the Inner City', p. 59.

17   Ibid.

18   Fagg, 'Incubator Hypothesis'.

19   Ibid, p. 37.

20   Ibid, p. 43.

21   M. Beesley, 'The Birth and Death of Industrial Establishments: Experience in the West Midlands Conurbation', *Journal of Industrial Economics*, 4 (1955) pp. 45–61.

22   Firn and Swales, 'New Manufacturing', p. 211.

23   Evidence is provided by the following three studies: P.E. Lloyd, 'New Manufacturing Enterprises in Greater Manchester and Merseyside', North West Industry Research Unit, Department of Geography, University of Manchester, Working Paper 10 (Manchester, 1980); M. Cross, *New Firm Formation and Regional Development* (Gower, Farnborough, 1981); and P. Johnson and D.G. Cathcart, 'New Manufacturing Firms and Regional Development: Some Evidence from the Northern Region', *Regional Studies*, 13 (1979), pp. 269–80. For a discussion, see C.M. Mason, 'New Manufacturing Firms in South Hampshire: Some Preliminary Survey evidence', Paper to Annual Conference of IBG, University of Southampton (January 1982).

24   Quoted in Beesley, 'Births and Deaths in West Midlands', p. 54.

25   R.A. Henderson 'An Analysis of Closures amongst Scottish Manufacturing Plants

between 1966 and 1976', *Scottish Journal of Political Economy*, 27 (1980), pp. 152–74.

26 P.J. Johnson, 'Policies Towards Small Firms: Time for Caution?' *Lloyds Bank Review* (12 July 1978), pp. 1–11.

27 R. Dennis, 'The Decline of Manufacturing Employment in Greater London', *Urban Studies*, 15 (1978), pp. 63–73.

28 Lloyd and Mason, 'Inner City Manufacturing: Greater Manchester'.

29 J.R. Firn and J.J. Hughes, 'Employment Growth and Decentralisation of Manufacturing Industry: Some Intriguing Paradoxes', Paper to the CES Urban Economics Conference, University of Keele (10–13 July 1973).

30 P. Elias and G. Keogh, 'Industrial Decline and Unemployment in the Inner City Areas of Great Britain: a Review of the Evidence', *Urban Studies*, 19 (1982), pp. 1–15.

31 Lloyd and Mason, 'Inner City Manufacturing: Greater Manchester', p. 80.

32 P. Gripaios, 'The Closure of Firms in the Inner City: The South-east London Case 1970–75', *Regional Studies*, 11 (1977), pp. 1–6; and P. Gripaios, 'Industrial Decline in London: an Examination of its Causes', *Urban Studies*, 14 (1977), pp. 181–90.

33 Reported by R. Dennis, 'The Decline of Manufacturing Employment'.

34 C.M. Mason, 'Manufacturing Decentralisation: Some Evidence from Greater Manchester', *Environment and Planning A*, 13 (7) (1981), pp. 869, 884.

35 G.P.F. Steed, 'The Changing Milieu of a Firm: a Case Study of a Shipbuilding Concern', *Annals of the American Association of Geographers* (1968), pp. 506–25.

36 Ibid, p. 507.

37 Ibid, p. 507.

38 See, for example, K. Young, 'The Problems of Economic Strategy', in K. Young and C. Mason (eds), *Urban Economic Development: New Roles and Relationships* (Macmillan, London, 1983).

39 See, for example, Keeble, *Industrial Location*; Gripaios, 'Industrial Decline in London'; and Dennis 'Decline of Manufacturing Employment'.

40 M.W. Dawson, W.F. Lever, and J.F. Malcolm, 'The Inner City Employment Problem in Great Britain 1952–1976: a Shift-share Approach', *Urban Studies*, 17 (1980), pp. 193–210. For an argument by Cameron that the decline of manufacturing in the conurbations cannot be explained by industrial structure factors alone, see G.C. Cameron (ed.), *The Future of the British Conurbations: Policies and Prescriptions for Change* (Longman, London, 1980).

41 Mason, 'New Firms in South Hampshire'; and Lloyd, 'New Enterprises in Greater Manchester and Merseyside'.

42 It follows from our argument at this point that the subjective aspects of the urban industrial milieu can be conceptualised within the assumptive world framework described in Chapter 2 of this book. We hope to pursue this possibility in our future work.

43 Confederation of British Industry, *Small Firms and the Inner City Problem*, Report by a working party of the CBI Smaller Firms Council (chairman Nigel Vinson) (CBI, London, 1979), p. 2.

44 Fothergill and Gudgin, *Unequal Growth*, p. 121.

45 Ibid, p. 123.

46 Ibid, p. 113.

47 According to Cameron, in *The Future of British Conurbations*, it is no longer the case that firms must seek close physical proximities in order to achieve agglomeration economies, and technical linkages are, he argues, 'the principal justification' for manufacturers' locating in the conurbations. Along with falling transport costs, he identified as a key factor in this process the growing tendency for industries to be organised around three or four corporate groupings 'which provide the necessary externalities for the individual production unit from within the corporate organisation' (p. 63), leaving industry free to consider a wide range of locational options. Empirical evidence is provided by, for example, A.G. Hoare, 'Industrial Linkages

and the Dual Economy: the Case of Northern Ireland; *Regional Studies*, 12 (2) (1978), pp. 167–80.

48 K.D. George, 'A Note on Changes in Industrial Concentration in the United Kingdom', *Economic Journal* (March 1975), pp. 124–8.

49 Ibid, p. 125.

50 I.J. Smith, 'The Effect of External Takeovers on Manufacturing Employment Change in the Northern Region between 1963 and 1973', *Regional Studies*, 13 (1979), pp. 421–37.

51 M.J. Healey, 'Plant Closures in Multiplant Enterprises: The Case of a Declining Industrial Sector', *Regional Studies*, 16 (1) (1982), pp. 37–51.

52 Ibid, pp. 42–3.

53 R. Leigh and D.J. North, 'Regional Aspects of Acquisition Activity in British Manufacturing Industry', *Regional Studies*, 12 (2) (1978), pp. 227–45.

54 Ibid, p. 240.

55 Ibid, p. 240.

56 P. Dicken and P.E. Lloyd, 'Inner Metropolitan Industrial Change, Enterprise Structures and Policy Issues: Case Studies of Manchester and Merseyside', *Regional Studies*, 12 (2) (1978), pp. 181–97.

57 P. Dicken and P.E. Lloyd, 'The Corporate Dimension of Employment Change in the Inner City' in C. Jones (ed), *Urban Deprivation and the Inner City* (Croom Helm, London, 1979), p. 55.

58 Dicken and Lloyd, 'Manchester and Merseyside', p. 194.

59 See however for some unequivocal arguments W.W. Daniel, *Whatever Happened to the Workers in Woolwich?* PEP Broadsheet 537 (Political and Economic Planning, London, 1972); and CDP, *The Costs of Industrial Change* (CDP, London, 1977).

60 D.B. Massey and R.A. Meegan, 'Industrial Restructuring Versus the Cities', *Urban Studies*, 15 (1978), pp. 273–88.

61 Ibid, pp. 274–5.

62 J. Westaway, 'The Spatial Hierarchy of Business Organisations and its Implications for the British Urban System', *Regional Studies*, 8 (1974), pp. 145–55. See also A. Schultz, *Local Politics and Nation States* (Clio Books, Santa Barbara, Cal., 1979), pp. 118–20; and D.J. Forsyth, 'Foreign-owned Firms and Labour Relations: a Regional Perspective', *British Journal of Industrial Relations*, 11 (1973), pp. 20–8.

63 Westaway, 'Spatial Hierarchy'.

64 J.B. Goddard, 'Office Development and Urban and Regional Development in Britain', in F.W. Daniel (ed,), *Spatial Patterns of Office Growth and Location* (John Wiley, London, 1979), p. 5.

65 P. Dicken, 'The Multiplant Business Enterprise and Geographical Space: Some Issues in the Study of External Control and Regional Development', *Regional Studies*, 10 (1976), pp. 401–12.

66 N. Thrift, 'Unemployment in the Inner City: Urban Problem or Structural Imperative? A Review of the British Experience', in D.T. Herbert and R.J. Johnston (eds), *Geography and the Urban Environment* (John Wiley, London, 1979), p. 145.

67 R.E. Caves, 'International Corporations: The Industrial Economics of Foreign Investment', *Economica* (February 1971), pp. 1–27; K.P.D. Ingham, 'Foreign Ownership and the Regional Problem: Company Pérformance in the Mechanical Engineering Industry', *Oxford Economic Papers*, 28 (1) (1976), pp. 133–48.

68 See 'UK Multinationals', *Labour Research* (January 1980), pp. 2–4. For a full discussion of the consequences of UK overseas investment on domestic employment, see Ann D. Morgan, 'Foreign Manufacturing by UK Firms'; and Stuart Holland, 'Comment', in Blackaby, *De-industrialisation*, pp. 78–101.

69 See Keeble, 'Industrial Geography', *Progress in Human Geography*, 2 (2) (1978), pp. 318–23.

70 P. McDermott and D. Keeble, 'Manufacturing Organisation and Regional Emp-

loyment Change', *Regional Studies*, 12 (2), pp. 247–66.
71 Leigh and North, 'Acquisition', p. 242.
72 See, for example, Thrift, 'Unemployment in the Inner City'.
73 D.E. Keeble, 'Industrial Decline in the Inner City', p. 106.
74 Keeble, *Industrial Location*, p. 14.
75 *Ibid*, p. 19.
76 Fothergill and Gudgin, *Unequal Growth*.
77 Mason, 'New Firms in South Hampshire'.
78 See D.E. Keeble, 'Industrial Decline, Regional Policy and the Urban-rural Manufacturing Shift in the United Kingdom', *Environment and Planning A*, 12 (1980), pp. 945–62.
79 Fothergill and Gudgin, *Unequal Growth*, p. 63.
80 D.E.C. Eversley, 'Employment in the Inner City' (mimeo, 1975), p. 9.
81 Keeble, *Industrial Location*, p. 288.
82 P. McLoughlin, *Regional Policy and the Inner Areas: a Study of Planners' Attitudes*, Department of Geography Paper No. 64, University of Reading (Reading, 1978).
83 See B. Moore and J. Rhodes, 'The Effects of Regional Economic Policy in the United Kingdom', in M. Sant (ed.), *Regional Policy and Planning for Europe* (Saxon House, Farnborough, 1974); M. Sant, *Industrial Development, Movement and Regional Development: the British Case* (Pergamon Press, Oxford, 1975).
84 Keeble, 'Industrial Decline', p. 955.
85 Ibid, p. 957.
86 S. Fothergill, M. Kitson and S. Monk, 'The Role of Capital Investment in the Urban-rural Shift in Manufacturing Industry', University of Cambridge, Department of Land Economy Industrial Location Research Project Working Paper 1 (Cambridge, 1982) summary.
87 Keeble, *Industrial Location*, pp. 255, 258.
88 D.B. Massey, 'In What Sense a Regional Problem?', *Regional Studies*, 13(2)(1979), pp. 233–43.
89 Keeble, 'Industrial Decline', p. 953.
90 Massey and Meegan, 'Industrial Restructuring', p. 287.
91 C. Jones, 'Population Decline in Cities', in C. Jones (ed.), *Urban Deprivation and the Inner City* (Croom Helm, London, 1979), M. Warnes, 'Decentralisation of Employment from the Larger English Cities', Department of Geography Occasional Paper No. 5, Kings College (London, 1977).
92 F.W. Hayden, *Factors Influencing the Location of Industry*, GLC Research Memorandum RM 528 (London, 1978), p. 4.
93 See, for example, the discussion in L. Weatheritt and A.F. Lovett, *Manufacturing Industry in Greater London*, GLC Research Memorandum RM 498 (London, 1976).
94 J. Salt, 'Housing and Labour Migration', *Estates Gazette* (30 June 1979), pp. 1281–3.
95 H. Carter 'Structure and Scale in the City System', in M. Chisholm and B. Rodgers (eds), *Studies in Human Geography* (Heinemann for SSRC, London, 1973).
96 A.G. Hoare, 'The Sphere of Influence of Industrial Location Factors', *Regional Studies*, 7 (3) (1973), pp. 301–4, 313.
97 For which see M. Chisholm, 'Freight Transport Costs, Industrial Location and Regional Development', in M. Chisholm and G. Manners, *Spatial Policy Problems of the British Economy* (Cambridge University Press, Cambridge, 1971).
98 D.E. Keeble, 'Industrialisation of the Metropolis: the North-West London Case', *Transactions of the Institute of British Geographers*, 44 (1968), pp. 1–54; and D.E. Keeble, 'Local Industrial Linkage and Manufacturing Growth in Outer London,' *Town Planning Review*, 40 (2) (July 1969), pp. 163–88.
99 Ibid.
100 A.M. Hammer, *Industrial Exodus from the Central City* (D.C. Heath, Lexington, Mass., 1973).
101 Hayden, 'Location of Industry'.

102   Fothergill, Kitson and Monk, 'Role of Capital Investment'; see also Fothergill and Gudgin, *Unequal Growth*, p. 172.

103   Scott, 'Location Patterns'. Norcliffe has extended Scott's arguments to cover not only metropolitan areas but the entire space economy in order to provide a framework within which to examine the growth of non-metropolitan industry. He stresses the costs of the two key factors of production, labour and capital, distinguishing in particular between fixed and circulating capital costs – that is, the costs of buildings, equipment and vehicles on the one hand, and 'the physical inputs to production – raw materials, partly processed goods or finished products' on the other (p. 6). In outline, his approach suggests that 'the metropolitan core is an area where labour and circulating capital costs are low, but fixed capital costs are high. In the suburbs, high labour costs, fairly low fixed capital costs, and low circulating capital costs attract a very different group of industries. Labour and fixed capital costs are low in non-metropolitan areas, although circulating capital costs are beginning to rise with increasing separation from the metropolis. And finally, in the periphery, all factor costs are high except for the circulating capital costs of processing local resources'. G.B. Norcliffe, 'Industrial Location and the Theory of Production', Paper to the Annual Conference of the IBG (Southampton, January 1982). This model seems to fit the Canadian case, where labour-intensive industries are found in the inner city, warehousing and assembly in the suburbs, and fabricating branch plants in non-metropolitan areas. Probably the spatial patterning of such factor costs and their relative importance will vary between economies.

Chapter 5

1   G. Lomas, 'London's Service Industries: The Scope for Further Development in Perspective', paper presented to Regional Studies Association Conference on Post-industrial London: Economy and Employment (1979). For a broad general review, see D.R.W. Knight, A. Tsapatsaris and J. Jaroszek, *The Structure of Employment in Greater London, 1961–1981*, GLC Research Memorandum RM501 (London, 1977).

2   G. Gudgin, I. Branskill and S. Fothergill, *New Manufacturing Firms in Regional Employment Growth*, Centre for Environmental Studies Research Series No. 39 (London, 1979); P.W. Daniels, *Office Location: an Urban and Regional Study* (Bell, London, 1975).

3   J. Gottman, *The Evolution of Urban Centrality: Orientations for Research*, Oxford University School of Geography Research Paper No. 8 (Oxford, 1974), p. 17; see also G. Manners, 'The Office in Metropolis: an Opportunity for Shaping Urban America', *Economic Geography*, 50(2) (April 1974), pp. 93–110.

4   Lomas, 'Post-industrial London'.

5   Manpower Services Commission, *Mismatch in London* (mimeo, 1979).

6   See P. Damesick, 'Offices and Inner Urban Regeneration', *Area*, 11 (1979), pp. 41–7.

7   Quoted in S.V. Pearson, *London's Overgrowth and the Causes of Swollen Towns* (C.W. Daniel, London, 1939), pp. 39–40.

8   See G.E. Bate, *And So Make a City Here* (Thomason's Hounslow, 1948); P.G. Hall, *The Industries of London Since 1861* (Hutchinson, London, 1962); J.E. Martin, *Greater London: an Industrial Geography* (Bell, London, 1966).

9   H.W. Richardson and D. Aldcroft, *Building in the British Economy Between the Wars* (Allen & Unwin, London, 1968), p. 308.

10   B. Hillier, Introduction, in T. Makertich and P. Makertich, *Façade: a Decade of British and American Commercial Architecture* (Matthews Miller Dunbar, London, 1976).

11   M. Ash, *A Guide to the Structure of London* (Adams & Dart, Bath, 1972); see also Hall, *Industries of London*, pp. 133–9.

12   *Evening Mail* (20 July 1973).

13   For an excellent brief review of the rise and fall of the Great West Road, see S.

Vines, 'Fading of a Thirties Dream', *Observer* (11 January 1981).

14 Daniels, *Office Location*, p. 177; see also London Regional Manpower Intelligence Group, *Employment Profile of Hounslow* (MSC, London, 1981).

15 Daniels, *Office Location*; See also P. Cowan, *The Office*.

16 Keeble, 'Industrialisation of the Metropolis', pp. 4–5.

17 Ibid, p. 3.

18 This and the following passage are based on the company reports of the respective companies for the years in question.

19 Brent Chemicals International, *Annual Report* (1974).

20 Brentford Nylons, *Annual Reports*.

21 A. Lief, *The Firestone Story: a History of the Firestone Tyre and Rubber Co* (McGraw Hill, New York, 1951), especially pp. 209, 367.

22 *Financial Times* (15 November 1979).

23 *Financial Times* and *Middlesex Chronicle* (16 November 1979).

24 *Brentford and Chiswick Times* (18 July 1974).

25 South East Joint Planning Team, *Strategy for the South East: 1976 Review* (HMSO, London, 1976), paras 4.12–4.35; C. Howick and T. Key, *The Local Economy of Tower Hamlets: an Inner City Profile*, Centre for Environmental Studies, Research Series No. 26 (London, 1978); P. Wood, 'Industrial Changes in Inner London', in Clout, *Changing London* pp. 38–49; Gripaios, 'Industrial Decline'; Gripaios, 'Closure of Firms'.

26 Community Development Project, *The Costs of Industrial Change* (CDP Inter-Project Editorial Team, London, 1977), p. 29.

27 London Borough of Greenwich, *Industrial Riverside Local Plan: Issues and Opportunities* (1979).

28 Daniel, *The Workers of Woolwich*, p. 1.

29 Southwark Trades Council and Southwark CDP, *Employment in Southwark: a Strategy for the Future* (The Trades Council, London, 1976).

30 Ibid, p. 33.

31 *Economist*, 20 May 1978, p. 102; 10 June 1978, p. 72; 28 October 1978, p. 60; Tate and Lyle, *Annual Report 1978*.

32 Tate and Lyle, *Annual Report 1978*.

33 Tate and Lyle, *Annual Reports 1979–80*.

34 Tate and Lyle, *Annual Report 1978*; *Economist*, 20 October 1978, p. 60; South East London Industrial Consultative Group, *Chairman's Annual Report 1976/7*.

35 Dennis, 'Decline of Manufacturing'.

36 For a general discussion, see Department of the Environment, *Industrial Renewal in the Inner City: an Assessment of Potential and Problems*, Inner Cities Research Programme Report No. 2 (DoE, London, 1980). See also Steed, 'Changing Milieu of a Firm'.

37 Southwark Trades Council, *Employment in Southwark*, p. 29.

38 SEJPT, *1976 Review*, paras. 4.30–4.31; see also G. Bramley, 'The Inner City Labour Market', in Jones, *Urban Deprivation*, pp. 63–91.

39 See D.J. Smith, *Unemployment and Racial Minorities* (Policy Studies Institute, London, 1981).

40 For a general discussion, see D. Palmer and D. Gleave, 'Employment, Housing and Mobility in London', *London Journal*, (Winter 1981) pp. 177–193.

41 Eversley, 'Rising Costs and Static Incomes'.

42 See M. Crawford and D. Dawson, 'Are Rates the Right Tax for Local Government?', *Lloyds Bank Review*, 145 (July 1982), pp. 15–36.

43 A 1907 cartoon in the London Municipal Society collection at the Guildhall Library, London, shows anxious industrialists towing mobile factories away from a London over which hangs the fog of high rates, leaving behind unemployed workers.

44 An industrialist in one of our case-study authorities complained that 'We once employed 900 [here] but now down to 300 . . . We've been restricted in every

possible way, and we've built up in Derby . . . We've felt, too, that we weren't wanted in the borough. To give one example, it's taken us a full year to get planning permission for a fence . . . We've had an adjacent car park for 30 years but no way will we be given permission to use it as a car park. It still finally has to be put down in two years' time back to agricultural use. This is frankly totally absurd. We're going to spend maybe £20,000 or £25,000 in making it a good amenity for the borough, it will help us to attract labour and so on, but our premises, many of them, are hopelessly out of date. On the other hand, if the rates increase over the next three years as they have over the last three years we'll be paying more than £100,000 in rates, yet we get no consideration about difficulties, getting large lorries down to the factory, and so on . . . we were asking for assistance about "no parking" in this very small road that comes down to the factory. But it's been discarded and there's no reason why it should be considered.'

45   J.J. North and J. Gough, 'The Impact of Local Authorities on Manufacturing Firms: Recent Experience in London', in Young and Mason, *Urban Economic Development*, pp. 155–183.

46   Dennis, 'Decline of Manufacturing', p. 47.

47   SEJPT, *1976 Review*; C.D. Foster and R. Richardson, 'Employment Trends in London in the 1960s and their Implications for the Future', in D. Donnison and D. Eversley (eds), *London: Urban Patterns, Problems and Policies* (Heinemann, London, 1973).

48   Dennis, 'Decline of Manufacturing', p. 59.

49   Ibid, p. 59.

50   Ibid, p. 57. For some inner/outer contrasts in decline in the number of factories, see J.E. Martin and J.M. Seaman, 'The Fate of the London Factory: Twenty Years of Change', *Town and Country Planning* (November 1975), pp. 492–5.

51   See Martin, *Industrial Geography*, p. 144, for the long-term westward drift of London's manufacturing.

52   For the significance of the Heathrow complex for employment in outer west London, see Kendall *et al.*, *Fourth Terminal at Heathrow*; for the impact of the recession in air transport upon Heathrow's employment, see LRMIG, *Employment Profile of Hounslow*, pp. 3–4. Heathrow's influence on west London firms is not entirely benign, and there is evidence that, while the benefits of the airport are experienced on a regional scale, firms in the immediate vicinity suffer problems of labour competition and noise. See A.G. Hoare, 'The Spheres of Influence of Industrial Location Factors', *Regional Studies*, 7(1973), pp. 301–14.

53   Bossard, 'Comment'.

Chapter 6

1   See P.J.O. Self, *Town Planning in Greater London*, Greater London Paper No. 7 (London School of Economics, London, 1970); J.M. Hall, 'A Mighty Maze: But Not Without a Plan', *London Journal* 2(1) (May 1976), pp. 117–26.

2   The following account is based upon extensive interviewing and observation and unrestricted access to policy and case files. The authority is not identified, and no specific citations are given in order to preserve the confidentiality of these sources. An abbreviated version of part of this chapter first appeared as K. Young, 'The Problems of Economic Strategy', in Young and Mason, *Urban Economic Development*.

3   *Evening Standard*, 14 February 1972.

4   Department of the Environment, *Local Government and the Industrial Strategy*, Circular 71/77 (1977), para. 3.

5   For thoughtful discussions of the significance of, and constraints upon, the use of intelligence, see A. Pettigrew, 'Information Control as a Power Resource', *Sociology*, 6 (1972), pp. 187–204; and H. Wilensky, *Organisational Intelligence: Knowledge and Policy in Government and Industry* (Basic Books, New York, 1967).

6   For a discussion of the ways in which the subsequent case decisions were affected

by inter- and intra-departmental conflicts, see Young, 'Problems of Economic Strategy'.

Chapter 7

1 As with Chapter 6, the account which follows is based on extensive interviewing, observation and unrestricted access to files. Once again, no specific citations are made, and the authority is not identified.

2 W. Morris, *News from Nowhere* (1890), quoted in the London Borough of Southborough 1973 plan for South Reach.

3 For the complexities of status and powers under the Inner Urban Areas Act 1978, see R. Hambleton, 'Implementing Inner Cities Policy: Reflections from Experience', *Policy and Politics*, 9(1)(1980), pp. 51–71; R. Hambleton, M. Stewart and J. Underwood, *Inner Cities Policy: Management and Resources*, Working Paper 13 (School for Advanced Urban Studies, Bristol, 1980); M. Stewart and J. Underwood, 'New Relationships in the Inner City', in Young and Mason, *Urban Economic Development*, pp. 131–51.

Chapter 8

1 For further discussion, see Young and Mason, *Urban Economic Development*, Chapter 10.

2 For government concern on this point, see Department of the Environment, *Local Authority Assistance to Industry and Commerce: a Consultation Paper* (DoE, London, 1982).

3 J. Rosenau, 'Intervention as a Scientific Concept', *Journal of Conflict Resolution*, 13(2) (1969), p. 149.

4 R. Little, *Intervention: External Involvement in Civil Wars* (Martin Robertson, London, 1971) p. 1.

5 Oakeshott, *Human Conduct*, pp. 52–3.

6 T. Shibutani, *Improvised News: a Sociological Study of Rumor* (Bobbs-Merrill, New York, 1966), p. v.

7 Marris, *Loss and Change*, p. 105.

8 Ibid, p. 122.

9 Ibid, p. 122.

10 For multiple boundedness, see R.O. Warren and L.F. Weschler, 'Governing Urban Space' (mimeo 1975).

11 J. Raban, *Soft City* (Hamish Hamilton, London, 1974).

12 U. Neisser, *Cognitive Psychology* (Appleton-Century-Crafts, New York, 1967), A. Strauss, *Images of the American City* (Free Press, New York, 1961). For more recent work on urban imagery, see the papers collected in R.M. Downs and D. Stea (eds), *Image and Environment* (Edward Arnold, London, 1973); and D. Pocock and R. Hudson, *Images of the Urban Environment* (Macmillan, London, 1978).

13 A. Buttimer, 'Social Space in Interdisciplinary Perspective', *Geographical Review*, 59 (July 1969), pp. 417–26. C. Steinitz, 'Meaning and the Congruence of Urban Form and Activity', *Journal of the American Institute of Planners* (July 1968), pp. 233–47.

14 K. Boulding, *The Image* (Michigan University Press, Ann Arbor, 1956) p. 143.

15 Parkes, 'Psycho-social Transitions', p. 104.

16 Young and Kramer, *Strategy and Conflict*, p. 229.

17 See Schon, *Beyond the Stable State*, for a discussion of the potency of 'ideas in good currency'.

18 See especially K. Kumar, *Prophecy and Progress: The Sociology of Industrial and Post-industrial Society* (Penguin, Harmondsworth, 1978).

19 J.D. Stewart *The Responsive Local Authority* (Charles Knight, London, 1974) p. 126. See also J.D. Stewart, 'The Government of Cities and the Politics of Opportunity', *Local Government Studies* (January 1975); and, more generally, A. Grey, 'Organising for Corporate Planning', *Local Government Studies* (October 1972).

20 Stewart, *The Responsive Local Authority*, p. 95.

21 See Horton and Finnegan, *Modes of Thought*, especially pp. 11–31; and F.R. Kluckhohn and F.L. Strodtbeck, *Variations in Value Orientations* (Row, Peterson, Evanston, 1961).

22 R.P. Neilsen, 'Communicating with and Motivating High Fatalists', *American Journal of Economics and Sociology*, 32 (4) (October 1973), pp. 337, 338. For a study of some cognitive aspects of bureaucratic innovation, see A.L. Stinchcombe, *Creating Efficient Industrial Administrations* (Academic Press, New York, 1974).

23 For further discussion, see K. Young, 'Environmental Management in Local Politics', in D. Kavanagh and R. Rose (eds), *New Trends in British Politics* (Sage Publications, London, 1977) pp. 141–65. See also the discussion of decision objects and decision consequences in R.P. Wolff, *The Poverty of Liberalism* (Beacon Press, Boston, 1968) pp. 86–93.

24 The following passage is abridged from Young, Mason and Mills, *Urban Governments*, pp. 41ff.

25 For a discussion of the powers available to local authorities in the economic field, see Young, Mason and Mills, *Urban Governments* pp. 78–87.

26 The London Borough of Wandsworth developed a co-operative enterprise with support from the rate fund under the general powers conferred by s. 137 of the Local Government Act 1972.

27 In 1981/2 the penny rate product in Westborough was close to £500,000, and in Southborough two-thirds of this figure.

28 See S.B. Sells, 'An Approach to the Nature of Organisational Climate', in Tagiuri and Litwin, *Organizational Climate*, pp. 83–103. Climate is used throughout the volume in a rather wider sense than our own usage of culture, which Tagiuri, in an extensive discussion of terminology and usage, sees as an ingredient of climate. See Tagiuri, 'The Concept of Organizational Climate', ibid, pp. 11–34.

29 See, generally, Hewitt and Hall, 'Social Problems', and D. Sims, 'A Framework for Understanding the Definition and Formulation of Problems in Teams', *Human Relations*, 32 (11) (1979), pp. 909–21.

30 For an excellent review of the field, see D.G. Myers, 'Polarizing Effects of Social Interaction', in H. Brandstatter (ed.), *Group Decision-Making* (Academic Press, New York, 1982), pp. 125–61.

31 See D.G. Pruitt, 'Choice Shifts in Group Discussion: an Introductory Review', *Journal of Personality and Social Psychology*, 20 (3) (1971), pp. 339–60; J.H. Davis and V.B. Hinsz, 'Current Research Problems in Group Performance and Group Dynamics' in Brandstatter, *Group Decision-Making*, pp. 1–20.

32 Pruitt, 'Choice Shifts . . .'; see, generally, the other papers presented in the *Journal of Personality and Social Psychology*, 20 (3) (1971), and those presented in the *European Journal of Social Psychology*, 2, (3) (1972).

33 Myers, 'Social Interaction', pp. 133–8.

34 It is worth recalling at this point the low morale which prevailed in Southborough's planning department in the early 1970s and the attempts made by junior officers to improve their organisational climate and achieve a greater sense of significance in policy development, for which see above pp. 109–110. Interestingly, almost precisely similar attempts were being made by a group of junior planners in Westborough in 1980. Some, but insufficient, support appeared to be available for a request to establish a 'junior officer working party' to reduce hierarchical relations and increase confidence, morale and efficiency and 'cross fertilisation'. The language of that debate in Westborough precisely echoes that recorded in Southborough ten years earlier.

35 The extent to which change in the composition of the councillor body is a prerequisite of culture change in local authority organisation is neither immediately obvious nor necessarily a common factor as between authorities or different areas of policy. For some further remarks on the impact of councillor dispositions in the race relations field, see Young and Connelly, *Policy and Practice*, pp. 158–9.

Index